†

The Dramatizing of Theology

The Dramatizing of Theology

Humanity's Participation in God's Drama

Matthew S. Farlow

Foreword by
Paul Louis Metzger

☙PICKWICK *Publications* • Eugene, Oregon

THE DRAMATIZING OF THEOLOGY
Humanity's Participation in God's Drama

Copyright © 2017 Matthew S. Farlow. All rights reserved. Except for brief quotations in critical publications or reviews, no part of this book may be reproduced in any manner without prior written permission from the publisher. Write: Permissions, Wipf and Stock Publishers, 199 W. 8th Ave., Suite 3, Eugene, OR 97401.

Pickwick Publications
An Imprint of Wipf and Stock Publishers
199 W. 8th Ave., Suite 3
Eugene, OR 97401

www.wipfandstock.com

PAPERBACK ISBN: 978-1-5326-0385-3
HARDCOVER ISBN: 978-1-5326-0387-7
EBOOK ISBN: 978-1-5326-0386-0

Cataloguing-in-Publication data:

Names: Farlow, Matthew S. | Metzger, Paul Louis, foreword.

Title: The dramatizing of theology : humanity's participation in God's drama / Matthew S. Farlow ; foreword by Paul Louis Metzger.

Description: Eugene, OR : Pickwick Publications, 2017 | Includes bibliographical references and index.

Identifiers: ISBN 978-1-5326-0385-3 (paperback) | ISBN 978-1-5326-0387-7 (hardcover) | ISBN 978-1-5326-0386-0 (ebook)

Subjects: LCSH: Balthasar, Hans Urs von, 1905–1988. | Barth, Karl, 1886–1968. | Theology—History—20th century. | Theology—Methodology.

Classification: BT28 .F37 2017 (print) | BT28 .F37 (ebook)

Manufactured in the U.S.A.   06/28/17

To you, Kristin, Kayla, and Jacob, this book is dedicated.
Love you Crazy Insane Jesus Love!

Contents

Foreword by Paul Louis Metzger | xi
Acknowledgments | xv
Abbreviations | xvi

Introduction | 1
    §1 The Drama of the Day | 1
    §2 Parameters of the Stage | 3
        §2.1 Parameters of the Concepts Relating to the Stage | 5
            §2.1.1 *Theology* | 5
            §2.1.2 *Participation* | 7
            §2.1.3 *Performance* | 8
            §2.1.4 *Theatre and Drama* | 12
                §2.1.4a THEATRE | 12
                §2.1.4b DRAMA | 14
            §2.1.5 *Introduction to the Parameters of Dramatic* | 15
        §2.2 Parameters of Being and Becoming:
        Our Theological Performance | 17
    §3 The *Becoming* of the Project | 21

Chapter One—The Act and Being of God | 23
    §1 Introduction | 23
    §2 The Event of God's Action | 25
    §3 God's Being-in-Act | 27
        §3.1 God for Us | 28
        §3.2 Participation in God's Being and Act | 31
    §4 God's Unity and Distinction in the Event of Revelation | 33
        §4.1 God the Father | 36
        §4.2 God the Son: The Objective Reality of Revelation | 38

§4.3 God the Spirit: The Subjective Reality of Revelation | 41
§5 Triune Revelation and Its Theological Importance | 46
§6 The Action of Theology as Exposed through the Theo-Drama | 48
  §6.1 Humanity's Participation in the *Theatrum Gloriae Dei* | 49
  §6.2 Recognition and Employment of the Theatricality of
       God's Action | 51

Chapter Two—Theological Expression | 56
  §1 Introduction | 56
  §2 The Narrative Model of Theology | 58
    §2.1 The Importance of the Narrative | 60
    §2.2 Narrative Movement: Dramatizing the Narrative | 62
  §3 The Dramatic Model of Theology | 66
    §3.1 The Benefits of Drama for Theology | 70
      §3.1.1 *Understanding our Humanity through
             a Dramatic Model* | 71
      §3.1.2 *The Expression of the Text and of Life
             through Performance* | 76
    §3.2 Performative Reality of a Dramatic Mode | 82
    §3.3 Framing the Action of a Dramatic Model | 84
  §4 Theological Performance | 86

Chapter Three—Dramatic Model of Theology | 90
  §1 Introduction | 90
  §2 Incorporation into the Normative | 92
    §2.1 Dramatic, Performative Foundation of Theology | 93
    §2.2 Theological Movement: Dramatization | 96
  §3 Christ as the Universal and Theological Focal Point | 97
    §3.1 Christ as Center, Midst and Periphery of Performance | 98
    §3.2 Theological Enactment | 100
  §4 Characteristics of a Dramatic Model of Theology | 102
    §4.1 The Performance of Language in a Dramatic Model
         of Theology | 105
    §4.2 Suiting the Action of the Word to the Action
         of the Drama | 107
  §5 State of Theology Today | 109

§5.1 Explicit Belief in and Use of the Dramatic | 110
§5.2 Movement of Language in a Dramatic Model
of Theology | 112
§6 Development and Movement of Theological Language | 115
§6.1 Vanhoozer and The Drama of Doctrine | 116
§6.2 The Drama of the Biblical Story in Bartholomew
and Goheen | 117
§6.3 Performing the Faith: Stanley Hauerwas | 118
§6.4 Incarnational Performance of Theology through
a Dramatic Model | 119
§7 Performance and Person as Exposed through a Dramatic Model
of Theology | 120
§7.1 Performance and Personhood Rooted in Christ | 121
§7.2 From Our *Analogia Relationis* towards the
Ideal Becoming the Real | 123

Chapter Four—Imagining the Real | 125
§1 Into The Real | 125
§2 Embedded in God | 128
§2.1 Imagining the Real: Our Performance in Christ | 128
§2.2 The Threefold Movement of Revelation, Invitation
and Reconciliation | 130
§2.2.1 *Revelation of Being* | 131
§2.2.2 *Invitation to Humanity* | 132
§2.2.3 *Reconciliatory Performance* | 134
§3 Theology's Use and Recognition of Its Imaginative Powers | 136
§3.1 The Result of a Rationalistic Theology: The Re-Imagining
of Theology | 140
§3.1.1 *Imaginative Products: A Look at Augustine* | 140
§3.1.2 *Negative Reception of the Imagination* | 144
§3.2 Today's Theological Imagining | 145
§4 Imagining the Real | 148
§4.1 Overcoming the Unimaginative | 148
§4.2 Realizing Our Mission: The Becoming of the Real | 151
§4.3 Realization of Our Participatory Mission | 153
§4.4 Realizing the Possibilities Through our Interactions | 155
§5 Relational Reality | 157

§5.1 Identity of Mission | 157
§5.2 Relation of Being | 160
§6 Elevation of the Real | 162
§7 Imaginative Movement towards the Actuality of
   Our Faithful Performances | 164

Chapter Five—Performative Reality | 167
   §1 The Opening Movement | 167
   §2 Dramatic Movement | 168
      §2.1 Performance within the *Theologica Dramaticas* | 168
      §2.2 Dramatizing Theology | 172
   §3 Beyond Theatre into *Theologica Dramaticas* | 175
      §3.1 Discovery of Identity | 175
      §3.2 Driving the Dramatic | 177
         §3.2.1 *In Perspective: Investigating Balthasar's Approach* | 178
         §3.2.2 *Performative Foundation* | 181
      § Theological Interlude: *The Person of the Spirit in the Theo-Drama* | 183
   §4 The Character of Theology: A Performative Reality | 187
      §4.1 Strange Dichotomy | 187
      §4.2 Redemptive Reality | 191
   §5 Theological Performance | 195
      §5.1 Moving towards the Core of Performance | 195
      §5.2 Eucharistic Improvisation | 197
      §5.3 Today's Performance within the Play of Yesterday and Tomorrow | 201
      §5.4 The Final Word: Love | 203

Concluding Remarks | 207
   §1 What's Done Cannot Be Undone | 207
   §2 The Truth Shall Set You Free | 209
   §3 How Now Shall We Live? | 211

Bibliography | 215
Author Index | 227
Subject Index | 229
Scripture Index | 233

Foreword

"ACT WELL YOUR PART; there all the honour lies." Alexander Pope penned these famous lines in his celebrated "An Essay on Man." Kant admired the piece. Early on in his career, Voltaire loved it. However, he later denounced Pope's essay for what he took to be a false optimism and passivity on humanity's part.

Regardless of what one makes of Pope's work, Matthew Farlow plays his part well in *The Dramatizing of Theology*. Farlow rehearses and performs with skill his lines for God's dramatic presentation on the world's stage. He does so without projecting a false sense of optimism or passivity. Rather, Farlow accounts for the tragicomedy of salvation, which includes all humanity in dynamic and interactive terms, including theologians!

Farlow calls on the theological actors' guild to do more than argue logical points or narrate stories, however important. If, as he argues, salvation is God's drama in which we participate, theologians should call on their fellow humans not simply to reflect upon or contemplate salvation, but to share or participate in what Hans Urs von Balthasar refers to as the *Theo-drama*.

Farlow makes explicit this implicit feature in Karl Barth's work, showing how participation is a key embedded feature in the *Church Dogmatics*. *The Dramatizing of Theology* highlights especially Balthasar's explicit treatment of the divine drama in his multi-volume masterpiece titled *Theo-Drama*. While reenacting the various movements, Farlow goes further, making explicit its implications for daily life and cultural engagement in every sector of society. He understands that the best dramatists and playwrights, such as Shakespeare, involve every sector of society in their plays; moreover, they capture the imaginations not simply of the high and lofty in the box seats or front rows, but also the masses in the back of the auditorium, and in a cathartic way. After all, it is not enough for some to witness the drama; we must all experience and live it. This is even more true of the Theo-drama, which Christian Scripture reenacts. The church's theologians should follow suit.

The theologian who responds to Balthasar's call shines the stage light on God's revelation, invitation, and reconciliation. Farlow highlights the importance of living into the ideal reality, which is our identity in the God-Man, Jesus Christ. As we respond in obedience, the ideal becomes real, or realized in our lives, through the outpouring of God's Spirit. The triune God includes our stories and weaves them into the drama of salvation. Humans do not simply observe as spectators, or serve as pawns or props on the stage of God's dramatic production. Rather, we are vital participants, who can improvise in response to God's revelation, invitation, and reconciling activity in history.

In no way does the *Theo-drama* intrude or overpower us, or deny the tragedy of our existence by offering us a false sense of hope as hype. However, there is no hysteria either. The theologian is called to engage life openly and honestly, not unlike Jacob who wrestled with God and won.

The reader might find interesting that Dr. Farlow wrestled in college, where he also majored in Shakespearean literature. Wrestling does not allow for bystanders, whether innocent or not. One cannot sit back and allow others to struggle on one's behalf. So, too, with Shakespeare; it is not enough to read his works; they call for performance. Even in his theological studies and now in his work as a pastoral theologian, Farlow models and makes explicit what the *Theo-drama* entails: enacting the reality of the ideal in seeking to respond well to God's invitation.

Farlow's *Dramatizing of Theology* will unsettle those dramatists who would make theology subservient to theater; if the whole creation is the theater of redemption, we must all come to terms with the reality that God is the ultimate playwright. For Farlow, the emphasis is rightly on "Theo" in Theo-drama, while still applauding and proclaiming the singular importance of the dramatic presentation.

Not only will some dramatists find this work unsettling, but also it will make the arm-chair as well as limelight theologian uneasy. If one reads this work well, one will rise from one's seat and perform, both as a theologian, and as a fellow human, with the rest of the characters gathered for the production. One will seek to tear down invisible and visible walls: walls that separate the stage from the rest of the theater, as well as the podium, platform and pulpit from the rest of the classroom and sanctuary; walls that separate the academy and church from the surrounding world, as well as glass ceilings that separate the various sectors of society. No one is a spectator; we must all participate; we must all wrestle and struggle to play our parts well together as one liberated and cathartic community in the tragicomedy of life.

Revelation, invitation and reconciliation account for God's divine in-breaking, where God steps off the stage into our lives. In Jesus' incarnation and our inclusion through the Spirit, God invites us into his ongoing divine work of reconciliation. We do not simply imitate, repeat, or go so far as to replace God's activity; rather, we share in it, even unto death. But there is more.

As with Shakespeare, there are tragedies that end with death, and comedies that end with marriage. In the *Theo-drama*, there is no division. Once again, the wall comes down. Christ's death gives rise to resurrection and the Marriage Supper of the Lamb. As Farlow shares, life is the ultimate tragicomedy, as the triune God transforms profound suffering and incorporates our history into the drama of redemption. The Spirit and the Bride say, "Come!" Ultimately, our wrestling match with death will give way to the sacred dance of eternal life, as we share in the Eucharistic marriage feast whose encore is the Eschaton.

—Paul Louis Metzger

Acknowledgments

It is first acknowledged that this project is a blessing from God and as such, the hope is that it will be a light in revealing the all-consuming love of the Father, Son and Holy Spirit to a world in need of Christ's reconciliatory performance.

My parents have been long-standing supporters of my theological quest during my Masters and PhD degrees. They have supported me and Kristin in a multitude of ways and we are exceptionally grateful for their love, support and guidance. Indeed, both of mine and Kristin's families have been supportive through their continuous offerings of encouragement and love, and for this we are grateful.

This book stems from my time at the University of St Andrews, Scotland. Thus, I must acknowledge my gratitude to Trevor Hart for his supervision and guidance, as well as to Michael Partridge who came on late in the game so as to fill out the depth and strength of my project. I am thankful for the willingness of both to share their wisdom. I wish also to thank ITIA, and specifically, Dr Gavin Hopps, for the intellectual stimulation granted on a weekly basis. As for Dr Hopps, well the friendship he offered to me and my family was truly a blessing. A word of thanks is necessary for the insightful and mind-stimulating discussion and comments offered by Dr Ivan Khovacs via the Viva Voce.

Finally, as cliché as it sounds, it is true, words simply do not have the depth of meaning, the depth of gratitude, or the depth of love to express my feelings of acknowledgement and thanks for my family. Kristin, Kayla and Jacob are the embodiment of Christ's love that brings daily strength to my life. Through my beloved family, my life is and has been daily drenched in the Insane Love of Jesus. This whole journey has been one that has seen its ups and downs, but has never been one that I have questioned as through the presence of my wife and children, I have always found the strength and courage to press on towards the goal.

Abbreviations

Hans Urs von Balthasar
All works published by: San Francisco: Ignatius Press.

SI	*The Scandal of The Incarnation*, trans. John Saward. 1990.
Ep	*Epilogue.* 2004.
ET	*Explorations in Theology* vols. I-IV (1989-94).
GL	*The Glory of the Lord*, trans. Erasmo Leiva-Merikakis, vol. I, *Seeing the Form.* 1983.
LAC	*Love Alone is Credible.* trans. D.C. Schindler. 2004.
MWR	*My Work: In Retrospect*
TD	*Theo-Drama: Theological Dramatic Theory* vols. I-V. (1988-98).
TL	*Theo-Logic*, vols. I-III. (2000-2005).
TH	*A Theology of History.* 1994.
TKB	*The Theology of Karl Barth: Exposition and Interpretation.* trans. Edward T. Oakes, SJ. 1992.
PR	*Prayer.* 1986.
PT	*Presence and Thought: Essay on the Religious Philosophy of Gregory of Nyssa.* 1995.
UC	*Unless You Become Like This Child.* 1991.

Karl Barth

CD	*Church Dogmatics*, ed. G. W. Bromiley and T. F. Torrance (Edinburgh: T&T Clark, 1956-76).
DO	*Dogmatics in Outline* (Harper Perennial, 1959).
EvanT	*Evangelical Theology: An Introduction* (New York: Holt, Rinehart and Winston, 1963).
GHN	*God Here and Now*, trans. Paul M. van Buren (London: Routledge Classics, 2003).
GA	*God in Action* (New York: Roundtable Press, 1963)
HofG	*The Humanity of God*, trans. John Newton Thomas and Thomas Wieser (USA: John Knox Press, 1960).
LJC	*Learning Jesus Christ Through the Heidelberg Catechism* (Grand Rapids, Mich: Eerdmans, 1981).
T & C	*Theology and Church*, trans. Louise Pettibone Smith (New York: Harper & Row, 1962)
WGWM	*The Word of God and the Word of Man*, trans. Douglas Horton (New York: Harper, 1957).

Introduction

> For theology is not adjunct to the drama itself: if it understands itself correctly, it is an aspect of it and thus has an inner participation in the nature of the drama (where content and form are inseparable).[1]

§1 The Drama of the Day

LIFE IS INHERENTLY DRAMATIC, and as Hans Urs von Balthasar maintains, "God does not want to be just "contemplated" and "perceived" by us, like a solitary actor by his public; no, from the beginning he has provided for a play in which we must all share."[2] This project takes seriously the need for theology to share in God's play, a play that is rooted in the being of God, and according to both Karl Barth and Balthasar God is Being-in-act. Through revelation, God confronts humanity and this confrontation, it will be argued, is dramatic. According to Balthasar, God's revelatory action "can only appear in its full stature—if it is presented as being dramatic *at its very core*."[3] Throughout this book we will investigate the claim that awareness of this dramatic reality is illumined most effectively through the *dramatizing* of theology. God has revealed to humanity His desire for its participation in His drama. As Balthasar writes:

> Theology has at its disposal various degrees of intensity of such participation as well as various literary themes and patterns, enabling it to represent revelation's dramatic character, and each of these embraces one aspect of the unique, archetypal and inexhaustible drama. Of course, this presupposes that theology understands itself to be involved in and committed to the drama which—according to the Bible—is taking place.[4]

---

1. Balthasar, *Theo-Drama*, vol. II, 151. Hereafter cited as *TD* followed by volume and page number.
2. Balthasar, *My Work*, 97.
3. *TD* II, 51.
4. *TD* II, 151.

If life is indeed inherently dramatic, then it would be advantageous to understand how, as Balthasar notes, "all the elements of the drama can be rendered fruitful for theology." For as Balthasar continues, "God's revelation is not an object to be looked at: it is his action in and upon the world, and the world can only respond, and hence "understand," through action on *its* part."⁵ Drama's fruitfulness for theology stems from the elements present in both the theatrical drama as well as the world drama whereby comparisons are made and insights can be obtained through the interplay of this relationship so as to further illumine God's action.

As a whole, the focus of this project is the return to theology's core, which as argued throughout this project, is dramatic. "It is not a question of recasting theology into a new shape previously foreign to it," but, the recognition that, as Balthasar continues, "Theology itself must call for this shape; it must be something implicit within it, manifested explicitly too in many places. For theology could never be anything other than an explication of the revelation of the Old and New Covenants, their presuppositions (the created world) and purposes (its infusion with divine life). This revelation, however, in its total shape, in large-scale and in small-scale matters, is dramatic."⁶ I am arguing that theology's *return* to its foundation moves beyond any simple "enrichment of language" so as to bring to light the drama intrinsic to the revelatory invitation extended by God through Christ's reconciliatory performance. God's drama is understood in part through biblical hermeneutics, exegesis and the like, yet the claim of this project is that the central action, the locus of authority, and thus, the foundation of the Theo-drama is Christ through the Spirit, rather than other model's such as the one employed by Kevin Vanhoozer when he states that Scripture is the "authorized version of the theo-drama . . . and the locus of authority."⁷ This project's intention is for theology not simply to acknowledge a "turn" towards the dramatic, which quite often results in a "mere quarrying of drama to enrich the language of theology,"⁸ but instead, to embrace and enact a faithful *return* to the core action and foundation of its object—God.

This project is situated in the recent movement of our theological endeavors that recognize the profundity of the dramatic and its ability to illuminate God's action and call to action from theology, the Church and society.⁹ Moving forward from the seminal work of Balthasar, and set forth

---

5. *TD* I, 15.
6. *TD* I, 125.
7. Vanhoozer, *Drama of Doctrine*, 239.
8. Khovacs, "Divine Reckonings," 33.
9. Some current examples are: Harris, *Theater and Incarnation*; Hart and Guthrie,

in the context of the theologies of Balthasar and Barth, this project argues that it is through the *dramatizing* of theology that theology is best equipped to illumine God's desire for humanity's participation in His *Theo-drama*. As Balthasar writes, "If there *is* such a thing as theo-drama and if it is fundamentally the event of God becoming man and his action on the world's behalf, there must be dramatic ways (legitimately so) of presenting it . . . And such forms of presentation, to which we now turn our attention, must yield conclusions with regard to the nature of this same theo-drama."[10]

The primary focus of the Theo-drama is the action of God that then illumines the secondary focus, His interaction with His creation. As Balthasar argues, Christ "is the living framework within which every human destiny is acted out; every human destiny is judged by his perfection and saved by his redeeming meaning." Thus, continues Balthasar, by grace each of our roles on stage can be "recognized as a dramatic action within the dramatic action of Christ, in which case the actor becomes 'fellow actor', a 'fellow worker' with God (1 Cor 3:15)."[11] Tracing the thoughts of Balthasar and combined with Barth's argument that, "Revelation is reconciliation, as certainly as it is God Himself: God with us; God beside us, and chiefly and decisively, God for us,"[12] I will argue that God's revelation, invitation and reconciliation, which I call His threefold movement, is a unified act that reveals to humanity His role and performance on the world's stage. This performance startles humanity, and thus, theology, out of their "spectator's seat," being dragged onto the stage." And as Balthasar writes, "the distinction between the stage and auditorium becomes fluid, to say the least."[13]

§2 Parameters of the Stage

Throughout the book the terms theology, participation, performance, theatre and drama will be used and furthered unpacked. The sense in which these terms are being employed does indeed overlap while retaining distinction between each of the terms. This is to say that many of the terms intersect and interact with another, but in so doing, do not lose their

---

Faithful Performances; Hauerwas, *Performing the Faith*; Horton, *Covenant and Eschatology*; Johnson and Savidge, *Performing the Sacred*; Quash, *Theology and the Drama of History*; Vanhoozer, *Drama of Doctrine*; Wells, *Drama of Christian Ethics*; and Wright, *New Testament and The People of God*.

10. *TD* I, 112.
11. *TD* III, 87.
12. *GA*, 17.
13. *TD* II, 17.

distinct and particular appeal. This is exactly the case for theology and theatre, which are intimately related through a third, and prior element called drama. Both theology and the theatre mediate in action. For theology, this action is revealed through the action of God, that is, His revelation, invitation and reconciliation, and for the theatre, the intertwining action of all involved—producers, directors, actors, stage crew, audience and the like. This relationship illumines the thoughts put forth by Peter Brook that, "anyone interested in processes in the natural world would be greatly rewarded by a study of theatre conditions."[14] Theatre does indeed offer a tremendous wealth of possibility for theology. Commenting on the relationship between theology and theatre, Balthasar writes:

> through the theatre, man acquires the habit of looking for meaning at a higher and less obvious level. And at the same time it dispels the disheartening notion that this higher level is no longer dramatic but a static level where nothing happens and which relativizes all events beneath and external to it . . . To that extent the theatre is making its own contribution to fundamental theology.[15]

The interplay of relationship between theology and theatre continues to offer ways in which a person can see himself in the *other*, or as Balthasar writes, "portrayed by another; in this 'mask' the 'person' both loses and finds himself." Balthasar concludes the thought by writing that if revelation is "the ultimate precondition on the basis of which existence (and its reflected image, drama) can experience tragedy—and not a tragedy which dissolves in meaninglessness—the path is clear for us to get a view of the dramatic elements inherent in revelation."[16] If theatre, then, through its dramatic elements, can and does promote a glimpse of the world's existence in the realm of the divine might it be advantageous for theology to intentionally and explicitly employ the instrumentation of the theatre? As Balthasar remarks, "thus arises our task, which is to draw an instrumentarium, a range of resources, from the drama of existence which can then be of service to a Christian theory of theo-drama in which the 'natural' drama of existence (between the Absolute and the relative) is consummated in the 'supernatural' drama between the God of Jesus Christ and mankind."[17] Following the model of theology laid out by Balthasar, I argue that it is through the aid of the theatre that theology entertains the possibility of furthering its path

14. Brook, *The Empty Space*, 111.
15. *TD* I, 20.
16. *TD* I, 123.
17. Ibid., 130.

towards obedience and *returning* to its core, both of which are illumined and enacted through its (theology's) *action* which is best expressed and apprehended through the *dramatizing* of theology. The *dramatizing* of theology is theology's movement from the "reading" and "exegesis" of the Bible to its *performance*. Christian performance is the application and implementation of God's Word *in action*.

§2.1 Parameters of the Concepts Relating to the Stage

The terms given in this section, and employed throughout the project are indeed complex. Thus, this section is more of an outlining of the parameters of the given terms. Of course, each of the listed terms will be further developed throughout the project.

§2.1.1 Theology

In the context of this project the understanding of theology is close to that of Barth and Balthasar. It is true that Barth and Balthasar sit on opposite sides of the Church pews, so to speak; however, even while there remains some disagreement between the Protestant and Catholic understandings of nature and grace, this did not create a chasm large enough to dissuade compatibility between the Barth and Balthasar. The answer for compatibility rests within an intense Christological perspective and analogy. Concerning the latter, the analogy of being (properly rescued from neo-Thomism and stripped of the concept of "pure nature") and Barth's "analogy of faith" (that is, a relation between God and creation grounded and sustained solely in the event of saving grace) are "two ways of understanding the one revelation of God." Thus, Balthasar concludes, "we are . . . permitted to unite and harmonize the inalienable demands of the Church as promulgated above all by Vatican I with the essential insights of Karl Barth without artificial or forced syncretism" by affirming both "the absolute priority of grace and revelation and the relative priority of nature and its faculties."[18]

Both men have an intense Christological perspective that permeates throughout the whole of their respective work. At one point Barth wrote of Balthasar that in Balthasar's writing, I have "found an understanding of the concentration on Jesus Christ attempted in the *Church Dogmatics,* and the implied Christian concept of reality, which is incomparably more powerful

---

18. *TKB*, 382–83. Covenant and analogy are further discussed and unpacked throughout the project.

than that of most of the books (on my theology) which have clustered around me."[19] With regards to Christology, both weighted their theology in the reality of the covenantal relation of God and humanity as revealed most concretely in Jesus. As John Webster notes, "what drew their differing accounts into proximity was a conjunction of instincts about the structure of Christianity. Both considered that the central theme of Christian truth is the covenantal relation of God and humankind; both insisted that the metaphysics of that relation must be thoroughly informed by salvation-historical considerations."[20] Because of the explicit covenantal relation of God and humanity, both Balthasar and Barth believed that theology is a question and response of obedience to the *action* of God in Christ through the Holy Spirit.

Theology is an activity that we participate in, it is "an activity proper to the very essence of faith, and one in which faith engages naturally and inevitably, therefore wherever it is to be found."[21] Theology is the action of faith that confronts each of the participants on the world's stage. It is important to realize, claims Balthasar, that the understanding that faith seeks (the *intellectus fidei*) will be false if it "claims to be the last word or fails to take into account the encounter between creature and God and the obedience this encounter calls for."[22] The encounter between God and humanity is the essence of faith; it is the reality of grace. Thus, with this in mind, theology is, writes Barth, concerned with "the encounter between man and the Word of God."[23]

Theology, then, taken from the dramatic understanding from Balthasar and the revelatory foundation set forth by Barth, is based upon the relational revelation of God to His creature; a revelatory invitation that seeks a participatory response from the creature. Our response is the inquiry into what it means to be human. Because of our creation in the image of God, each one of us is involved with God, humanity and life. From a Christian standpoint, then, through our theological foundation and essence we participate in God's drama in a number of different ways and at a number of different levels of interaction, and while the ways of participation occur through a multitude of avenues, the point to be emphasized is that we all theologically participate as actors upon the world's stage. This type of interaction and participation could be considered to be theology with a small "t." As Hart

---

19. *CD* IV/1, 768.
20. Oakes and Moss, *Cambridge Companion*, 250.
21. Hart, *Faith Thinking*, 7.
22. Balthasar, *Theology of Karl Barth*, 138.
23 *CD* I/2, 791.

notes, "while we may not all be formally trained as theologians, we are all nonetheless engaged in "theology" to the extent that Christian faith for us forms an integral part of that picture."[24] For instance, if as is claimed in this project, humanity is created in the image of God, then at some level, all upon the world's stage engage with God (the *Other*) and with their neighbor (the *other*). This engagement/interaction is emphasized and investigated throughout the book. However, in chapter five I take a more concrete look into the ways in which our lives, or better yet, our performances, intersect. Such intersection on the stage, as is argued, highlights that all upon this stage are at some level "theologians" who each have their particular parts to perform.

With this said though, the project as a whole concerns itself primarily with those who practice theology within the contexts of the academy and Church leadership all the while recognizing that the profundity of this drama is realized when each of us comes to embrace our own faithful performances. Thus, one might call the theology practiced by the "trained" or "professional" theologians as being (T)heology with a capital T or theology proper. Faithful theology is carried out by the theologians of the academy and Church who through the Spirit's movement are obedient to the call to make known the possibility and profundity revealed through the encounter between humanity and the Word of God.

It is argued in this project that a crucial and historical need for theologians in Church leadership and the academy has always been to illumine how through the act of God, as Barth notes, "the Word of God thus becomes the word of man. It is not an insignificant word. Indeed, it is a supremely significant word. Yet it is still the word of man."[25] Theology is founded in God's revelatory event that continues to illumine the primary fact that the truth of revelation points to a personal rather than a propositional foundation. This is significant because it is through the dramatic that this foundation is best presented; created in the *imago Trinitatis*, humanity is beckoned to respond relationally to God's threefold movement.

§2.1.2 Participation

Christianity is a "*praxis*," writes Balthasar. It tells us "how we should act" and our theology must "drag Christianity out of the scholar's study" so as to set it "on the world stage where it is to act."[26] It is true that some parts

---

24. Hart, *Faith Thinking*, 1.
25. *CD* I/1, 266.
26. *TD* I, 33.

of theology's overall work are and must be done in the "scholar's study," but there is more, and must be more in our theological praxis. What is being argued is that theology should seek to elevate the call towards action; action that finds the fullness of its performance through its participation in Christ's eternal action. Participation is, writes Balthasar, the recognition that "the creature is meant ultimately to live, not over against God, but in him. Scripture promises us even in this life a participation—albeit hidden under the veil of faith—in the internal life of God: we are to be born in and of God, and we are to possess his Holy Spirit." One of the purposes of the Holy Spirit's indwelling, continues Balthasar, is "to enable men to participate in the relations between the Divine Persons; and *relations* are precisely what these Persons are, wholly and entirely."[27] Human participation is its involvement in and following of God's actions of faith, hope and love so as to encourage and enliven the on-going drama of reconciliation and redemption on the world's stage. Participation, then, as used throughout this manuscript is humanity's involvement with God in His drama; an involvement that is brought to light through the event of God's revelatory act in Christ through the Spirit. Through God's threefold movement, humanity is enabled to participate in the theatre of God's glory.

§2.1.3 Performance

Marvin Carlson writes that everyone at some time or another is, "conscious of 'playing a role' socially, and recent sociological theorists have paid a good deal of attention to this sort of social performance."[28] The general question, then, is: what is performance? What exactly is meant when we call a vehicle high performance or speak of someone making a performance out of a situation, or criticize the slow performance of the computer, or call ourselves performers, or congratulate one another for a fine performance?

The term performance has a "long history and wide range of meanings in everyday English usage," writes Barbara Kirshenblatt-Gimblett. These usages, Kirshnblatt-Gimblett continues, range from "high performance in technology and performance measures in management and finance to the legally defined performance requirements of contracts. Only recently has the word performance entered other languages, almost exclusively to designate performance art."[29] And while the word performance has only

---

27. *TD* V, 428.

28. Marvin Carlson, "What is Performance," in Bial, *Performance Studies Reader*, 72.

29. Barbara Kirshenblatt-Gimblett, "Performance Studies," in Bial, *Performance Studies Reader*, 47.

recently entered into use by other disciplines, its terminology is said to be rooted in ancient uses. Hart notes that the roots of performance have been linked to "*parfournir* (to accomplish entirely, achieve, complete)."[30] Thus, the complexity of this term rests in its generalized and particular uses today combined with its ambiguous past understanding.

While for many, performance directly relates to the specific action of a character on stage, many analysts of society, write Simon Shepherd and Mick Wallis, "argue that within the everyday there is a constant interplay of personal and social bodies (performances)."[31] Performance is understood to be our engagement with reality on a daily basis, and in this sense, the study of performance has become a means of examining and assessing the profundity of the day's actions. The actions of the day have been identified by Schechner as the "performances in everyday life," actions such as daily greetings, professional roles, family life, theatre, dance, athletics and the like. Performance is, writes Schechner, "a broad spectrum of activities including at the very least the performing arts, rituals, healing, sports, popular entertainments, and performance in everyday life."[32] Performance insists on being recognized not simply as an act or action, but as a self-conscious action undertaken by the performer that as stated before, so often becomes accomplished and performed subconsciously or as second nature.

Stanley Wells maintains that, "it is in performance that the plays lived and had their being. Performance is the end to which they were created."[33] Performance is, according to Schechner, "the whole constellation of events, most of them passing unnoticed, that take place in/among both performers and audience from the time the first spectator enters the field of performance—the precinct where the theatre takes place—to the time the last spectator leaves."[34] Performance then, in this context is an inclusive term referring to the entirety of the "theatre experience" on the occasion of a particular presentation of a particular play, and, it should also be noted that performance, in its inclusiveness, also includes the writing of the play, the development of the play, its rehearsal, and the like. The term's importance, maintains Bial, can be attributed to the fact that "the idea of the world as performance has become increasingly relevant throughout the last century."[35]

---

30. Hart and Guthrie, *Faithful Performances*, 5.
31. Shepard and Wallis, *Drama/Theatre/Performance*, 121.
32. Schechner, "Introduction," in Bial, *Performance Studies*, 7.
33. W. B. Worthen, "Disciplines of the Text: Sites of Performance," in Bial, *Performance Studies Reader*, 13.
34. Schechner, *Performance Theory*, 70–71.
35. Bial, *The Performance Studies Reader*, 59.

Theologically, the term performance has come into use, writes Hart, "as theology has sought models to help it understand better aspects of Christian faith's own peculiar situation with respect to a text, a text which must be "brought to completion" through forms of embodied action in which it is 'interpreted' faithfully for a world (and not just a world) which looks on as it does so."[36] The bringing to completion of the text follows the foundation of faith which is manifested through our living out the Biblical principles. That is, as Max Harris writes, "the transformation of text into performance is found at the very heart of the Christian faith. The proclamation that 'the Word became flesh' (John 1:14) suggests that speech became spectacle, that God, if you will, dropped himself incarnate into the atmosphere of the world, no longer hidden within the 'shell' of what he had said or spoken into being, but seen in the flesh in his full life and color."[37] Theologically, performance elevates the *action* of the script ultimately through the inter*action* between God and us, as well as our interaction with one another.

The phenomenon of performance-based talk within the realms of theology is arguably a "new" phenomenon occurring within the past twenty years or so. As Hart notes,

> the metaphor was proposed first by writers concerned with the nature of biblical interpretation, a discipline that had become somewhat hide-bound by the dominance of historical-critical models which, by their emphasis on the antiquity and essential "strangeness" of the biblical text, tended to exalt (or relegate) it to the status of a valuable artefact, but thereby easily lost sight of its role as a living Word to the Church. Interestingly, it was not New Testament scholars proper who first advocated the model, but systematic theologians and patristic scholars, whose own work was necessarily concerned with Scripture as possessed of contemporary as well as historical significance, and with the ways in which, over the centuries, it has been "played out" variously within the living traditions of the Church.[38]

The immediacy of performance in correlation to theology is evidenced by the fact that the Biblical text calls for more than observation, analysis or interpretation. "If Christian faith is from start to finish a performance," notes Stanley Hauerwas, "it is so only because Christians worship a God who is pure act, an eternally performing God."[39]

36. Hart and Guthrie, *Faithful Performances*, 2.
37. Harris, *Theatre and Incarnation*, 1.
38. Hart and Guthrie, *Faithful Performances*, 4.
39. Hauerwas, *Performing the Faith*, 77.

Even amidst the complexities concerning the term performance, though, what will be argued throughout the book is that we as humans are social beings, and as we negotiate life—at all times, but not always consciously or overtly—we perform. For the sake of this project, and in light of the aforementioned uses of performance, it is important to set the parameters in which this project employs and unpacks the term throughout these pages.

First, it is understood that performance is "an activity done by an individual or group in the presence of and for another individual or group."[40] Furthermore, the particular aspect of performance for this thesis is that of our action, primarily with God, and our interaction with Him; and secondarily, our interaction with one another. Thus, while it is being argued that our conscious actions are what constitute the foundation of our performances, as stated before, this does not deny the fact that daily performances, which at one time might have required a completely conscious engagement, can and do often occur after time subconsciously, even becoming ritualistic or habitual. Needless to say though, Christian performances are rooted in a conscious determination and decision to respond to Christ's invitation so as to perform alongside and with Him.

Secondly, performance is understood to be a deliberate or intentional undertaking in life. That is, as Schechner writes, "performance is . . . more consciously 'chosen.'"[41] What is claimed, then, from a Christian perspective is that this conscious choice is our response to God's invitation to deliberately act *with* Him. God desires and expects a consciously chosen decision by His creation in response to His invitation. Thus, the performative actions primarily investigated throughout this project are those with regard to the Christian identity.

Finally, our performances are to be understood and measured against the *ideal* performance of God in Christ through the Spirit. As Carlson highlights, "all performance involves a consciousness of doubleness, through which the actual execution of an action is placed in mental comparison with a potential, an ideal, or a remembered original model of that action."[42] Theologically, this ideal, as is argued throughout this project, is Christ's performance as He represents what a *perfected* performance looks like, what the human is meant to be. Christ's performance is the ideal as it is based upon His undeniable obedience to the will of the Godhead, and thus, He (Christ) remains the *ideal* of our human performances. According to

---

40. Ibid., 22 n. 10.
41. Schechner, *Performance Theory*, 98.
42. Carlson, "What is Performance," in Bial, *Performance Studies Reader*, 73.

Carlson, "performance is always a performance *for* someone, some audience that recognizes and validates it as performance even when, as is occasionally the case, that audience is the self."[43]

§2.1.4 Theatre and Drama

Through the interplay of theology, drama and theatre, we gain the possibility of coming to understand better the interplay of relationships between ourselves and God, as well as ourselves and one another. Historically though, the wealth of assistance offered through the theatre has, as Balthasar remarks, been "hardly noticed by theology up to now—which can be used to portray God's action."[44] In the next two sub-sections, I will attempt to provide a few definitions of each term (theatre and drama), before presenting the way in which each term is employed and unpacked throughout the book. Let us now turn to the parameters employed to the given terms of theatre and drama.

§2.1.4A THEATRE

The theatre, Balthasar points out, will always survive precisely because, "life manifests a fundamental urge to observe itself as an action exhibiting both meaning and mystery."[45] This only emphasizes the natural relationship between theology and the theatre, as theology seeks to understand our interaction with God and our neighbor, while the theatre enables us to attain an understanding of ourselves, through its (theatre) ability to exhibit and/or present life. As Brook notes, "there is no doubt that the theatre can be a very special place. It is like a magnifying glass, and also like a reducing lens."[46] Recognizing the theological need for the theatre, this project draws upon the overarching theatrical interactive experience and its connections that draw upon the human need for community and interaction. However, though Brook might view the theatre as a lens into society, Richard Southern remarks that while "drama may be *the thing done*, theatre is *doing*. Theatre is act."[47] As opposed to drama being the action that fills the theatre, Southern makes the theatre the act itself claiming that it is the results that

43. Ibid.
44. *TD* I, 17.
45. *TD* I, 78.
46. Brook, *Empty Space*, 110.
47. Quoted in Styan, *Drama*, 144.

make the theatre act as opposed to the embodiment of an action. While it is agreed that because the theatre includes the drama and de facto contains an intrinsic element of act, for the sake of the book, the theatre is recognized more along the lines of understanding that acknowledges the theatre as the place of interaction between all its participants.

The theatre, throughout my argument, is understood as encompassing both performance and production as it is the place in which the drama is enacted. Johnson and Savidge write, "theatre derives from the Greek *theatron*, which is literally 'seeing place.' Theatre generally refers to the place of performance or production aspects of the art."[48] The theatre presupposes the presence of actors, an audience and a stage, as it is through their interaction that the essence of the drama is presented. The theatre, while being a place in the world, is not the world, but the place in which the action—the drama—of the world takes place.

My use of the term, theatre, fundamentally recognizes that the theatre is to the world what theology is to the Church. That is, the theatre presents life to the world so that they—the audience—might critically examine it. J.L. Styan writes of the theatre, that it is "designed expressly to touch and involve an audience, a segment of society, that audience and that society must in part control the kind of activity found in the theatre."[49] The partial control of the audience upon the theatre is directly due to interrelationship of the theatre and society and is the reason why the theatre engages life most meaningfully in presenting to humanity what it means to play on the world-stage, instructing the soul, writes Khovacs, "with so plain an exposition of truth that "It stares at you in the face."[50] With this said, the theatre is the place of action, it is where the interaction of actor, director, writer, audience, stage hand, etc. plays out and thus, theologically it refers to realm of creation—heaven and earth.[51]

---

48. Johnson and Savidge, *Performing the Sacred*, 12.
49. Styan, *Drama*, 109.
50. Marcus Aurelius, *Meditations*, XI.7.

51. In 1 Cor 4:9 "spectacle" is literally, "theatrical spectacle," a spectacle in which the world above and below is the theatre, and angels and men the spectators. The FBD, Faussett Bible Dictionary circa. 1888, further comments that "the theatre was anciently in the open air; semicircular; the seats in tiers above one another the stage on a level with the lowest seats. Besides the performance of dramas, public meetings were often in the theatre, as being large enough almost to receive "the whole city" (Acts 19:29); so at Ephesus the theatre was the scene of the tumultuous meeting excited by Demetrius. The remains of this theatre still attest its vast size and convenient position"(see entry 3549.01 under the "theatre" heading of no. 3549).

§2.1.4B Drama

As with theatre, so too with drama; a definition is intertwined in a complexity of meaning. Schechner writes that drama "can be taken from place or time to time independent of the person or people who carry it. These people may be just "messengers," even unable to read the drama, no less comprehend or enact it."[52] According to Schechner, drama represents the enactment of "a written text, score, scenario, instruction, plan or map."[53] The emphasis of action in drama is due to its Greek root of *drao*: to do, to act, to make. Needless-to-say, as R.A. Banks concludes, drama includes some or all of the following elements: written words; presentation or representation of life; interpretation for an audience; impact; enhancement and intensification of emotion and language; thought; spectacle; plot; and performance.[54] For the sake of this project, drama is meant to evoke the idea of action, specifically interaction between God and His creature and creature with creature. Furthermore, while drama might typically begin with the words on the page, the primary perspective employed is drama's emphasis of the dialogue and enactment of a script, plan or teaching. Drama, writes Banks, "moves off the page, through the imaginations of those who "realize" the words in performance and those who share the dramatic experience as audience and participants, into a new creation."[55]

The enactment of the words, or the script, further emphasizes the action of God through His event of revelation that invites us into this eternal performance through our own responsive action. The *dramatizing* of theology is the result of an intentional desire, and act, to participate in God's drama. Through the dramatic reality of God, who is *Being-in-act*, theology is called to participate in this action by continually guiding the Church back to her source. Scripture comes to life through our action on the world's stage. And while in this project I specifically focus on the performance of Scripture, I do recognize that God's drama is realized when our endeavors focus not only the enactment of Scripture, that is, the written texts, but also, through the performance of the Church historically. Looking through the history of the Church "how can we not think of the Theo-drama in light of the mediaeval Passion-and-Resurrection plays that made salvation visible in a drama (and the plays of the Antichrist and Judgment that showed forth its eschatological dimension); the centering of drama on the Mass in

---

52. Schechner, *Performance Theory*, 71.

53. Ibid., 71.

54. Cf. Banks, *Drama and Theatre Arts*, 1–13; Styan *Drama*, 26–30; Schechner, *Performance Theory*, 66–111.

55. Banks, *Drama and Theatre Arts*, 13.

the endings of the plays for Corpus Christi."[56] Through the likes of liturgy and the "martyr plays," participants throughout the Church's history have engaged God and one another. As Nichols notes, Balthasar is able to point to the "overflow of the Liturgy in the mystery plays of the Western Middle Ages; the deployment of mythological themes as pointers to the drama of Christ in the Spanish theatre of the sixteenth and seventeenth centuries, and the 'martyr plays' of the classical French stage."[57] God's drama also comes to fruition through the performances of the Church's tradition, creeds, and the like. The action or better yet, "performance" of the Church throughout history is an action that is simply the passing on of past performances, not always contained in the script, from one generation to another, but held to be essential to the drama as a whole. This is to say, that our theological endeavors should seek to account for the entirety of the action, dialogue and movement of God with humanity throughout the span of time.

God's involvement and participation with humanity, through the event of revelation, is best expressed through the language of the dramatic, yet, as Aidan Nichols notes, the church has "sometimes used drama to express the action-filled content of revelation, but her theologians have not in any all-embracing way (till Balthasar!) presented revelation as itself divine theatre."[58] Bearing this in mind, then, in conjunction with God's threefold movement of revelation, invitation and reconciliation, I will argue that it is important as the Church's theologians to realize our own threefold movement: first, to acknowledge God's revelatory act; second, moving out from this action and call, to recognize and accept our role upon God's stage; and third, to perform faithfully this role through the most efficient and effective means available. This, as will be argued, is aided and facilitated through the dramatizing of theology.[59]

§2.1.5 Introduction to the Parameters of Dramatic

The use of both the theatre and drama occurs through the chosen dramatist and their respective methods. However, it seems pertinent to offer a brief word concerning modern drama, which has, according to David Brown, had somewhat of a crisis of identity brought on through the invention of film. The new medium writes Brown, "appeared better able to achieve what at the time was considered one of the main aims of the theatre, perhaps its

56. Nichols, *No Bloodless Myth*, 23.
57. Ibid., 21.
58. Ibid.
59. Cf. chapter 5 §2.2.

primary aim, realistic portrayal."⁶⁰ Brown goes on to discuss the reaction to this "crisis" through his discussion of four types of theoretical analysis that were "generated in reaction to this crisis," and, as Brown concludes, "the four theories discussed here have usually been treated as rivals rather than as complementary, but there is no reason why insights should not be drawn from them all . . . It is precisely through performance pulling us now in one interpretative direction, now in another, that the possibilities old and new can be most easily accessed and developed. That way significant encounter is most likely to occur."⁶¹

While the dramatists and their methods referenced within this project do represent each of the four modern responses highlighted in Brown's writing: method acting (Stanislavski), drama as community experience (Reinhardt), estrangement or alienation, (Brecht) and a psychological dislocation (Artaud); the underlining unity and complimentary aspect throughout the manuscript, as presented through the dramatist, are the ideas of identity and existence. That is, within the context and argument of this project, two common themes run throughout each of the dramatists and the given examples from their works: identification and existence, specifically human existence. The dramatists referenced are those who intentionally examine the human condition of life; our identity and existence which as Esslin writes, is where the theatre illuminates "the human condition of man . . . confronted with basic choices, the basic situation of his existence."⁶² And while Brecht and Stanislavski seem to be on the complete opposite ends on the acting theories scale, their similarities warrant their use together within this project. That is, neither Stanislavski nor Brecht see life or art as sanguine or perfect, they both respected the different sides of human nature that motivate actors, plots, and real life. Brecht wanted just as much realism as Stanislavski did, the key difference being that Stanislavski wanted it from his actors whereas Brecht wanted it from his gritty, unyielding plays.

The dramatist and their methods acknowledged within this project are chosen because they leave their audiences no hiding space. As Artaud writes, "the action of the theatre is beneficial, for, impelling men to see themselves as they are, it causes the mask to fall . . . it invites them to take, in the face of destiny, a superior and heroic attitude they would never have assumed without it."⁶³ Each of the dramatists recognized expresses a belief

60. Brown, *God and Mystery*, 176.

61. Ibid., 184. Brown discusses two theories that are concerned with identification, looking specifically at K. S. Stanislavski and Max Reinhardt, and dislocation, looking specifically at Bertolt Brecht and Antonin Artaud (176–84).

62. Esslin, *Theatre of the Absurd*, 391.

63. Artaud, *Theater*, 31.

that the authenticity and impact of a performance stems from its embodiment of truth. The actors of the stage cannot simply *appear* to be playing their parts, doing nothing more than re-presenting the characteristics of life. Just as God desires an authentic response to His authentic invitation, so too does the stage. The actors of the stage, in order to be faithful to their performance, must recognize, writes Stanislavski, the difference between "the two words *seem* and *be*." It is through the quest of life's truth that the stage illumines the profundity of life, when the actors know, continues Stanislavski, that they (and the stage) must "have real truth" rather than being "satisfied with its *appearance*."[64]

§2.2 Parameters of Being and Becoming: Our Theological Performance

Throughout the centuries discussions of the correspondence between theology and the world quite often move along the trajectory of being—that is, what it is to be a human being, or better yet, who am I? This question is, argues Balthasar, answered only through theology for without the grounding of being in Absolute Being, the human subject is left in an abyss. As Balthasar writes, "I must will myself, but it is impossible for me to reach myself directly, for blocking the way is an unbridgeable abyss."[65] Who am I is the question we must all wrestle with so as to move closer and closer to the essence not of being in general, but what is means to be me. Balthasar maintains that it is when alone with his fate, that Oedipus must ask himself this very question. "All must ask this question, but each person can only ask it as a solitary individual."[66] Balthasar then draws from the thoughts of Plato who wrote that "No one who does not wonder about himself can be considered to lead a human life."[67] And then building from the work of Charles Dickens, Balthasar quotes a passage from chapter 3 that highlights the questioning nature of the human:

> A wonderful fact to reflect upon, that every human creature is constituted to be that profound secret and mystery to every other. A solemn consideration, when I enter a great city by night, that every one of those darkly clustered houses encloses its own secret . . . that every beating heart in the hundreds and

---

64. Stanislavski, *An Actor Prepares*, 157.
65. *TD* I, 481.
66. *TD* I, 483.
67. Plato, *Apol.* 38a. quoted by Balthasar, *TD* I, 483.

> thousands of breasts, there, is, in some of its imaginings, a secret to the hearer nearest it! . . . In any burial places of this city through which I pass, is there a sleeper more inscrutable than its busy inhabitants are, in their innermost personality, to me, or than I am to them?[68]

What these discussions elevate is the continued quest to understand being. It is in light of this that Balthasar emphasizes the reality of personhood (being) as that which cannot be apprehended apart from our being *in* Christ. The person (being) *in* Christ (Absolute Being) thus *becomes* who they are meant to be thereby recognizing God's idea of their being. It is, writes Balthasar, in Christ that "once and for all, the duality of 'being' and 'seeming' . . . is absolutely overcome."[69]

Humanity's performative reality hinges upon action as only the action itself, writes Balthasar, "will reveal who each individual is; and it will not reveal, through successive unveilings, primarily who the individual *always was*, but rather who he *is to become* through the action, through his encounter with others and through the decisions he makes."[70] The *becoming* of being illumines the dramatic foundation of life, and *if* theology is to remain true to its calling, it needs to be faithful to its object, Jesus Christ. In being faithful, theology is able to perform one of its essential roles, which, as Barth writes, is to refer the message of the Church back to its source, that is, its object, all of which is done *in* Christ through the Spirit.[71] The Theo-drama provides the means for theology to perform this mission, which is accomplished through the continued participation, of the academy and Church's theologians, with both the Church and society as well.[72] Through the action of theology, each human participant on the world's stage stands the possibility of coming to a deeper notion of who they are (being), and more importantly, who they are meant to be (becoming). The reality of our *becoming* is, as Balthasar points out, because "by its very essence, being is always richer than what we see and apprehend of it."[73]

68. Dickens, *Tale of Two Cities*, quoted by Balthasar, *TD* I, 484.

69. *TD* I, 647.

70. *TD* II, 11.

71. One of theology's critical tasks is to refer the message of the Church back to its source. Thus, Barth writes, "I believe the Church as the proclaimer and the hearer of the divine Word . . . the Church could not ever be exempt from seeking after the Word and asking for the Holy Spirit which alone leads it to all truth" (*Theology and Church*, 285, 295).

72. Again, as stated earlier, though the primary focus of this thesis is on theologians of the academy and Church and their respective roles in the Theo-drama, the belief remains that all of creation is involved at some level in God's drama.

73. *TL* I, 131.

Through its role of referring the Church back to Christ, theology is able, then, to participate with the Church, in magnifying the profundity of life found *in* Christ rather than a life found simply looking *at* Christ and examining Him. Life *in* Christ is revealed through a continual *becoming*, and thus, just as life unfolds through its *becoming*, so too does this book. Concerning our *becoming* or rehearsal of life, Balthasar writes, that "if a man truly recollected his past, he would be open to his future, he would be on the way to the free, limitless life of eternity, where God makes it easy for the one who strives to step over the threshold. This step is not only something to which God invites us, it is something we rehearse through our whole life in the world."[74] It is understood, then, that the *becoming* of theology is recognized through its continual action. The call for the dramatizing of theology today is explicitly due to the reality that Christian theology is rooted in Christ through the Spirit—such is the nature of a reality that is "action, not theory."[75] If, then, God is *act*, today's theology must respond in kind through its own action. That is, I am arguing that theology should be act if it is to be faithful to God who is act.

Erich Auerbach writes of the profound difference between the drama of the Bible contra "narrated reality," when he states, "far from seeking like Homer, merely to make us forget our own reality for a few hours, it (the Bible) seeks to overcome our reality: we are to fit our own life into its world, feel ourselves to be elements in its structure of universal history."[76] The world of the Bible is illumined and enacted on the stage of creation, and if the reality of God's drama is truly that which transforms our reality, then the path forged by Balthasar in his *Theo-Drama* is one good specific instance of the general way in which the theological academy and Church need to move so as to enter into the profound performance of the Father, Son and Spirit.

Humanity is created in the image of a Trinitarian God who is *act*, and as Barth writes, "He is who He is in His works," that is, continues Barth, "God is who He is in the act of His revelation . . . God's Godhead consists in the fact that it is an event—not any event, not events in general, but the event of His action, in which we have a share in God's revelation."[77] I will argue that Christian performance is the application and implementation of God's Word *in action*. The point to be made is that the foundation of theology's *dramatization* is an action that recognizes the nucleus of God's action, for the Church and theology, is that which frees our endeavors from the dilemma of trying to create a theological system. The movement of

---

74. *TD* V, 116.
75. *TD* I, 66.
76. Auerbach, *Mimesis*, 14.
77. *CD* II/1, 260, 263.

theology deeper into the action of God represents the proper response to His invitation for participation. Regarding Balthasar's Trinitarian theology, which makes theology's movement possible, Nichols writes, "the doctrine of the Trinity is not the result of reason working through the materials of general experience. It has been disclosed to us only in and by the Word made flesh ... Only if God, eternally, from everlasting, and internally, in his own interior life, is Father, Son and Holy Spirit, can we get the hang of the drama played out in the life of Jesus."[78] Recognizing God's disclosure and action allows theology to remain faithful to the ongoing enactment of the drama, drawing on and continuing the drama, as witnessed in the Biblical script, through an intentional engagement with the Church and the world, so as to participate in Christ's transfiguring of history.[79]

According to Balthasar, because of the encompassing performance of God, "human life, both personally and socially, will also be shaped by it."[80] In light of this, it is first recognized that this is a theological project; it is not a study of drama from a theological perspective, but an attempt to acknowledge the intersection and interaction between theology, and drama, so as to recognize, and make known, some of the profound ways in which this relationship lends to the advancement of our theological deeds.

The project builds upon a theological foundation seeking to show that theology, like life, is inherently dramatic. Drama can assist theology in our endeavors that examine not only the question of what it means to be a participant in God's drama, but also, to guide our understanding and engagement in God's action on the world's stage. From drama, theology is given further ways to explore life, for as Antonin Artaud notes, drama is, "not confined to a fixed language and form, not only destroys false shadows but prepares the way for a new generation of shadows, around which assembles the true spectacle of life."[81] Through the interplay of relations between theology, drama and theatre, this project seeks to help theology, once again, recognize its own dramatic foundation, so as to witness the *becoming* of its faithful performance.

---

78. Nichols, *Divine Fruitfulness*, 167.

79. See for instance Wright, *New Testament and the People of God*, 41–42, 45, 350 (Hereafter *NTPG*).

80. *TD* II, 164.

81. Artaud, *Theatre*, 12.

§3 The *Becoming* of the Project

In chapter 1 I reckon with Barth's account of revelation, which as he writes, "it is not a state, but an event."[82] This act of God is significant as it is what roots all of our theological efforts. Thus, if God's involvement is itself an event, happening and constantly active, it is important, as I argue that theology consciously determines to participate in this event. The understanding of being is found in Absolute Being and through the event of revelation God distinctly and profoundly, writes Barth, "reveals Himself. He reveals Himself *through Himself*. He reveals *Himself*."[83] The obvious importance, then, of theology seeking to understand God through His Being-in-act is that through such knowledge, we come closer to understanding the essence of being thereby moving towards the realization of our faithful performances.

Chapter 2, then, takes God's revelatory event and seeks to realize the proper orientation of how best theology can participate in God's Being-in-act. Chapter two highlights two common models of theology: narrative and dramatic. The hope is to establish an effective way for theology to illumine God's interaction with us, and our participation in this event. According to Balthasar, the "mobility"(*Bewegtheit*) of the inner-Trinitarian life requires from theology, the "language of *event* for its evocation, and that the "eventfulness" of the triune God founds the possibility of the becoming that typifies the world."[84] The discussion is furthered through the action and *becoming* of the narrative which ultimately illumines the *becoming* of the human, that is, our movement towards what it means to be human. What the chapter intends to show is that theology should be appropriate to its matter; and if both Barth and Balthasar's assessments are correct: that God is Being-in-act (Barth), and that there must be a dramatic way of presenting God's revelation (Balthasar), then, the movement of the narrative to the drama seems the natural progression.

Chapter 3 moves deeper into Balthasar's belief that the profundity of the drama is realized in the drama of Christ, to the extent that humanity is, Balthasar maintains, "prepared to cooperate in being inserted into the normative drama of Christ's life, death and Resurrection."[85] Investigating the implications of this idea, the chapter argues that it is through the *dramatizing* of theology that theology returns to its core, which is dramatic. Theology should continue to push towards the fullness of its participation in Christ

---

82. *CD* IV/1, 7.
83. *CD* I/1, 296.
84. *TD* V, 67.
85. *TD* II, 50.

by the Spirit, so as to perform faithfully its *mission* as exemplified by the incarnational performance of Christ. Through, then, the narrative *becoming* the drama, we are further exposed to the potentialities of our performance in Christ through the Spirit.

Chapter 4 explores the idea raised by both Barth and Balthasar that we are who we are through our becoming. According to Barth, the Christian *in* Christ not only finds being, but in and of themselves "they are always in the process of becoming."[86] And as Balthasar maintains, "we can say that everything that is in process of becoming . . . attains its definitive shape, ultimately in full participation in the life of the Trinity."[87] If this is indeed the case, how then, does this *becoming* affect our theological practices? The chapter continues the movement of the book through its illumination of humanity's *becoming*. In other words, through an allowance and better understanding of the imaginative essence of our being, we can realize the profundity of our particular performances in Christ through the Spirit. That is, as Balthasar, notes since "in God we shall see how man was intended to be, and in man we shall see how God reveals himself to him."[88]

Chapter 5 argues for the continued theological need of its interaction with the Church and the world, so as to illumine that the core of Christian theology falters, if it rests upon the essence of "God with us" as being only a statement, teaching, or proposition. In fact, "God with us" is the expression of the dramatic act of God Himself—an act that invades humanity so as to bring about reconciliation. Theology realizes its faithful performance first, through the revelation of God, second through His invitation to participate in His act, which theologically, is best expressed to the Church dramatically, and third, through the willingness to imagine the *real* of the human, in light of the *ideal* of Christ's reconciliatory performance. In Christ's incarnational performance, God actively participates in "our being, life, and activity and therefore obviously our participation in His."[89] The chapter argues that such interaction plays out through the multiple scenes—intersecting narratives—of the characters on the world's stage, thereby allowing the realization not only of what our performances are, but what they are *becoming*. The *becoming* of our performances is the realization of our being; it is the realization of our faithful performances.

---

86. *CD* IV/2, 307.
87. *TD* V, 101.
88. *TD* V, 392.
89. *CD* IV/1, 13.

Chapter One—The Act and Being of God

> God is who He is in the act of His revelation. God seeks and creates fellowship between Himself and us, and therefore He loves us.[1]

§1 Introduction

"GOD WITH US," IS, as Karl Barth indicates, at the "heart of the Christian message;" it is, continues Barth, the "description of an act of God, or better of God Himself in this act of His . . . It is not a state, but an event . . . it stands in a relationship to our own being and life and acts." And as Barth concludes, "the whole being and life of God is an activity both in eternity and in worldly time, both in Himself as Father, Son and Holy Spirit, and in His relation to man and all creation."[2] Drawing from this *active* reality, then, chapter one has as its focus, the questions: Who is the God who reveals Himself, and what then are the implications on our theology? We do not know God Himself otherwise than as acting God, and in this action, "we have to understand a divine action, and therefore an event—not a reality which is, but a reality which occurs."[3] The occurring reality of God's eternal act, according to Barth, is an invitation to participate in His reconciliatory action. God is active, and through His love, He brings together humanity with Himself, and secondly, humanity with one another (Matt 22:37-9). As Barth notes, "God is not idle but active, for the love of God in Jesus Christ is decisively, fundamentally and comprehensively His coming together with all men and their coming together with Him."[4] Being *in* God is the result of God's revelation, it is our exposure to His love, which not only exposes us to His Being, but most importantly, invites humanity to participate in His Being. This is significant theologically,

1. *CD* II/1, 257.
2. *CD* IV/1, 7.
3. *CD* II/2, 548.
4. *CD* IV/1, 103.

because as John Thompson writes, revelation conveys God as he is, "it is God in his being and action who is both object of faith and the content of our thinking in theology. It is for this reason that Barth puts revelation and the Trinity at the forefront of his *Dogmatics* . . . In other words this doctrine determines the whole content and structure of theology."[5]

Theologically, then, the being and act of both the Church and the academy can be fruitful when focused on God's Being and act. According to Barth, "we can regard His (God's) self-unveiling in every instance only as His act in which He reveals Himself to a man who is unable to unveil Him, showing Himself indeed in a specific form, but still unveiling Himself."[6] Because of the importance of revelation, and its opening up of God's Being and Act to humanity, this chapter begins with Barth's theological understanding of this event and seeks to unpack the implications of his findings. In commenting on Barth's theology, Balthasar writes, "He (Barth) knew that the task of theology was not only to say something proper about the content of revelation but also somehow to convey to us how utterly, stupendously dramatic the event was that is now reaching our ears."[7]

This chapter seeks to explore the truth of God's Being and Act as witnessed through His event of revelation. Commenting on God's revelatory action Balthasar insists that this event, "challenges the believer, takes him over and appoints him to be a witness—bearing witness with his whole existence. Otherwise he is no real 'witness to the truth.'"[8] Our attempt to "bear witness" with our "whole existence" will guide the exploration of the chapter, such exploration that begins first at the axiom of revelation—the Triune God. With the event of revelation humanity steps into the reality of its own *created* intention, that is, as Barth writes, "we (humanity) recognize ourselves, not as in the mirror of an idea of man, but as in the mirror of the Word of God which is source of all truth."[9] The chapter then moves directly into the discussion of God's Being-in-act. If God's Being is act, how are we to respond theologically? From this section the chapter moves into the discussion of God's unity and distinction in the event of revelation. It is within this section that the particular roles of the persons of God are examined. Moving from God's unified and distinct action in revelation, the next section attempts to understand the event of Triune Revelation and its theological importance for our theological endeavors. The chapter concludes through

5. Thompson, *Holy Spirit*, 2.
6. *CD* I/1, 321.
7. *TKB*, 82.
8. *TD* II, 57.
9. *CD* II/2, 550.

an initial look into the action of theology as exposed through the Theo-drama. If Barth's understanding of revelation as an "event" (something dynamic and active) and, indeed, of God Himself as having His Being-in-act, is true, then theology, as an engagement with God in and through His "event" of revelation, is bound to be dynamic and active itself.

The argument of this project is that if true to its object, theology cannot be anything but dramatic, as the Theo-drama seems to emerge naturally from the model of theology as exposed by Barth. While Barth did not go forth into the Theo-drama, Balthasar did. Building, then, from Barth and Balthasar, the project seeks to illumine the need for the *dramatizing* of theology which is nothing more than a return to its core. That is, the intentional move towards participation in the Being and act of God as revealed through His threefold movement of revelation, invitation and reconciliation.

§2 The Event of God's Action

The action of God in revelation takes life, and as Barth observes, "sets it into crisis, shaking its false foundations, and bringing to bear upon it the very Goodness of God."[10] Through such a shaking, our theological endeavors begin to understand the confrontation between Creator and creature; an *interaction* whereby the creature is, writes Barth, "confronted by the mystery comparable only to the impenetrable darkness of death, in which God veils Himself precisely when He unveils, announces, and reveals Himself to man, and by the judgment man must experience because God is gracious to him, because He wills to be and is his God."[11] If it is true that God is who He is as revealed through His event of revelation, the query remains, who is this God? Naturally arising from this initial question is the one that inquires as to how our understanding who God is will affect our theological endeavors; What is the appropriate response of theology? However, in attempting to find answers to the aforementioned, it is important to keep in mind the particularity involved in God's revelatory act, so as not to stray from the essence of the event of revelation. According to Barth, "to its very deepest depths God's Godhead consists in the fact that it is an event—not any event, not events in general, but the event of His action, in which we have a share in God's revelation."[12]

Revelation is the unmasking of God's hiddenness; it is the self-revealing of life, which, writes Barth, highlights the fact that the "definition we

10. *TC*, 12.
11. *H of G*, 37.
12. *CD* II/1, 263.

must use as a starting-point is that God's being is *life*," and as Barth continues, the essence of life comes from the essence of God which is seen in His revealed name, that is, seen in "His being and therefore His act as Father, Son and Holy Spirit."[13] Life revealed in and through God is the gracious act of the Trinity; it is the very event that exposes humanity to who this God is that the Bible proclaims as being "God with us." In the event of revelation, writes Barth, "God is the revealer, the act of revelation, the revealed; Father, Son and Holy Spirit. God is the Lord active in this event. We say 'active' in this event, and therefore for our salvation and for His glory, but in any case active."[14] The event of revelation is the indivisible act of the Godhead for the sake of creation; it is the act of God Himself "in unimpaired unity yet also in unimpaired distinction as Revealer, Revelation, and Revealedness."[15] Revelation is the unified movement of the Father, Son and Holy Spirit—the drawing in of humanity by means of God's own act. God moving to man "means God with the man for whom salvation is intended and ordained as such, as the one who is created, preserved and over-ruled by God as man."[16] This action is the fulfilment of God's love that ultimately presents itself in His desire for reconciliation. According to Barth, "God is He who, without having to do so, seeks and creates fellowship between Himself and us. He does not have to do it, because in Himself without us . . . He has that which He seeks and creates between Himself and us. It implies so to speak an overflow of His essence that He turns to us."[17] This overflow presents to theology, to the Church and to the world, God's active essence that continues to move towards the completion of His will, that is the fullness of reconciliation. It is through God's act that reconciliation occurs. As Barth notes, "Reconciliation has been made and accomplished . . . reconciliation is the truth of God Himself who grants Himself freely to us in His revelation."[18] If this is the case, then because of the event of revelation, humanity owes everything to God, as it is only from God's *interaction* and initiation that humanity gains the possibility of sharing in the presence of God and thus, finding life.

The absolute truth of God's eternal act as unfolded through His revelation and played out in His invitation and reconciliation is, as is argued throughout this manuscript, the action that empowers and guides the action of theology and thus, the Church. God's Being is, writes Barth, "the event

13. Ibid., 263, 273.
14. *CD* II/1, 263.
15. *CD* I/1, 295.
16. *CD* IV/1, 9.
17. *CD* II/1, 273.
18. *GA*, 17.

of his self-disclosure, his radiance as the Lord of all lords, the hallowing of his name, the coming of his kingdom, the fulfilment of his will in all his work."[19] Such action is the overflow of love and grace, as it is by the grace of God and only by the grace of God that God is not only knowable to us, but where we come to understand His desire for fellowship. This understanding builds directly from the idea espoused by Barth when he writes that in revelation "God seeks and creates fellowship with us, He wills and completes this fellowship in Himself . . . He is Father, Son and Holy Spirit and therefore alive in His unique being with and for and in another . . . He does not exist in solitude but in fellowship."[20] Through His desire to create fellowship, we come to witness glory of His Being and the unity of His action. Through the event of revelation, theology is exposed to the unified Being and act of God, thereby providing the foundation for today's theological endeavors.

§3 God's Being-in-Act

Revelation is the event that reveals the reality of God's Being-in-act. As Barth writes, "our first and decisive transcription of the statement that God is, must be that God is who He is in the act of His revelation."[21] Through the event of revelation, theology encounters the object of its focus, thereby having revealed the foundation and essence of its theological pursuits. That is, through revelation theology witnesses the Being and act of God and is called not only to share in this event, but also, to expose the Church and the world to the Creator of all. Concerning the reality of who God is, Barth writes:

> In the development and explanation of the statement that God is we have always to keep exclusively to His works (as they come to pass, or become visible as such in the act of revelation)—not only because we cannot elsewhere understand God and who God is, but also because, even if we could understand Him elsewhere, we should understand Him only as the One He is in His works, because He is the One and no other . . . We are interpreting the being of God when we describe it as God's reality, as "God's being in act."[22]

---

19. *EvanT*, 9.
20. *CD* II/1, 275.
21. *CD* II/1, 262.
22. *CD* II/1, 260, 262.

If Barth's claim is true, that God is Being in *act*, it seems then, that the most effective way for theology to proceed, is to emulate its object, to seek for self-involvement in the action of God. As Barth claims:

> Seeking and finding God in His revelation, we cannot escape the action of God for a God who is not active. This is not only because we ourselves cannot, but because there is no surpassing or bypassing at all of the divine action, because a transcendence of His action is nonsense. We are dealing with the being of God: but with regard to the being of God, the word "event" or "act" is *final*, and cannot be surpassed or compromised.[23]

From Barth's account of God's Being-in-act, there follow two primary factors for our theological pursuits: 1) God's Being-in-act means that God is for us; and 2) God's Being-in-act invites humanity to participate in His Being *in* Christ through the Spirit. Commenting on the importance of God's Being-in act for Barth, Thompson writes, "God's being in revelation is a being *in action*, again an important and central aspect of Barth's whole theology. God is revealed as a living, dynamic, active God."[24] Thus if Barth's idea that "God is not idle but active," is correct, and if it is the case that theology's object is this God whose Being is act, what then is the impact on our theological endeavors?

§3.1 God for Us

God for us means that we are able to experience and share in the fruits of His eternal act. Barth writes that through reconciliation, God grants to humanity, "not merely to see, but actively to share in the harvest which follows from the sowing of reconciliation. In willing this and not something supposedly better, Jesus Christ confirms Himself and His whole being and action. From all eternity He is not alone, but He is the Elect of God in whom and with whom creation is also elect."[25] In discussing the contribution of Barth to our theological understanding of God, Bruce McCormack writes, that "God's being for Barth is a being-in-act; first, as a being-in-act in eternity and then, corresponding to that, as a being-in-act in time . . . God's essence is not hidden to human perception. It is knowable because it is constituted by the act of turning towards us. God in himself *is* God 'for us.'"[26] This turn-

---

23. Ibid., 263.
24. Thompson, *Holy Spirit*, 16.
25. *CD* IV/3, 332.
26. McCormack, *The Cambridge Companion*, 99.

ing toward us exemplifies the truth of God being for us such that He is for all eternity, our God. As Thompson writes, for Barth, "since the Holy Spirit brings God to us and leads us to know him, the Spirit also makes known to us that from all eternity God is *our* God."[27] God for us occurs according to Barth, "because in all His modes of being He is equal to Himself, one and the same Lord . . . He can meet us and unite himself to us, because he is God in His three modes of being as Father, Son and Spirit, because creation, reconciliation and redemption, the whole being, speech and action in which He wills to be our God, have their basis and prototype in His own essence, in His own being as God."[28] God being *for* us is the manifestation of His love for humanity; it is the dynamic movement of God to us.

This love expressed through God's Being in action presents to theology the reality of our interaction and understanding of the Trinity. As Thompson notes, from Barth's thoughts on the Trinity, it follows that "there is a dynamic movement in God who is never to be conceived in static terms . . . God is life, movement and relationship, fellowship and love as such in himself and this he communicates to us as Father by the Son and in the Spirit. The love of God, the grace of Christ and the fellowship of the Spirit are God in action for our good and salvation."[29] God's Being-in-act is assuredly an act *for* us; He is *Deus pro nobis* expressed in Christ's incarnational act and through the action of the Spirit in His pouring out of love into our hearts. As Barth insists, "when God of His own will raised up man to be a covenant-member with Himself, when from all eternity He elected to be one with man in Jesus Christ, He did it with a being which was not merely affected by evil but actually mastered by it."[30] God for us is the expression of His love through the eternal event of revelation. That is, "revelation is always reconciliation and atonement."[31]

God's Being for us is manifested through His eternal will of fellowship as expressed through His covenantal relationship with humanity. It is through this relationship that humanity is exalted. In other words, as McCormack writes, "to *exist* in covenantal relationship to God means the exaltation of the human."[32] The exaltation of the human is the continual movement of God towards man; it is the epitome of His Being-in-act as fulfilled and exposed in Christ's incarnational self-giving to the creature.

---

27. Thompson, *Holy Spirit*, 29.
28. *CD* I/1, 383.
29. Thompson, *Holy Spirit*, 23.
30. *CD* II/2, 163.
31. Thompson, *Holy Spirit*, 17.
32. McCormack, *The Cambridge Companion*, 107.

According to Barth, "The act of revelation as such carries with it the fact that God has not withheld Himself from men as true being, but that He has given no less than Himself to men as the overcoming of their need, and light in their darkness—Himself as the Father in His own Son by the Holy Spirit."[33] Barth's account of God in His revelation seems to instantiate that our theological practices, if they seek to move in the same direction as God, should insist upon active practices that elevate the reality of action that ultimately seeks to elevate the *other*, that is, to be *for* the other. As Barth remarks, "we can regard His (God's) self-unveiling in every instance only as His act in which He reveals Himself to a man who is unable to unveil Him, showing Himself indeed in a specific form, but still unveiling Himself."[34]

Through the event and act of God, then, humanity is awakened to the foundation of what it means to be human, which, as revealed through God's act, is ultimately played out through our incorporation into the inner-love shared and poured out by the Father, Son and Holy Spirit. Of this action of God, the reality of "God with us," Barth writes:

> God makes Himself the means of His own redemptive will, but He is obviously more than this means. And in making peace by Himself He obviously gives us more than this peace . . . more than the preserving and assuring to us of our creaturely being and this as our opportunity for salvation. For when God makes Himself the means of His redemptive will to us, this will and ourselves attain our goal. What is at first only God's gracious answer to our failure . . . is—when God Himself is the help and answer—His participation in our being, life and activity and therefore obviously our participation in His; and therefore it is nothing more nor less than the coming of salvation itself, the presence of the *eschaton* in all its fullness.[35]

God's own act is the very act of love that continues to draw humanity into participation in His Being and act. As Irenaeus once wrote, "in this God differs from man: God makes, man is made . . . so man, being in God, will always advance toward God."[36] Through God's Being-in-act humanity is witness to the eternal movement of love through the revelatory act of Christ. God *for* us creates and communicates His love; it creates and communicates

---

33. *CD* II/1, 261.
34. *CD* I/1, 321.
35. *CD* IV/1, 13.
36. Irenaeus, Against *Heresies* IV.11.2.

"his own fellowship to us," and as Thompson continues, exalts us to "participate in the divine life, communion and love."[37]

§3.2 Participation in God's Being and Act

Humanity's act, then, is its response to the God of all creation, for as Stanley Hauerwas notes, "to act is to share in the divine life, for human reality exists solely within God's reality . . . any action we perform entails an actualization of the divine act in our own temporal and finite context . . . because all this life *is* God's act."[38] Sharing in the divine life is sharing in the event of revelation; it is a sharing in the act of God, which ultimately results in our further knowledge of the God who reveals Himself through this event. Knowledge of God is "bound to the objectivity of God just as it is bound to this definite object who is the God who gives Himself to be known in His Word . . . The fact that man stands before the God who gives Himself to be known in His Word, and therefore to be known mediately, definitely means that we have to understand man's knowledge of God as the knowledge of faith."[39]

The realization of humanity's participation in God's Being and act stems from the self-revealing of God, such a revealing that actualizes knowledge of God through our participation in His Being-in-act. Expounding upon this reality, Barth states that the revelation of God, "in which man's fulfilment of the true knowledge of God takes place, is the disposition of God in which He acts towards us as the same triune God that He is in Himself, and in such a way that, although we are men and not God, we receive a share in the truth of His knowledge of Himself."[40] This reality—the reception and participation in God's self-revealed knowledge—is the action and presence of the Trinity which rests within the dynamic interaction between Creator and creature, through God's revelation, invitation and reconciliation.

God's revelatory act not only reveals His Being-in-act, but also includes the "self-involvement" of humanity. It is on the basis of this revelation that humanity can and must, "participate in the knowledge of God," which continues Barth, "in its truth is indeed wholly and utterly God's self-knowledge. He can and must, therefore, participate in the truth. On the basis of revelation, man and his views and concepts, which in themselves and as such are impotent, can and will participate in the truth of the goal to which the way

---

37. Thompson, *Holy Spirit*, 23.
38. Hauerwas, *Performing the Faith*, 86.
39. *CD* II/1, 12.
40. *CD* II/1, 51.

here entered leads."[41] Through the Son, (the Way, the Truth, and the Life), and by the Spirit, (the guide unto Truth), humanity enters into the eternal communion of love thereby coming to know God, and thereby coming to the potential knowledge of itself, that is, the answer to what it means to be human.

Participation in the Being and Act of God occurs when theology is obedient to its calling, so as to assist the Church in her commission of revealing the Word of God to the world. Knowledge of the human is obtained only through God who is, as He is the foundation of our being. Barth insists that the reality of God—that God is—is something that humanity must not only hear, but reckon with. "What God according to His word wills with men and from men," writes Barth, "is that they should and must hear, believe, know and reckon with this; in great things and small, in whole and in part, in the totality of their existence as men, they should and must live with the fact that not only sheds light on, but materially changes, all things and everything in all things—the fact that God is."[42] It is in light of this revelation and reality that the Church is called to make known to the world the Being and act of God. The profundity of participating in God's Being and act occurs when the Church makes known that "God is." As Barth writes, The Church is "true to its commission when taught and bound by the Word of God and for the sake of it, it says this directly or indirectly but unequivocally to itself and to the world."[43]

The truth of God's Being and act as declared through the fact that "God is" is that which is revealed through the event of revelation. This event is where "the being of God declares His reality: not only His reality for us—certainly that—but at the same time His own, inner, proper reality, behind which and above which there is no other."[44] From the act of God—His seeking and creating fellowship—humanity is given the ability to participate in God's redeeming act. In being called into covenant with God—that is, the co-partner of God through His seeking and creating fellowship—humanity is enveloped in God's Being-in-act, through Christ by the Spirit. According to Barth, the ability for humanity to participate in God's Being and Act is the fullness of His acting on us so that we might have a greater knowledge of His Being. Our participation in and response to His revelation is an act of His grace. Barth writes:

---

41. *CD* II/1, 201–2.
42. Ibid., 258.
43. Ibid.
44. *CD* II/1, 262.

God is known only by God. We do not know Him, then, in virtue of the views and concepts with which in faith we attempt respond to His revelation. But we also do not know Him without making use of His permission and obeying His command to undertake this attempt. The success of this undertaking, and therefore the veracity of our human knowledge of God, consists in the fact that our viewing and conceiving is adopted and determined to participation in the truth of God by God Himself in grace.[45]

§4 God's Unity and Distinction in The Event of Revelation

In our continual pursuit of apprehending the fullness of revelation so as to further our understanding of who this God is that is *for* us, the next step is twofold: first we will look at the unified act of God in revelation; second, we will move to the distinct roles of the three modes of Being. This movement from God's oneness to His threeness will give valuable insight as to what it means not only that God is for us, but also, both the complexity and the profundity of our participation in His Being. That is, the goal of this section is to expose us further to the God revealed through the event of revelation.

It is from the continual experience of and investigation into the event of revelation that theology gains a communal and active perspective, a perspective specifically based upon the action of the Triune God. Such a perspective comes to light through the idea posited by Gregory of Nazianzus, who writes of the Triune God, "No sooner do I conceive of the One than I am illumined by the splendor of the Three; no sooner do I distinguish them than I am carried back to the One."[46] The act of revelation is the self-revealing reality of God's pluriform activity "ad extra." Drawing from the argument made by Barth, God's unity (His oneness) within allows for His external acts to present the distinct parts of each of the "three modes of being" while never being separated from the other two. As Barth writes, "Thus to the same God who in unimpaired unity is the Revealer, the revelation and the revealedness, there is also ascribed in unimpaired differentiation within Himself this threefold mode of being."[47] This pattern of oneness and yet distinction provides the relational model for theology, informing us that while each of us most assuredly has a role to play, these roles are not in isolation.

45. *CD* II/1, 179.
46. Gregory of Nazianzus, *Oration* 40.41.
47. *CD* I/1, 299.

Humanity is meant for fellowship, as the seriousness of "God with us," writes Barth "carries with it in all seriousness a 'We with God.'" From this relational reality we are exposed to the essence of our own true being. That is, as Barth insists, "We with God" means that "we are directly summoned, that we are lifted up, that we are awakened to our own truest being as life and act, that we are set in motion by the fact that in that one man God has made Himself our peacemaker and the giver and gift of our salvation."[48]

The significance of Barth's theological understanding of God through the event of revelation plays out when our own pursuits recognize not only God's transcendence, but also His immanence. In other words, our theological understanding of revelation is furthered through Barth, who posits that the act of revelation is, "God's reality in that God Himself becomes present to man not just externally, not just from above, but also from within, from below, subjectively."[49] Again, this point harkens back to the aforementioned idea of Barth when he remarked that revelation reveals that "God does not exist in solitude but in fellowship."[50] The unified act of God is realized through the distinct action of each person of the Godhead. Whatsoever the Father does, so too do the Son and the Spirit. Furthermore, divine action is not only Trinitarian, but it also includes human actions; thus, writes Gunton, "All divine action, and that includes the actions in which human beings are granted a measure, begins with the Father, takes shape through the Son and reaches its completion in the Spirit."[51] The act of God's Being revealed through the event of revelation is *one* act, as the Father never acts independently of the Son or the Spirit. The work of the Trinity for and in creation is the act of God's self-unveiling through the unified act of His revelation. This is an act in which "God from all eternity willed to become man in Jesus Christ for our good, did become man in time for our good, and will be and remain man in eternity for our good. This work of the Son of God includes in itself the work of the Father as its presupposition and the work of the Holy Spirit as its consequence."[52]

The unity of action in God's "opera ad extra" is the manifestation of the intra-Trinitarian Oneness—the Father is in the Son, the Son in the Spirit, the Spirit in the Father. Concerning such subjectivity present within God, Miroslav Volf concludes, "being in one another does not abolish Trinitarian plurality; yet, despite the abiding distinction among the persons, their

---

48. *CD* IV/1, 14.
49. *CD* I/1, 451.
50. *CD* II/1, 275.
51. Gunton, *Act and Being*, 113.
52. *DO*, 65.

CHAPTER ONE—THE ACT AND BEING OF GOD

subjectivities do overlap. Each divine person acts as a subject, and at the same time the others act as subjects in each person, which is why Jesus can utter paradoxically, 'My teaching is not mine'" (John 7:16).[53] Thus, the full significance of the aforementioned reality—the aspects of "mine" and "not mine"—find their meaning in and through the unified and Trinitarian Being-in-act of God as revealed through the unity of His revelation.[54] Through God's unity (oneness) as well as His distinction (threeness), humanity is witness to and invited into the free act of God. Barth writes that "the Father of Jesus Christ who according to the witness of Scripture is revealed in Jesus His Servant has the qualities of a Lord of our existence. The witness to Him leads us to a place where the miracle of creation can be seen. It bears witness to the holy God, the God who alone is God, the free God."[55]

Realization of the miracle of creation is realization that God is the creator and source of all; He is the source of relations as the One God who exists in eternal Trinitarian communion. It is in His complete unity that God involves humanity through His event of revelation, an event such that as Barth maintains, "God always meets us, as we have seen, in varying action, in one of His modes of being or, more accurately, as distinguished or characterized in one of His modes of Being." Such a meeting does not imply distance nor separation in God, but quite the contrary, as Barth continues "surely as the relatively different revelation of the three modes of being points to a corresponding difference in themselves, so surely it also and specifically points to their unity in this distinction."[56] Revelation is a unified act of both grace and obedience that gives life eternal while exposing us to the Being of God. According to Barth, revelation is an act that "in the three modes of being—that which makes them *modes* of being—can be indeed

---

53. Volf, *After Our Likeness*, 209.

54. In the foregoing discussion of God's plurality, that is, His threeness, there must be the concern to guard against the aspect of tri-theism in any discussion of plurality. There are not three objects/subjects of faith as this would mean three gods. Furthermore, as Barth writes, "the triunity of God does not mean threefold deity either in the sense of a plurality of Gods or in the sense of the existence of a plurality of individuals or parts within the one Godhead" (*CD* I/1, 350). God is unified in Himself while eternally present in the three modes of being of Father Son and Holy Spirit. As Barth states, Father, Son and Spirit are the one, single, and equal God . . . The subject of revelation as attested in the Bible is the one Lord, not a demi-god, either descended or ascended" (*CD* I/1, 381). Thus, while there is an aspect and realness of subjectivity within the Godhead, it must be understood that such subjectivity is not of the same kind of subjectivity humanity experiences. Human subjectivity is that which is limited and can be objectified whereas Divine subjectivity—the subject of revelation is, "the subject that remains indissolubly subject. One cannot get behind this subject" (*CD* I/1, 381).

55. *CD* I/1, 390.

56. *CD* I/1, 362.

derived from the concept of revelation."[57] Building, then, from the thoughts of Barth, such an act as the event of revelation is the event of the Father, Son and Spirit that not only draws humanity into a "sharing" of this act, but provides the foundation for our theological practices.

Accordingly, revelation is apprehended as God's unity which is an action that is presented also in its distinction. That is, while God is one, He is, writes Barth, "God three times in different ways, so different that it is only in this threefold difference that He is God, so different that this difference, this being in these three modes of being, is absolutely essential to Him, so different then, that this difference is irremovable."[58] Allowing for this premise to be our guide, it seems natural for us to move from the previous discussion of the One into a discussion concerning each of the three distinct modes of being.

§4.1 God The Father

Our understanding of God the Father builds from Barth's statement that "the eternity of the fatherhood of God does not mean only the eternity of the fellowship of the Father with the Son and the Spirit. It also protects the Father against fusion with the Son and the Spirit."[59] Such fellowship reminds our theological endeavors of the communal and relational reality of God. This reality not only elevates theology's relational need, but also the need for distinction. From this "eternity of fellowship" within the Trinity, humanity is able to recognize the Being of God the Father precisely because of the Being of God the Son and God the Spirit. Through Jesus, humanity comes to recognize God the Father of the Son as being Father of all. Concerning this fatherly revelation, Barth writes, "God as the Father of Jesus Christ can be our Father because even apart from the fact that He reveals Himself as such He already is the One He reveals Himself to be, namely, the Father of Jesus Christ, His Son, who as such is Himself God."[60] God reveals Himself through the communion of His Being so that by such an event, humanity is invited into the reconciliatory performance of God, and reconciled.

Humanity's apprehension of its gracious creation continues through the recognition of the Father as the eternal grounding of Fatherhood. This realization is apprehended through the self-demonstration of God whereby humanity comes to grasp, writes Barth, the "knowledge of God the Father

57. Ibid., 363.
58. Ibid., 360.
59. Ibid., 397.
60. Ibid., 390.

as our Lord, because in eternity God is the Father of His own eternal Son and with Him the source of the Holy Spirit."[61] Humanity is enveloped by the relentless pursuit by the Father through the sending of the Son which is perfected in and through the Holy Spirit. God is the One who loves and acts in freedom. Through such an understanding and recognition, humanity is opened to the sovereignty of God as manifested through the Father "ultimately willing himself." This is to say that God's willing of Himself is His offering of Himself to humanity, which is, writes Barth, "primarily a determination of love." This is the very love "of the Father and the Son in the fellowship of the Holy Ghost."[62]

Indeed, to recognize the unity of act—God in His Triune self-revelation—is to also recognize the distinction, or better yet, the particularity within the Godhead, for while the Father and Son are in one another their distinction remains, and must remain intact. Humanity comes to know—to recognize—the Father as He is the One whom Jesus reveals. Barth writes, "God the Father wills neither our life in itself nor our death in itself. He wills our life in order to lead it through death to eternal life. He wills death in order to lead our life through it to eternal life. He wills this transition of our life through death to eternal life. His kingdom is this new birth," and He is continues Barth, "the Lord of our existence."[63]

As mentioned earlier, from the Father comes the sending forth of the Son. God the Father is the one who gives being to all beings, the one to whom humanity looks when it looks upon the Word, the image of the unseen God.[64] The presentation of the Father by the Son is established through the reality that God is the foundation of life and the initiator of such giving. Barth notes that "God alone as He who He is by Himself, and therefore as the eternal Father of His eternal Son, is properly and adequately to be called Father."[65] Through His self-giving by the Son, the Father reveals His love and Being to His creature. From this overflow and giving by the Father, humanity comes to recognize the mode of being—the person of the Father in the Son through the Spirit. It is through the mutual acts of reciprocity and self-giving towards humanity that God reveals His acceptance of creation thereby revealing His desire not only to invite or even draw humanity into

---

61. *CD* II/1, 48.
62. *CD* II/2, 169.
63. *CD* I/1, 388.
64. Jenson, *Triune Identity*, 76.
65. *CD* I/1, 393.

His act, but hope of our participation, that is, our mutually reciprocated and active acceptance of His reconciliatory offer.[66]

§4.2 God the Son: The Objective Reality of Revelation

Jesus is the object of the self-revealing of God, He is the image of God and is in turn, "the Ground of all other being."[67] As Torrance writes, "In Jesus Christ the Truth of God has already been made relevant to man and his need, and therefore does not need to be made relevant by us ... [T]he closer theological instruction keeps to the *humanity* of Jesus Christ, the more relevant it is to the humanity of the receiver."[68] It is the argument of this project that our theological practices should be led by the revealed Word of God, the "*vere Deus vere homo* and with it the revelation of God as a whole is not an intellectual but a spiritual reality."[69] Through such a reality, Christ's in-breaking confronts humanity, thereby opening us to and drawing us deeper into the presence of God. Christ is the very essence of the divine and human being brought together. As Kurt Richardson notes, "In this his being, we have not only the objective revelation of the Triune God in the life of a historical human being but also the condition by which communion between God and humanity is re-established."[70] It is in Christ that humanity glimpses the purest form of the human—humanity glorified—as in Christ, the divine and human are determined and related to each other in such a form that remains the determinative and conclusive form for humanity. The opening up of humanity to the Godhead occurs in Christ, for His very humanity is that of all human beings. Christ is the perfected purpose that humanity moves toward in its incorporation into His incarnational act, so as to be able to participate in God's Being. Barth writes:

> When we say Jesus Christ, this is not a possibility which is somewhere ahead of us, but an actuality which is already behind us ... This is where all Christian knowledge and life derive their emphasis, or they are not what they give themselves out to be. It

---

66. God's offer to humanity, His giving and receiving, is His acceptance of humanity rather than His blocking of humanity. This offer, if "accepted" or "blocked" profoundly affects the movement not only of the stage, but also of the understanding of our own performances. The ideas of acceptance and blocking are unpacked and discussed in chapter 4 §4.
67. Origen, *John* 1.17; quoted by Jenson, *Triune Identity*, 75.
68. Torrance, *Theology in Reconstruction*, 26.
69. *CD* I/2, 178.
70. Richardson, *Reading Karl Barth*, 165.

is equally important to remember that this fact is an event. The act of God in which it is a fact, and without which it would not be, is completed; but it is completed in its occurrence as the act of God—a being which does not cease as such to be a becoming: *et homo factus est*. To celebrate Christmas is to think of the *perfectum* but with a remembrance, and indeed in the face and presence, of the *perficere* in which alone it is always actuality . . . Jesus Christ is the name at whose remembrance the event arises as such, so that if Christian knowledge and the Christian life are worthy of the name they can never lose their astonishment at participation in the act of that becoming which—as the Son of God once became man in time—can never become past or cease to be His act.[71]

Revelation finds its purity in action through the God-man who acts on behalf of both God and man. Such understanding leads Balthasar to write, "Christ is, though he has a human nature, a divine Person." Because of His Being—fully divine, fully human—Christ has opened God to the world. Balthasar continues in saying that "in this movement of descent (God) has determined the course of every mode of ascent of man to him. Christ is the one and only criterion, given in the concrete, by which we measure the relations between God and man, grace and nature, faith and reason."[72] Because of the self-revealing act of the Godhead, theology has been presented with the way to lead the Church in its witness to the world thereby exposing the world to God and His love and grace. God's grace and love poured out is an act that the Church (and humanity) is very much a part of, because as Barth teaches us, "the humanity (of Christ) only has reality through and in the Word, so too the Word only has reality through and in the humanity."[73]

Reality comes to humanity through the divine act of self-giving in the God-man—Jesus Christ. Humanity knows God through His humanity just as God knows Himself, for as Barth remarks, "the only begotten Son of God and therefore God Himself . . . has become the bearer of our flesh and does not exist as God's Son from eternity to eternity except in our flesh. Our flesh is therefore present when He knows God as the Son of the Father, when God knows Himself. In our flesh God knows Himself."[74] According then to Barth, the knowledge of God is actualized through the action of God, that is, the self-giving of God Himself, for in and through such action humanity comes to know God as the Son does.

71. *CD* IV/2, 46.
72. *ET* I, 162.
73. *CD* I/2, 166.
74. *CD* II/1, 151.

It is through Christ that humanity comes to familiarize itself with the Father as Jesus did not "proclaim the familiar Creator God and interpret Him by the unfamiliar name of Father. He revealed the unknown Father, His Father, and in so doing, and only in so doing, He told us for the first time that the Creator is, what He is and that He is as such our Father."[75] The revealing of the Father by the Son occurs only because the Son is wholly God and wholly human. As Irenaeus wrote, "Christ did not at that time descend upon Jesus, neither was Christ one and Jesus another: but the Word of God—who is the Saviour of all, and the ruler of heaven and earth, who is Jesus, who did also take upon Him flesh, and was anointed by the Spirit from the Father—was made Jesus Christ."[76] Jesus is the fullness of revelation, He is the One in whom humanity sees the revealing of the Creator and Sustainer of life. Barth concludes that "the true humanity of Jesus Christ is, therefore, the execution and revelation, not merely of *a* but *the* purpose of the will of God, which is not limited or determined by any other, and therefore by any other happening in the creaturely sphere, but is itself the sum of all divine purposes, and therefore that which limits and determines all other occurrence."[77] The making into flesh of the fully divine is the very action that propagates the presence and declaration of the Godhead. Barth further posits that, "The work of the Son or Word is the presence and declaration of God,"[78] such a declaration heard by humanity through the presence of the Holy Spirit. This act of declaration and hearing is the fact of revelation while also being the event, the act, of reconciliation. This very event is found *only* in Christ through the Spirit yet this centrality of action does not deny the essential and underlying fact that because of Christ's action, humanity is gifted the profound opportunity to participate *in* Christ through faith and obedience. The fulfilment of grace is the fullness of act. This is to say that when humanity becomes a *hearer* and *doer* of God's invitation and reconciliation, it (humanity) comes to witness the perfection of its own act. As Barth writes:

> The fact and form of the coming of God's Word to man so that man becomes a hearer and doer of it, the fact that Jesus Christ the Son of God acquires many brothers and His eternal Father

---

75. *CD* I/1, 391.

76. Irenaeus, *Against Heresies* III.9.3.

77. *CD* IV/2, 31. Again, while Christ's historical performance confronts the stage not with *a* version of God's eternal purpose for humanity, but *the* purpose, it does not discount each of our own particular and distinct performances. The relation of Christ's performance and its purpose to each of our own particular performances is unpacked further in chapter 4 §2.

78. *CD*, I/1, 409.

> many children, the fact of the fulfilment of grace: these very facts constitute an integral part of the biblical testimony to revelation . . . we can say, not only that "*God* with us" is a fact, but also, and included in the former statement, that "God with *us*" is a fact . . . God's revealedness among us and in us really comes to us in revelation. It is part of revelation . . . Not God alone, but God and man together constitute the content of the Word of God attested in Scripture . . . The Holy Spirit acting upon man is also God. Hence his work upon us is also revelation, and knowledge of him is knowledge of revelation, and therefore rests upon knowledge of the witness to revelation.[79]

The reality of the self-revelation of God in the God-man through the Spirit is the "mystery of Christmas." It is a mystery that "is of God's revelation to us and our reconciliation to God."[80] In this mystery, this self-revealing, humanity is enveloped by the action and outpouring of the Trinity and enabled to enact the multitude of desired embodied performances that seek to participate in the Revelation (Christ) and with the Revealedness (the Holy Spirit) among us. Through the outpouring of the Holy Spirit into humanity, writes Richardson, "an entirely new freedom to know and to be for God is created within the human subject, a freedom that corresponds to the original divine freedom to be for human beings."[81] From this freedom and action of God, humanity is enabled to participate in the theatre of God's glory. This participation is enabled, directed and secured by the Godhead who is present in the unity of Word and Spirit—the Two Hands of God.[82]

§4.3 God the Spirit: The Subjective Reality of Revelation

While Christ is the "objective reality of revelation," according to Barth, it is the Holy Spirit, he writes, who is the "subjective reality of revelation."[83] The second of the "Two Hands of God," the Holy Spirit, is God Himself to the degree that "in an incomprehensibly real way, without on this account being any the less God, He can be present to the creature and in virtue of

---

79. *CD* I/2, 207.
80. *CD* I/2, 186.
81. Richardson, *Reading Karl Barth*, 165.
82. In the fourth book of his *Against Heresies*, Irenaeus writes, "That One God formed all things in the world, by means of the Word and the Holy Spirit . . . For with Him were always present the Word and Wisdom, the Son and the Spirit, by whom and in whom, freely and spontaneously, He made all things, to whom also He speaks, saying 'Let Us make man after Our image and likeness'" (IV.20.1).
83. See *CD* II/1, §13 and §16.

this presence of His, effect the relation of the creature to Himself, and in virtue of this relation to Himself grant the creature life," writes Barth.[84] Just as the Son reveals the presence and power of the Godhead, so too does the Spirit. The action of the Spirit is manifested through His revealing of the perfecting relationship between Father, Son and humanity. That is, the Spirit is the perfecter, the guarantor of salvation, as humanity is in need of such guarantee through and from God's self-revealing.

Revelation is God's reality in that, "He does not merely come to man," but "encounters Himself from man. God's freedom to be present in this way to man, and therefore bring about this encounter, is the Spirit of God, the Holy Spirit in God's revelation."[85] The Spirit is in the world, guiding our actions while fulfilling the personal outpouring of Triune love. It is in light of such an outpouring that Barth suggests that, "man's freedom for God is actualized in the Holy Spirit."[86] Freedom realized in the act of faith and obedience, then, comes through humanity's being acted upon (directed) by the Spirit. Commenting on the Pauline formula of "in the Spirit," Barth writes that such a position, a reality, "describes man's thinking, acting, and speaking as taking place in participation in God's revelation."[87] Thus, through the Spirit, humanity is freed to love and obey God in Christ, because the act of the Spirit gives to humanity the ability, capacity, and capability of true faith, which theologically speaking, it will be argued, is a *performed* faith. Following along the ideas proposed by Barth, it is through the guidance of the Spirit that humanity is able to recognize God's invitation to participate in His reconciliatory act. By being acted upon and taken into the event of revelation, the person, writes Barth, is "revealed to himself as the child of God." And this work, this enactment upon, Barth writes, is indeed the "work of the Holy Spirit, or the subjective reality of revelation."[88]

The Spirit's role in the act of revelation not only guarantees humanity's participation in God's revelation, and thus, knowledge of God, but the act of the Holy Spirit is also, the "Yes to God's Word which is spoken by God Himself for us, yet not just to us, but also in us." Concerning the work and role of the Spirit, Barth continues that in this act of the Spirit, the "Yes to God's Word," is the "mystery of faith, the mystery of the knowledge of the Word of God, but also the mystery of the willing obedience that is well-pleasing

---

84. *CD* I/1, 450.
85. Ibid., 451.
86. *CD* I/2, 209.
87. *CD* I/1, 453.
88. *CD* I/2, 238.

to God. All these things, faith, knowledge and obedience, exist for man "in the Holy Spirit."[89]

Life in every sense exists for humanity "in the Holy Spirit," as it is the Holy Spirit who actualizes the love of Christ through His (the Spirit's) indwelling, thereby allowing humanity's participation in God's revelation. Barth draws from the Augustinian influence with regard to the act of the Spirit, and ventures close to the line of thought that solely attributes the concept of love to the Holy Spirit. This is to say, the Spirit *is* the love of the Father and the Son poured out into the hearts of believers rather than being the *person* who is doing the pouring. The point is that attributing love to the Spirit is correct, but as a *total* characterization of His Being renders the Spirit to a love-relationship rather than a person. As Tom Smail points out, Barth does have the tendency to follow the line of Augustine in his account of the person of the Spirit. "While Augustine was of course formally Trinitarian," writes Smail, "he often presented the Holy Spirit as the "bond of love (*nexus amoris*)" between the Father and the Son, a relationship between two persons, rather than himself a person."[90] This trajectory of the Spirit *as* the love poured out de-personalizes the Third Person of the Trinity.[91] Instead of reading Romans 5:5 as "the love poured out *by* the Spirit," Augustine read *into* the passage, thereby rendering that the Spirit *is* the love poured out.[92] There is no denying the fact that the Spirit is indeed love, just as the Son and the Father, for 1 John 4 clearly states that "God is love." However, while each person is specifically love, the Spirit in particular is the One who pours out the love of the Godhead as is stated by Paul in his letter to Romans; He is not the only person of the Godhead who *is* love. Furthermore, the Spirit is the actualization of love for humanity, as His act in revelation is to elucidate the self-revealing acts of the Father and the Son. As such, God's self-revealing is a Triune action; an action that stems from the Father, mediated in Christ, while being made comprehensible by the Spirit. The Spirit, in being God himself, acts, writes Barth, both as "Creator and as Reconciler, as the Lord of the covenant. As this very Lord, however, he now dwells, has dwelt, and

---

89. *CD* I/1, 453.

90. Smail, *Giving Gift*, 43.

91. See the discussion in chapter 5, §"Theological Interlude" of this book for a more complete discussion concerning the problematic influence of Augustine's attribution of the concept of love to Spirit. For further reading of Augustine, see Augustine's *De Trinitate*, particularly book XV.

92. For further evidence and discussion of this argument, see Colin Gunton, chapter 3, *The Promise of Trinitarian Theology*, specifically 48–55.

will dwell in men. He dwells not only *among* them but also *in* them by the enlightening power of his action."[93]

Again, while Barth does allow the Augustinian influence to guide his doctrine of the Spirit, his thought goes beyond the point of simply recognizing the Spirit as *only* being love. As Barth remarks in regards to the person of the Holy Spirit, it is the "Lord who sets us free. As such He is the Holy Spirit, by receiving whom we become the children of God, because, as the Spirit *of* the love of God the Father and the Son, He is so antecedently in Himself."[94] The Spirit for Barth is not exclusively the love being poured out as tends to be the case for Augustine. Instead, Barth's doctrine of the Spirit recognizes Him as the Being who acts as the "quickening power in which Jesus Christ places a sinful man in His community and thus gives him the freedom, in active self-giving to God and his fellows as God's witness, to correspond to the love in which God has drawn him to Himself and raised him up."[95] In the progression of his writing, Barth illumines how it is the Spirit who acts in love—the very love shared by the Father and the Son—so as to expose the self-giving reality of God's self-revealing. So in *CD* IV we find Barth stating, "In this self-giving to man He is God in all His freedom and glory . . . What he (man) cannot win by desiring and seeking, he has already attained . . . in the power of the self-giving in which he may respond to the love of God. He *himself* is the one who is loved by God. He *himself* is the one to whom God has given Himself in His Son, and gives Himself as He gives him His Holy Spirit."[96] The Holy Spirit is the person of God who gives Himself to humanity while pouring out the self-giving, self-revealing love that God is in Himself from all eternity, thereby empowering the ability for us to participate in God's Being-in-act.

In a further example of Barth's move beyond solely attributing the Spirit as the concept of love, Barth writes that the Spirit must be realized as the one "whose existence and action make possible and real (and possible and real up to this very day) the existence of Christianity in the world."[97] The Spirit opens up humanity to the Godhead, as it is the Spirit who brings clarity to the event of revelation, thereby ensuring humanity's relationship with God. Commenting on Barth's theology of the Spirit, Thompson notes that for Barth the Holy Spirit makes possible our participation and relationship with God. "Our incapacity and utter inability to be one because

---

93. *EvanT*, 54.
94. *CD* I/1, 448; my italics.
95. *CD* IV/2, 727.
96. Ibid., 750.
97. *EvanT*, 55.

Chapter One—The Act and Being of God

of sinful human nature," writes Thompson, "means that the Holy Spirit is the positive power uniting God and humanity; it is nothing in us that does so." Thompson continues in saying that "Barth points out in a way that has scarcely been mentioned in any writings on the subject that the traditional manner of relating God and humanity in the incarnation *anhypostatia* and *enhypostasia* is real by the Holy Spirit. Pneumatology plays a key role in Christological doctrine."[98]

To apprehend the essence and reality of God clearly, humanity is in need of the person of the Spirit. So, as Barth states, the event of revelation has "clarity and reality on its subjective side because the Holy Spirit, the subjective element in this event, is of the essence of God Himself."[99] Barth's movement beyond the binding of the Spirit to the concept of love is further realized through such understanding of the Spirit being the one, who according to Barth, "makes us ready to listen the Word, that He Himself intercedes with us for Himself, that He Himself makes the speaking and hearing of His Word possible among us."[100] Therefore, might it be adjudged that the Spirit be thought of more along the lines of the one from whom humanity finds, amongst other things, the power of our imaginative capabilities?[101] Indeed, the Spirit surely does illumine love—that of the Father and the Son, as well as the love from the Godhead unto humanity (cf. Rom 5:5)—yet from His personal presence, humanity not only sees the work of the "recreating Spirit," but, through the Spirit we are set free, sanctified and transformed. Smail writes that the Spirit is:

---

98. Thompson, *Holy Spirit*, 42–3.

99. *CD* I/1, 466.

100. *CD* I/2, 221.

101. Admittedly the language of imagination is not used by Barth, but the concept being employed here does build upon the idea suggested by Barth that it is the Spirit who clarifies and makes ready the reception of God's revelation. It is the Spirit that allows for the eternality of time to enter into the temporality of time. Thus, John McIntyre writes, "The Spirit enables the believing readers to re-enact the past . . . Because in re-enacting that past not only are we enabled to stand where the saints and prophets, as well as the sinners and the perjurers stood, we are also introduced to that dimension of their lives and situations which made them worthy to be recorded and to have any meaning for us." Furthermore, the life of Jesus is not recorded and revealed simply to be read. Instead, the life of Christ confronts humanity through the action of the Spirit such that "many a person having read or heard of Jesus" account of the harvest being plentiful but the reapers few, has heard Jesus" words as if he or she were present, and responded to the appeal as if it were intended solely for them." Thus, the understanding of the Spirit as awakening our imaginative powers follows as McIntyre states, "what Barth used to describe as the Bible *becoming* the Word of God, bridging the gulf between then and now, so that God quite articulately speaks to them now out of a past which has miraculously been contemporanized" (McIntyre, *Shape of Pneumatology*, 272–73).

> the artist who shapes his people into countless creative portrayals of the risen Lord. First, with Jesus he changed the crucified humanity into the risen humanity in a way that preserved its identity but brought it to its fulfilment. Then, secondly in us, he takes the human material that makes you you and me me and, in a way that is authentic to what God made us and that preserves our created identity, he sets us free from our falleness and begins to sanctify and transform us into yet another portrait of Christ.[102]

Building then, from the foundation laid by Barth, and these thoughts given by Smail, might our theological account of the Spirit continue to press forward toward the fullness of our theological *becoming*? That is to say, if theology recognizes the power of the Spirit's direction for the world's stage, through His power to illumine the freedom of the stage, the possibility exists for our participation in God's Being-in-act through our imagining the hope of the eschaton enacted today. Today's theological endeavors might be further elevated if they begin to recognize such thoughts as those fostered by John McIntyre. McIntyre states that the Holy Spirit is, "God's imagination let loose and working with all the freedom of God in the world, and in the lives, the words and actions, of the men and women of our time."[103] Through the presence of the Spirit and His active role in revelation, humanity enters into and participates in the truth of the Godhead. From the Holy Spirit, writes Barth, humanity is given "an ability or capacity which is given to man as the addressee of revelation and which makes him a real recipient of revelation."[104] Humanity's imaginative reality is profoundly illumined and made clear by the Spirit. For those who have ears, let them hear what the Spirit says, as it is the Spirit who "guarantees man what he cannot guarantee himself, his personal participation in revelation."[105]

§5 Triune Revelation and Its Theological Importance

It is being argued that based upon the unified act of God that reveals both His act and His Being as illumined by Barth, theology is exposed to its proper role with regards to the Church and to the world, a role that should seek to be act. As Barth states, "God has conjoined Himself with man, existing in his own activity, and He has conjoined man existing in his own

---

102. Smail, *Giving Gift*, 180.
103. McIntyre, *Faith, Theology and Imagination*, 64.
104. *CD* I/1, 456.
105. *CD* I/1, 453.

activity with Himself. God is not idle but active. For good or evil, therefore, man must be active too."[106] Again, if what Barth is claiming to be the reality of our relationship with God, that it must be active, it seems that theology is true to our calling if we too respond through action on our part. This action manifests itself in the encouragement and call for the Church and humanity to respond positively to God's self-revelation by an intentional and active participation in His Being-in-act. God's self-revelation is, as Balthasar insists, "an initial glimpse of the divine Trinity," and as he continues "it is clear that the Trinity, and not Christology, is the last horizon of the revelation of God in himself and in his dramatic relationship with the world."[107] Revelation is the act of the Triune God that continues to this day to reveal the essence of His communal and relational being. In other words, as Barth remarks, "*God* reveals Himself. He reveals Himself *through Himself.* He reveals *Himself.*" And, as Barth continues, "If we really want to understand revelation in terms of its subject, i.e., God, then the first thing we have to realize is that this subject, God, the Revealer, is identical with His act in revelation and also identical with its effect. It is from this fact . . . that we learn we must begin the doctrine of revelation with the doctrine of the Triune God."[108] What must not be missed nor overlooked when speaking of revelation is the foundation in which it begins, God. This God, who is Father, Son and Holy Spirit, is relational; and from His love, He continually seeks and creates fellowship with humanity.

One of the main arguments stemming from this project, as it makes particular reference to the theologies of Balthasar and Barth, is that it is imperative for theology to recognize that its own foundation and purpose cannot be understood apart from Triune revelation; that is, the form which "God Himself in His revelation has assumed in our language, world, and humanity." This very form is, as Barth continues, "what we hear when with our human ears and concepts we listen to God's revelation, what we perceive (and can perceive as men) in Scripture, what proclamation of the Word of God actually is in our lives—is the thrice single voice of the Father, the Son, and the Spirit. This is how God is present for us in His revelation."[109] No amount of Christian theology can be done apart from the Being-in-act of the Godhead, for from the Triune God comes the truth of life; truth, as is being argued, that is made evident in revelation. Concerning Barth's notion of Christian theology, specifically "theological objectivity," Christoph

---

106. *CD* IV/1, 103.
107. *TD* V, *The Last Act*, 56.
108. *CD* I/1, 296.
109. *CD* I/1, 347.

Schwöbel writes, "this notion of 'theological objectivity' is developed in the context of emphasizing the need for doctrinal theology. This doctrinal theology is not based on received truths of traditional doctrine, but on the truth of God which is made self-evident in revelation, and which is the ground for the formulation of doctrine."[110]

Revelation opens theology up to the reality of God through the knowledge of His Being-in-act. Concerning our knowledge of God through His act, Barth writes that "the knowledge of God can be understood only as the bestowal and reception of this free grace of God . . . in this act of His free grace God makes Himself object to us and makes us knowers of Himself, the knowledge of this object cannot be fulfilled in neutrality, but only in our relationship to this act, and therefore only in an act, the act which is the decision of obedience to Him."[111] If Barth's claim is correct, that our knowledge of God is grounded in His action, and thus, a corresponding action on our part, then the implications pressed upon our theological endeavors seem to call for the *active* response of theology and humanity.

The knowledge of God is what gives theology its proper perspective as the truth of our practices are apprehended through the proclamation and action of God (His objectivity) and not on knowledge based on human subjectivity. Expounding upon the idea of the inner truth of God, and thus our self-knowledge of who "God is," Barth avers that the "inner truth of the lordship of God as the one supreme and true lordship revealed and operative in His proclamation and action—the inner truth and therefore also the inner strength of His self-demonstration as the Lord, as this Lord, consists in the fact the He is in Himself from eternity to eternity, the triune God, God the Father, the Son and the Holy Spirit."[112] Taking Barth's concept of God's self-revealing, then, revelation in its primary form reveals to theology the Being and act of its object; and thus, if desiring to be obedient to God, it would seem that theology should seek to be just as God, "not idle but active."

§6 The Action of Theology as Exposed through the Theo-Drama

The object of theology and the Church is the God whose Being-in-act seeks and creates fellowship with humanity. Barth writes that God's being is revealed in "the sphere of His action and working as it is revealed to us in

---

110. Schwöbel, *Cambridge Companion*, 25.
111. *CD* II/1, 29–30.
112. *CD* II/1, 47.

His Word. God is who He is in His works."[113] If Barth's claim is true, that the answer to who God is, is found in His act in His revelation, and that through the event of revelation we come to recognize God as Being-in-act, then theology's response to this God is most effective if in and of itself it is also act. It is based on this that I am arguing that the *dramatizing* of theology provides the most effective model for theology.

This project takes Barth's understanding of God as Being-in-act and makes the explicit move into the dramatic. If theology is obedient to its calling, which according to Barth is the act that exists when it guides the Church to seek "again and again to examine itself critically as it asks itself what it means and implies to be a Church among men,"[114] then the most effective model of theology, I am arguing, is developed through the *dramatizing* of theology. In other words, the action of theology as exposed through the Theo-drama is nothing other than a return to its core, which is found only in the Act and Being of the Father, Son and Holy Spirit. Balthasar, who was heavily influenced by Barth, attempted to do just this, to explicitly move towards the realm of the dramatic. In this last section of the chapter we will take an initial look at how the action of theology is exposed through the Theo-drama.

§6.1 Humanity's Participation in the *Theatrum Gloriae Dei*

The world, writes Balthasar, "is the stage which has been set up for the encounter of the whole God with the whole man—'stage,' not as an empty space, but as the sphere of collaboration of the two-sided form which unites in this encounter."[115] The intensity of this encounter is dramatically played out through the incarnation of the Word. Again, referring to the world, Balthasar remarks that the world "as an expression and image of God can only be rooted in the Word; its inmost essence rests upon the Word." And because of God's will to incorporate humanity into His salvific action, humanity is graciously granted the ability to hear and receive God's gift. Continuing then from his thought of the world being rooted in the Word, Balthasar writes that it is in "this foundation that we enter the sphere of hesitation, the sphere in which the Word of God may be heard or not heard, received or not received, answered or not answered. This is what is meant by saying that the entire created universe has come into being in, through and

---

113. Ibid., 260.
114. *GA*, 44.
115. *GL* I, 303.

for the Word."[116] Humanity is meant for the Word. To put it another way, humanity is meant for a participatory role in Christ's reconciliatory action, thereby displaying God's glory through our own action, or what might be called the faithful performances on the world's stage. This all occurs precisely because God has so willed that humanity's act be in accordance with His. As Barth writes, "In this primal decision God did not remain satisfied with His own being in Himself" but from all eternity has "caught up man into the sovereign presupposing of Himself."[117]

The deepening of our theological understanding through the employment of the theatre and its dramatic language can elevate our conception and understanding of God's dynamic action in His drawing in of humanity into His Being-in-act. Thus, one might begin to understand the depth of humanity's performance as that which takes place in what Barth writes is "this theatre of the great acts of God in grace and salvation." Further expounding, Barth writes that "Even as God's creatures, and within the world of other creatures, caught up in the great drama of being, we are not in an empty or alien place . . . If we take this seriously, our eyes are open to the fact that the created world including our own existence fulfils that purpose and constitutes that *theatrum gloriae Dei.*"[118]

Drawing from Barth's own notion of the *theatrum Gloria Dei*, the next natural movement is, as is being argued, is into the explicit use and employment of the language of the theatre. Indeed, Barth himself does not readily use the category of the drama,[119] but Balthasar, being immersed in Barth's Being-in-act centered theology did make this move and played out such implications explicitly through his *Theo-Drama*. Now, moving forward through the dramatic perspective, I am arguing for the *dramatizing* of theology, so as to fulfil our participation in God's threefold movement, (revelation, invitation, and reconciliation). It is only because this theatre (i.e., *theatrum gloriae Dei*) is the place of witness of God's glory that the

---

116. *TD* V, 106.

117. *CD* II/2, 168, 176.

118. *CD* III/3, 48.

119. Interestingly enough, while Barth does not explicitly employ the theatre or its dramatic language consistently in his theology, he does draw on a common foundation through his use of "saga." Saga is the story of God's action as it is embodied in the truth of his will. In *Dogmatics in Outline* Barth writes that "if we are to give the biblical narrative a name, or put it in a category, then let it be that of saga" (51). And then in *CD* III/1, in his discussion of the history of creation Barth writes that "in what follows I am using saga in the sense of an intuitive and poetic picture of a pre-historical reality of history which is enacted once and for all within the confines of time and space" (81). The point to be made is that both saga and drama push for the action of the Biblical narrative, or as will be argued throughout this project, the *becoming* of the narrative.

profundity of participation does occur. That is, because God has so chosen to incorporate humanity into His threefold movement, the possibility of our own faithful performances remains a real possibility. Indeed, the drama is God's, in Christ through the Spirit; and through his *Theo-Drama*, Balthasar expresses the essential fact that such drama is real, active, and personally involved. It is dramatic precisely because it is enfleshed in the action and life of Jesus Christ, who is the fullness of revelation, and who draws us into His faithful performance through the personal and intimate direction of the Holy Spirit. For, as Balthasar notes, when Paul writes his letters, history witnesses that they "testify with his whole life to the truth of revelation, putting God's action at the center but including himself . . . the drama comes from God, via Christ."[120] It is the action of the Triune God in Christ through the Spirit that originates and sustains the world's stage, as through revelation humanity comes to bear the marks of Christ. That is, upon the hearts of hearers—upon the scripts of flesh, the actors become the letter of Christ—a living, breathing, acting doctrine, written not with ink, but with the Spirit of the living God.[121]

§6.2 Recognition and Employment of the Theatricality of God's Action

The Bible is the attested account of the revealedness of the event of revelation. It is, notes Barth, the "sign of the promise . . . the witness to God's revelation and to that extent as the Word of God by which proclamation is to be measured."[122] This act and event of God is such an act that either compels or repels, there is simply no neutrality concerning God's interaction with humanity. This interaction is the epitome of the dramatic, as it magnifies the call of the Creator on the creature. Thus, the employment and recognition of the theatricality of God's action allows for theology to understand better such a call. Just as the theatre is "like a magnifying glass, and also like a reducing lens" that, continues Peter Brook, "narrows life down. It narrows it down in many ways. It is always hard for anyone to have one single aim in life. In the theatre, however, the goal is clear,"[123] so too is theology to be

---

120. *TD* II, 57.

121. 2 Cor 3:2–3. "You are our letter, written in our hearts, known and read by all men; being manifested that you are a letter of Christ, cared for by us, written not with ink but with the Spirit of the living God, not on tablets of stone but on tablets of human hearts."

122. *CD* I/1, 288.

123. Brook, *Empty Space*, 110.

for the Church and society. The call is to magnify the reduction of life *into* Christ thereby ultimately realizing the *one* goal of God's performance, the reconciliation of the world's stage and the eternality of life. Reconciliation of the world's stage occurs when the actors do not simply speak their lines, but perform them. Balthasar writes:

> Proclamation of the word of salvation—which is incumbent upon us—will not elicit faith if the herald himself does not fashion his life into a dramatic word of testimony. Neither faith, contemplation nor kerygma can dispense us from *action*. And the libretto of God's saving drama which we call Holy Scripture is worthless in itself unless, in the Holy Spirit, it is constantly mediating between the drama beyond and the drama here. It is not a self-sufficient armchair drama; its very form shows it to be a multifarious testimony pointing to an action at its core that goes beyond all words.[124]

The realization of God's act is made *real* through theology's response to the Spirit, so as to participate faithfully in God's drama. It is a drama that reveals itself through God's revelation, a revelation that is, writes Balthasar, God's action "in and upon the world and the world can only respond, and hence "understand", through action on *its* part."[125] Much of today's theology however, fails to recognize fully the dramatic revelation of the Triune God. The argument of this project is that theology should continue to respond to God's call for participation, thereby awakening the Church and society to the invitation of God to participate in His reconciliatory performance.

The truth and foundation of revelation, and its focus on God's desire for reconciliation, remain securely rooted in the miracle and act of the "actual human existence of the Revealer of God who is God Himself."[126] From this revelation the truth of the world's stage is illumined; that the Father was in Christ reconciling the world to himself, that He invites every captive to participate through the Spirit in His life on earth, and that He promises to return for those who eagerly wait for Him.[127] For this all to be understood properly, theology should continue to emphasize that the action and event of the stage stem directly from the Godhead; that, as Barth writes, "we have to understand the very Godhead, that divine being and event and therefore Himself as One who takes part in it, in the light of the fact that it pleased

---

124. *TD* I, 22.
125. *TD* I, 15.
126. *CD* I/2, 187.
127. 2 Cor 5:20; Luke 4:18; Heb 9:28.

Chapter One—The Act and Being of God

God—and this is what corresponds outwardly to and reveals the inward divine being and event—Himself to become man."[128]

The action of the Godhead is the fullness and completeness of Being, a reality revealed through the event of revelation. Through God's threefold movement of revelation, invitation, and reconciliation that humanity is provided with the breadth of possibility so as to fulfil its faithful performance on the world's stage. It is the Word and Spirit that invite humanity on to the stage, thereby giving meaning and breadth to the life of the drama. What is being argued throughout this thesis is that theology is dramatic in character, and because of this, gains tremendous assistance from the theatre in the attempts to best communicate God's action.

God's action and presence through the Word and Spirit, sustains and supports the world's stage. Concerning God's interaction with humanity, Walter Eichrodt comments, "Word and Spirit are given an internal rationale in the relationship of Logos and Pneuma as Persons of the Trinity, in whom, emerging from the transcendent divine glory, the One God condescends to men and becomes conceivable to them, without in any way surrendering His absolute otherness."[129] Again, moving theology into the dramatic highlights the fact that, through the threefold act of the Godhead, humanity is awakened to our potentiality and profundity as found in and from the Being of God. Through the revelatory performance of Christ through the Spirit, humanity is able to apprehend its own meaning thereby participating in the salvific action of the Godhead.

As is being argued, the Church and academy can deepen their understandings and recognition of the foundational act and essence of the divine drama through the dramatizing of theology. This essence is realized through the Being and Act of God, which at times is separated through the focus on either the act or the Being of God at a given time. However, as Balthasar insists, "this separation is a profoundly anti-dramatic undertaking; theologically speaking, it is a regression to a static, essentialist theology which, in its doctrine of God, doctrine of man, Christology, and so forth, imagines it can say things about "beings" before the action of these beings is either ascertained (in the case of man) or at least revealed (in the case of God)."[130] Theology can realize the fullness of God only through His *being* and *act*, which is administered through the revelation of God. This revelatory act is initiated only in and from the action of Father, Son and Spirit. The dramatic revelation of God is *His* dramatic revelation. It is, as Barth writes:

---

128. *CD* IV/1, 129.
129. Eichrodt, *Theology of the Old Testament*, 80.
130. *TD* II, 12.

> the *Deus revelatus* who is the *Deus absconditus*, the God to whom there is no path nor bridge, concerning whom we could not say nor have to say a single word if He did not of His own initiative meet us as the *Deus revelatus*. Only when we have grasped this as the meaning of the Bible do we see the full range of its statement that God reveals Himself, i.e., that He has assumed form for our sake . . . To deny that is to deny revelation itself . . . The fact that God takes form means that God Himself controls not only man but also the form in which He encounters man . . . The divine Word is the divine speaking.[131]

God's love poured out for all humanity is an act of grace and love originating from the One who is "this loving God without us as Father, Son and Holy Spirit, in the freedom of the Lord who has His life from Himself."[132] Thus, He who defines reality enters into humanity so as to reorient the stage through love. This love pours out from God, who seeks and creates fellowship between Himself and us with such intensity that it searches out the depths of our being, while piercing through the superficial realm so as to thwart every attempt on humanity's part to make itself out to be the divine creator–displacing God for the sake of humanity. Even more, this dynamic action is the sweet whisper of reconciliation, it is the great "yes" that supersedes humanity's "no." The dramatic action of God through revelation is the all-conquering and all-consuming love of the Father, Son, and Spirit that insists on drawing humanity into participation upon the world's stage. Through this dramatic participation, the Church and her theologians enter into the Theo-drama, thereby making possible the proper perspective for the Church and the world at large.

Rather than allowing the Bible to remain a story to be observed, analyzed and commented upon, I am arguing that the proper role of theology in God's drama is to continue to remind the Church of her object, thereby exposing to the world the loving interaction of God with his creation. God's interaction in His drama is "an event, happening or action in which, through our knowing of certain this-worldly realities, we are drawn into a relationship with a reality lying beyond this world altogether."[133] The transcendent event of revelation is intricately involved with God's immanent love, as His being as God is not, writes Barth, "exhausted by this dialectical transcendence which, however strictly it may be understood, must always

---

131. *CD* I/1, 321.
132. *CD* II/1, 257.
133. Hart, *Regarding Karl Barth*, 17.

be understood with equal strictness as immanence."[134] Revelation is God's self-communication to His creation. Humanity is freely invited to participate in Christ's self-sacrificial (Eucharistic) and self-surrendering (eschatological) performance.

The determination of God for us is the eternal moving into time, the drama of history that beckons the participatory performance of the Church and her theologians. The revelation of God as witnessed and proclaimed in the Bible is the dramatic event in which humanity participates. Through creation, God has provided the people and the place for this grand drama to occur. The theatre of His glory reveals the interaction between the Creator and the creature. Theology today needs to be mindful of its object so as to realize and enact its faithful performance in God's drama. As Barth notes, "the event in which revelation occurs must be seen in connection with what has happened once for all in this act. All fulfilled time must be seen as filled with the fullness of this time."[135] The revelatory action of God is *dramatic* in its form and in its content. In light of this, then, it will be argued, the most effective theological mode of happening is through the *dramatizing* of theology.

---

134. *CD* II/1, 264.
135. *CD* I/1, 119.

Chapter Two—Theological Expression

> God does not play the world drama all on his own; he makes room for man to join in the acting. In other words: when God, acting in Jesus Christ, utters, expresses himself, his language must be intelligible to the world, or at least *become* intelligible through the divine Spirit, who teaches men's hearts to listen and to speak so that they can utter a word in reply.[1]

§1 Introduction

THE BIBLICAL SCRIPT REVEALS to humanity that the heart of the Christian message is "God with us." If, as Barth claims is true, this message is the description of God's act, "which is His being" and that this is linked with the fact that "God is to be found alone in His act because alone in His act He is who he is,"[2] what, then, is the most effective form of theological expression that will most effectively unpack God's Being-in-act? Indeed, the story of Scripture is recognized through our theological investigations and exegetical work. However, if left in this stage of investigation, there remains more than a tendency towards the elevation of detachment (observation, analysis, discussion, etc.) over against a contemplative and participatory reality. The reasons behind this could be said to be on the one hand, a lack of understanding scripture as being "revelatory in that sense by virtue of the fact that it *participates* in those things—persons and events—that we call revelation,"[3] and thus, calling for a participatory response. On the other hand, dwelling on observation, analysis, etc., over against participation might be the lasting effect of the inability to employ an appropriate theological model that invokes performance. Inevitably, the inability of *some* uses of theological language to emphasize God's call for participation has the effect of relegating God's revelatory performance

---

1. *TD* II, 91.
2. *CD* II/1, 272.
3. Gunton, *A Brief Theology of Revelation*, 108.

to nothing more than a story about God and humanity. This relegation runs the risk of projecting our ideas on God's Being-in-act, thus, falling prey to what Barth claimed could happen to theology if God's action and His expectation of participation are not kept central, that is, to "become either openly or secretly thoughts about ourselves."[4]

Theological endeavors that simply seek to define and discuss God's communication and to treat it as being "just" communication, fail to realize the character and purpose of Christ's faithful performance; a performance that seeks to incorporate the whole of humanity. This incorporation is the ultimate foundation of *becoming*; for, as Balthasar writes, the process of *becoming* "attains its definitive shape, ultimately in full participation in the life of the Trinity."[5] The revealing of God seeks incorporation, while always being the revelation of His performative Being.[6] Our full participation in the "life of the Trinity" is exposed through the act and Being of God as revealed in and through Scripture. Balthasar writes that through Scripture we are given the words of Jesus "actually uttered but formulated in an inchoate and preliminary manner, which are now fleshed out in a linguistic form appropriate to the new understanding."[7] The question then, if Balthasar is correct, is: what form or model of theology is appropriate?

This chapter builds upon Balthasar's use and insistence that the Theo-drama is a drama that God does not play all on His own. In our exploration of two common models of theology today, narrative and dramatic, the hope is to obtain a "linguistic form appropriate to the new understanding." In this chapter, we will look at each of these models of theology in the hopes of comprehending the most effective way in which theology can expose the realization that "God does not play the world drama all on his own; he makes room for man to join in the acting."[8]

---

4. *CD* II/1, 272.

5. *TD* V, 101.

6. The separation of revelation and divine discourse as attempted by Kevin Vanhoozer will be taken up in the next chapter. While Vanhoozer attempts to distinguish that this separating act is not to "displace Christ but to serve as a means for offering appropriately 'thick descriptions' of him," he ends up *telling* more *about* Christ as opposed to *interacting with* (showing in action) the profundity of Christ's performance through the revelatory action of the Godhead. Such action seeks to incorporate humanity into this performance—it does so through the definite means of Scripture, for sure, but does not attempt to act outside of Christ's performance for to do so would de-dramatize the drama making it nothing more than an expanded *divine discourse*. Cf. chapter 3 of this book; Vanhoozer, *Drama of Doctrine*, 44–50.

7. *TD* II, 106.

8. Ibid., 91.

Exploration into the ideas and employment of the narrative and the dramatic is important as the burden of the chapter—and book—rests within the ability to show that while both aspects are crucial to theology, it is through the *dramatizing* of theology that our faithful performances are realized. The first part of the chapter looks specifically into the narrative model of theology, which is one of the most common models of theology employed today. Secondly, the chapter takes up its argument and presentation of the *dramatizing* of theology by specifically looking into what a dramatic model of theology is. This section of the chapter presents an answer as to why we should use drama in modelling our theology; and it is a discussion of the positive influence the theatre can and should have on our theological practices.

§2 The Narrative Model of Theology

Our understanding of the narrative model and its language will benefit by highlighting some terms that have been theologically employed over the years. The use of narrative has a long theological tradition, and it is in this light that the discussion of narrative develops. The category of narrative, writes Hauerwas, "has been used, among other purposes, to explain human consciousness, to depict the identity of agents (whether human or divine), to explain strategies of reading (whether specifically for biblical texts or as a more general hermeneutic), to justify a view of the importance of 'story-telling' (often in religious studies through the language of 'fables' and 'myths'), to account for the historical developments of traditions, to provide an alternative to foundationalist and/or other scientific epistemologies, and to develop a means for imposing order on what is otherwise chaos."[9] The historical uses of narrative within theology show its tremendous impact and importance for our theological endeavors.

The use of narrative stems from its ability to connect us and our experiences to the experiences presented throughout the Bible. According to Johann Baptist Metz, "theology is above all concerned with direct experiences expressed in narrative language. This is clear throughout Scripture, form the beginning, the story of creation, to the end, where a vision of the new heaven and the new earth is revealed. All this is disclosed in narrative."[10] The significance, then, of narrative stems from its ability to connect the movements of history thereby allowing for closure, or rather, the connection of the beginning to the end. In other words, the strength of the narrative is

---

9. Hauerwas and Jones, *Why Narrative?*, 2 (hereafter cited as *WN*).
10. Metz in *WN*, 252.

drawn from the fact that the narrative, while intimately involved in a recounting or relating process, involves itself in the future, that is, the telling of what might or will happen, as well as in the realism of the present. The narrative use in theology has historically been played out through the two common forms of the lyric and the epic.

In his *Theo-Drama*, Balthasar discusses how the two most common forms of the narrative: epic and lyric are used theologically. At a very early stage writes Balthasar, "the river of Christian utterance splits into two streams: the lyrical . . . and the epic mode."[11] The epic tale or the epic story is understood to relate to a story incorporating myth, legend, folk tale and history. The aspect of the epic rounds out the fullness of the story as it contains characters, plot and some sort of incident—all of which are key elements in the narrative or novel. As Balthasar remarks, the epic's tendency is to restrict itself within the realm of description. Thus through the epic form of the narrative, theological language tends towards the descriptive attempts at "grasping the historical events as precisely as possible and describing them in their abiding 'universal significance.'"[12] Balthasar continues his assessment of the narrative in identifying that, in furthering our understanding of the narrative or story, there is the element of lyric which contains many of the same elements of the epic but tends, according to J.A. Cuddon, to "express the feelings and thoughts of a single speaker in a personal and subjective fashion."[13]

For Balthasar and his account of the lyric, "Lyrical means the internal motion of the devout subject."[14] Lyrical renderings of the story trace the trajectory of the emotional internal reality of the subject as realized and expressed through the events as they have happened throughout the span of time. The lyrical narrative is involved with the process of revealing reality, as it continually depicts or expresses the sentiments and occurrences of yesterday. Again, according to Balthasar, the lyrical narrative is the "vivid re-presentation, in its pristine originality, of what is a past event."[15] The profundity, then, of the narrative, both epic and lyrical, is that through the story of yesterday, as well as through the stories of imagined events and "histories" answers to today's existence are possibly recognized and made approachable; that is, the investigation into the past and the reading of its

---

11. *TD* II, 55–56.
12. *TD* II, 55.
13. Cuddon, *Dictionary of Literary Terms*, 225–35; 372–75.
14. *TD* II, 55.
15. Ibid.

story allows humanity to further its pursuit of the meaning of existence as it has been exposed throughout history, and in fiction and fantasy as well.

§2.1 The Importance of the Narrative

Narrative in many ways reveals life through its ability to draw us in, as often times we find similarities between our own narratives and the narratives of others. Because of the reality involved in narrative, humanity welcomes the epic tale of its history—laid out through events—as human history is discerned through such events. Concerning the events of history and their meaning, there is the continual need to realize the relational aspect of our stories. That is, as Michael Stanford writes, the "meaning of an event is not inherent in it, but lies rather in its relation to other events," thus bringing about its reliance upon narrative, as narratives are "stories that we tell about the significances that we find in history."[16] A man hanging on a cross does arguably have meaning, as it literally means that a man is hanging on a cross. However, the fullness of the specific God-man, Christ, being nailed to the Cross of Golgotha, finds the full meaning of this event through its relation to the events of the garden of Eden, OT prophesy and expectation, Israel's wandering and estrangement, Christ" birth and life, Herod's anger and slaughter, the religious leaders" hatred of Christ, the 1st century crucifixion of Him, and so on, all of which, while being individual narratives, are deeply interconnected in such a way that they each contribute to the entirety of the Biblical narrative and its meaning.

The importance of narrative is that it provides a structure of history, experienced in language that tells and retells these past significances thereby drawing a connection between our individual (particular) histories and those of life's history, and also providing a beginning and an end to the (grand) story. Alasdair MacIntyre posits that the narrative approach to understanding life is appropriate because "we all live out narratives in our lives, and because we understand our own lives in terms of the narratives that we live out, that the form of narrative is appropriate for understanding the action of others."[17] Through the narrative, humanity tells its history and is thus exposed to its foundation, which is the foundation of life, and history; this crucial use of the narrative marks an essential need of the narrative within theology.

Narrative, in its exposing humanity to its *purpose*, begins to draw out some clarity to life's meaning through its ability to allow the reader to

---

16. Stanford, *An Introduction to the Philosophy of History*, 197.
17. MacIntyre, *After Virtue*, 197.

construct a temporal reality in accordance with the movements of history's narrative. An important characteristic of narration is that it is at once, "linguistic, temporal and epistemological. Narratives concern the past. The earliest events recounted take on their meaning and act as causes *only* because of the later ones."[18] Narrative is not merely an attempt at constructing the reality of life's events, but "its structure inheres in the events themselves. Far from being a formal distortion of the events it relates, a narrative account is an extension of their primary features."[19] The apparent concreteness of narrative is directly connected to humanity's understanding of its own existence as that which is bound up in the world of stories. Many people view their lives as ongoing narratives; a collection of stories they tell and retell to themselves (and others) in the repeated attempts at life's meaning. Concerning this practice—the telling and retelling of our personal stories—Stanford writes that it is, (amongst other things), "an attempt to give meaning, both to our own lives and to the world about us. One may not see the meaning of one's own life as a whole, but one can find a meaning in this or that episode of the day's experiences."[20] The events of the personal (particular) story strung together only add to the fundamental quest of life's truth within the universal story of the human.

One novelty of narrative is that it serves to record the human experience, thereby emphasizing and telling of the events of history, as well as representing truth and moral issues that are critical to the societal anatomy of humanity.[21] A genuinely realistic narrative "does not borrow its form from literary tradition, but recovers it from the process of historical change; the plots and characters in realistic fiction (stories) show us what actually happened in history."[22] The recounting of past events offers the comfort of knowing that today is somehow connected to yesterday, beyond the simple chronological formula of time. The coherence of time and self-identity stems from the realization and recognition that through the narrative of time the individual gains a sense of their own identity.

From a Christian perspective, Jesus is the normative within the realm of faith, and it is His truth, and desire for interaction with His fellow participants, that underlies the reality of the personal narrative being that which lends to the further realization of the person. Richard Bauckham writes that a person's story is "integral to their identity, but also with the nature of a

18. Martin, *Recent Theories of Narrative*, 74.
19. Carr, *History and Theory*, 25:117.
20. Stanford, *An Introduction to the Philosophy of History*, 197.
21. Martin, *Recent Theories of Narrative*, 18–19.
22. Ibid., 62.

story: that it gains definitive meaning only in the light of its end, and that therefore even the provisional meaning we may find in it along the way depends on some kind of anticipation, explicit or implicit, of how it will end and what it will turn out to mean in the end."[23] The person's relation to Christ determines the theological meaning of each "individual" story. That is, first of all: are they *in* Christ's performance or attempting to create their own *original* performance? The importance, then, of theology recognizing the narrative's ability to connect life-stories, rests within God's expectation of theology to perform in accordance with His threefold movement (revelation, invitation and reconciliation), in Christ through the Spirit. It is this realness, the ability to connect stories and illumine meaning, as presented by the narrative, that continues to open each person up to the foundation of his/her personhood, as through the story people are presented with queries concerned with the reality of life's beginning and end. The reality of these specific events—the beginning and the end—connects directly to the reality of events in our own particular life stories, and thus, contributes to the process of comprehending identity through the on-going narrative. This reality, or the realism depicted through the narrative, is important in understanding who we are, as a "person's identity is not to be found in behavior, nor— important though this is—in the reactions of others, but in the capacity *to keep a particular narrative going*."[24] Thus, and this is the second point concerning our relation to Christ's performance: my identity is established and maintained through the story of me, my particularity as witnessed through Christ's particularity, as God has created each of us to "keep a particular narrative going." Indeed, these on-going stories intertwine with other stories, and necessarily so, as "No man is an island," but never is this intermingling the annihilation of the distinctness of our stories. Giddens comments that "the individual's biography, if she is to maintain regular interaction with others in the day-to-day world cannot be wholly fictive. It must continually integrate events which occur in the external world, and sort them into the ongoing "story" about self."[25]

§2.2 Narrative Movement: Dramatizing the Narrative

The need of a person for self-definition influences the ways in which humanity attempts to reconstruct the narrative of history, as to narrate is in some sense to know. Jeremy Tambling notes the interesting connection

23. Bauckham, *Cambridge Companion to Jesus*, 270.
24. Giddens, *Modernity and Self-Identity*, 54; italics in original.
25. Ibid., 54.

between narration and knowledge, writing that the "etymology of the word 'narrate,' relates to 'gnarus,' knowing (cp. 'cognoscere'): narrative is a way of knowing the world."[26] Knowledge of self and life are arguably contained within the narrative structure, as through humanity's stories the reality of life gains the possibility of its revelation. The contribution of the narrative is its relations to and recounting of life's events, in hopes of establishing a connection to a deepened meaning and understanding of life. Thinking back on Balthasar's argument concerning the epic and lyric dimensions, the hope is now to begin a movement into the dramatic. Commenting on the reality of the narrative becoming the dramatic, Wells writes that "the *dramatic* perspective synthesizes the strengths of the epic and lyric dimensions. Like the lyric, it does justice to the role of the subject, the way that events arise from the hearts and minds and actions of people, rather than from impersonal external forces. Like the epic, it perceives an object that has reason and validity beyond the subjectivity of the involved observer."[27] The narrative movement, then, is its dramatic use, in other words, the dramatizing of the narrative. Indeed, the narrative is given so as to teach and guide the Church, but must not stop there, as its teaching and guidance are incomplete until they reach participation in God's Being-in-act—His performance. This is to say that the word given in text is meant for performance—as indicated through the performative reality of the Incarnation. The movement of the narrative towards drama explicitly promotes a participatory reality in the on-going performances of the world's stage.

God has invited us into life's performance; He has "invited us to join with him in the grace of his movements, performing them just as he has taught us, so that we might awaken bodily and fleshly to a graceful performance that God is enacting in us and through us."[28] The theological use and understanding of the narrative *becoming* drama will procure ways of apprehending and thus, participating in life's truth.

Participating in life through the story is integral to the story's ability to account honestly for the characterization of both the social climate and the proper social being. Narratives "have traditionally provided an affirmation of social values," thereby establishing the validity of the narrative as the values which it highlights constitute our being as our ideas of "courage and cowardice, honesty and hypocrisy, justice, goodness, and fairness are all part of our social being."[29] What is more, in and through the narrative

26. Tambling, *Narrative and Ideology*, 94.
27. Wells, *Improvisation*, 47.
28. Hauerwas, *Performing the Faith*, 109.
29. Martin, *Recent Theories of Narrative*, 159.

there is also the possibility of new uses, innovation, creativity, and criticism of the current/accepted values and of current forms of "social being." The Bible does quite a bit of this through its narratives. Theology indeed needs the Biblical narrative, but must not remain limited to the text. There obviously is the need for interpretation and the like, but as Samuel Wells notes, theology must not "be just a verbal matter, written or spoken. It inevitably involves the organization of interpretation and its structuring into doctrine, but this exercise must always be a support to something else, not an end in itself. That something else is the embodiment of the text, the events it describes, its interpretation and systematic construal in the practices and performances of the community."[30] Bearing this in mind, the argument of this project is not for the abandonment of the narrative, but for the realization that God's act and incarnational performance call for a response from the entirety of the creation, as no one is outside of God's performance.

The movement of narrative towards drama, that is, and in particular, the theological recognition of its dramatic character, is what in the past has been identified as the dramatic use of the narrative, or the enactment of the narrative.[31] However, while recognizing the movement of narrative to drama, this project seeks to establish the intentional acknowledgement by theology of the theatre's profound possibilities for today's endeavors. Drawing from the argument once made by Alasdaire MacIntyre, Hauerwas writes that "human actions in general are but enacted narratives in which agents are at best but co-authors of their own narratives. The narrative of my life is but part of an interlocking set of narratives embedded in the story of those communities from which I derive my identity."[32] Christian faith is meant to be a participatory reality based upon the archetypal performance of Christ; this reality, as is being argued, is best illumined through the lens of the theodramatic.

The perpetuation of human knowledge is enhanced through narrative. Furthering this thought, the argument projected from this chapter maintains that the encouragement of the narrative *towards* the drama acknowledges this enhancement or "grasping together," but does not stop there. Instead, it moves into the expectation and realization of participation in the drama of life. Indeed, Christian faith must acknowledge the story of life, but theology must not allow it to remain here, it (theology) is to be true to its object Who is *act*. The drama of life is revealed through its *action* or better yet, its shared

---

30. Wells, *Improvisation*, 46.

31. See §4 of chapter 3 in this project, where examples of such uses by the likes of N. T. Wright, Theodore Wedel, Craig Batholomew and Michael Goheen, and Kevin Vanhoozer are discussed.

32. Hauerwas, *Performing the Faith*, 140.

actions and *interactions* before God. As Hauerwas notes, "Christian faith means that the church's witness is more than something spoken, debated, written about, discussed; it is a faith that is enacted, performed, fleshed out."[33] The fleshing out of faith is the theological movement that recognizes not only the need of the telling and re-telling of history, but the *becoming* of history. There exists a certain mutual belonging that oscillates between the narration of history and the fact of its *becoming*. According to Balthasar, what is dramatic about the movement or as we have called it, the *becoming* of history, is that this progress, "is not only that a spiritual being, an identity, can learn from the past, enrich himself in his present and plan his future; at each successive 'now,' he is able, through a free and responsible decision, to stamp the entirety of his finitude with a meaning that reflects, and is guaranteed by, the presence of the absolute (through conversion, for instance)."[34] It is when we pass on our stories that progress is made and the *becoming* of history is realized. For as Balthasar concludes in regards to the plan of world history, "progress can only be sought and found where the discoveries of one generation can be taken up and carried farther by the next,"[35] an action propagated through the continual telling of our stories.

A major theme, then, of this chapter is the desire for the narrative within theology to move to its fullness through its *becoming*. This process, this *becoming* "is what happens when words leave the page, when thoughts leave the mind, when actions ripple through other lives and cause further actions and furthers thoughts. It is what happens when narrative becomes drama."[36] This is not the denial of narrative within our theological endeavors, but the desire to overcome the subtle distance of the reader and author.[37] Writing of this distance, David Brown remarks that "the modern tendency is to treat words as though they were there simply to convey information, whereas the power of meditative practices lies precisely in their ability to force us beyond standing apart from the words into inhabiting what they are trying to convey."[38] Overcoming this subtle division occurs through the action (movement) of the narrative, an action that allows for the proper understanding of language's life-reflecting and life-forming capabilities. Indeed, a profound interconnectedness occurs between the writer and the

33. Ibid., 98.
34. *TD* IV, 88.
35. Ibid.
36. Wells, *Improvisation*, 46
37. For a further development of understanding the distance between the reader and the author of the narrative, see Martin, *Recent Theories of Narrative*, chapter 7.
38. Brown, *God and Mystery*, 67.

reader, the playwright and the audience; yet in saying as much, it is recognized that most often such interconnectedness occurs through the action and reality of our spoken deeds, that is, the intentional inhabiting of what the words are trying to convey.

Inhabiting the words is the "story breathed to life, the word made flesh." The importance, then, of the dramatic is, continue Johnson and Savidge, that it elevates the Biblical script to its performance calling, for each of us (the actors) to "tell the story by becoming the story."[39] The "becoming of the story" occurs, it is being argued, through the narrative *becoming* drama as it is rooted in the activity and action of dialogue and performance.[40]

§3 The Dramatic Model of Theology

The dramatic model of theology accepts the importance and power of drama and seeks to employ such energy and capability for its own endeavors. If Simon Shepherd and Mick Wallis are correct in writing that drama is "important and powerful because it can express the make-up of our species,"[41] then the assistance it (drama) can provide theology in ascertaining the answer to the question "who am I?" is invaluable. Furthermore, and specifically for theology, the ability to employ, and the special value of employing, a dramatic model is directly due to the dramatic way in which God has chosen to interact with humanity. According to Balthasar, "if there *is* such a thing as theo-drama, (however intangible it may be at its core), and if it is fundamentally the event of God becoming man and his action on the world's behalf, there must be dramatic ways (legitimately so) of presenting it, be they ever so indirect, risky, precarious, and ambiguous. And such

---

39. Johnson and Savidge, *Performing the Sacred*, 7, 58.

40. With this said, it is acknowledged that dialogue/speech deeds do not always have to occur between two "present" participants. For example, when reading a book, my mind's eye might begin to converse with the author or a character in the book, or when reading an essay I might engage with the thoughts of the author on how I agree or disagree with the points presented. Finally, when reading to someone, dialogue occurs on a multitude of levels, whether or not the listener is able to respond (I think of a baby or someone sick), as our lives interact through the movement of the narrative which is the opening up of the stage to the dramatic dimensions and realities of life. And this movement, the opening up of the stage, is brought about through the performance of the theatre, for as Peter Brook wrote, "I can take an empty space and call it a bare stage. A man walks across this empty space while someone else is watching him, and this is all that is needed for an act of theatre to be engaged" (*Empty Space*, 11). I thank Michael Partridge for raising the idea of the narrative and its dramatic function and ability when used as a means of interaction between peoples.

41. Shepherd and Wallis, *Drama/Theatre/Performance*, 60.

Chapter Two—Theological Expression

forms of presentation . . . must yield conclusions with regard to the nature of this same theo-drama."[42] The possibility and employment, then, of a dramatic model is a direct result of our encounter with God and His call on our lives and thus, our theology. The aim of the dramatic model is to bring "into center stage the *drama intrinsic to divine salvation.*"[43] This "drama" is the result of God's Being-in-act eternally for the sake of humanity, and it is this truth and action in which theology is called not only to expose, but also to participate in.

The move towards a dramatic model, that is, the action of the narrative *becoming* dramatic, is what is being called, the *dramatizing* of theology. However, this dramatization is not new. Nichols points out that the concept of the dramatizing of theology is an historical reality. Thus, how could we not think of and employ a dramatic model of theology when, writes Nichols, we consider:

> the mediaeval Passion-and-Resurrection plays that made salvation visible in a drama (and the plays of the Antichrist and Judgment that showed forth its eschatological dimension); the centering of drama on the mass in the endings of the plays for Corpus Christi and Calderon's *Great Theatre of the World*; the "postfiguration" of Christ's struggle in the martyrs in, say Corneille's *Polyeucte*—notably as seen through the eyes of Péguy; the way that Schiller (and more radically de-Christianized playwrights like Sartre and George Bernard Shaw) need the "laws of bronze" of the Church's teaching on faith and morals as the "absolute" against whose "necessity" their heroes can try their strength.[44]

Again, if is true, as Barth claims, that God is Being-in-act, and that through His dramatic revelation in Christ through the Spirit we have existence, might it then be concluded that our theological model should represent such dramatic action?

The dramatic model of theology follows the action of revelation and seeks to respond in accordance with this action. According to Balthasar, the dramatic model is a model steeped in the dramatic elements inherent in revelation. If, writes Balthasar, "revelation is the ultimate precondition on the basis of which existence (and its reflected image, drama) can experience genuine tragedy—and not a tragedy which dissolves in meaninglessness—the path is clear for us to get a view of the dramatic elements inherent

---

42. *TD* I, 112.
43. Nichols, *No Bloodless Myth*, 23.
44. Ibid.

in revelation itself."⁴⁵ The theological movement towards the drama is the intentional incarnation of the stories of the Bible. It is an enactment of and participation in these stories that on the one hand acknowledges the dramatic experience of the tragic, the joyous, the good, etc., while on the other hand realizes such experiences are all enveloped in the boundless grace of God. The stories of the Bible tell us as much, for as Barth writes, "in the Christian concept of the creation of all things the question is concretely one of man and his whole universe as the theatre of the history of the covenant of grace; of the totality of earthly and heavenly things as they are to be comprehended in Christ (Eph. 1:10)."⁴⁶ The Christian is called not simply to recognize such acts, but to participate in them. As Joachim Jeremias points out, "Jesus did not confine himself to spoken parables, but also performed parabolic actions."⁴⁷ Thus, for example, upon the reading or hearing of God's command to "love thy neighbor as thyself," or of the story told by Christ to His disciples concerning the "good Samaritan," a person would then enact the very principles being taught through their participation in Christ's eternal performance of love and reconciliation. Such enactment might be: the calling of an old friend to see how they are doing; the care of the outcast or down-trodden; the feeding of the poor at the local soup kitchen; the visiting of a prisoner; the clothing of the unclothed; or the invitation of a stranger to dine with you. The point to be made is that theology's role in God's drama is to elevate and dramatize God's call for participation in His work on earth. Thus, the movement or *becoming* of narrative to drama evokes the foundational element of participation harkening to God's revelatory and reconciliatory invitation, embodied and performed through His incarnational act.

A dramatic model of theology adheres to the Biblical reality that is itself inherently dramatic. "The nature of the events described in the Bible," writes Harris, "is often inherently theatrical. At the heart of the narrative is the transformation of Word into flesh."⁴⁸ The enfleshment of the Word stands at the center of the dramatic model as it represents the fullness of our theological performance. Drawing further from the thoughts of Harris, the dramatic model illumines the reality that "there is a transformation effected when word becomes performance . . . the Christian concept of God's mode of self-revelation is theatrical."⁴⁹ Through God's threefold movement of revelation, invitation and reconciliation, the transformation of the human is

---

45. *TD* I, 123.
46. *CD* III/1, 44.
47. Jeremias, *The Parables of Jesus*, 36.
48. Harris, *Theater and Incarnation*, 8.
49. Ibid., 12.

enacted; a transformation that invites us to comprehend God's performance so as to gain and to develop the fullness of our performance, and thus, our own *being-in-act*.

Focusing on performance is insightful for today's theological endeavors, because as Schechner writes, "performance is always embodied or embedded at particular places in specific times."[50] Specifically in a theological perspective, performance in this aspect can prove to be helpful if understood in light of Christ's particular performance in a particular place and a particular time that continues to remain the *ideal* and judge of all performances. What this means is that all action on the world's stage is confronted by God's particular action in Christ's performance.

Performance's foundation of action and interaction further highlights the interactive reality of God with His creature. As Trevor Hart notes, "performance is suggestive in theological terms because of the fundamental religious conviction that human life is indeed lived (a work "played out") not just in the sight or hearing of other people, but before a God who (however else he may be held to be involved in things) looks on and listens with great interest, and makes judgments about what he sees and hears. This conviction grants all life lived in terms of a "performative" aspect from beginning to end."[51] Christ's performance is the "ideal," or "original model" of the stage's action. This is so due to the fact that, as Balthasar writes, "the whole history of the human race, which is transformed in its whole nature by the hypostatic union, cannot ultimately stand over against Christ as independent of him; it will attain its final justification, its ultimate meaning, solely because it comes within the realm of the life and lordship of him to whom is given "all authority in heaven and on earth" (Matt 28:18).[52]

Christian personhood can only be claimed through participation *in* Christ. According to Balthasar, "this participation is what makes conscious subjects into persons in the Christian sense."[53] What this freedom of choice accentuates theologically is that our performances are not to be understood theoretically, but practically. Theological performances are the reality of Jesus" words "Go and do likewise" being acted and lived out on the world's stage. In other words, performance is to be taken as the conscious action with its trajectory centered *in* Christ that runs straight through to the eschaton. Performance is the epitome of Matthew 25, that is, the fulfilment of

50. Schechner, *Performance Studies*, 2.
51. Hart and Guthrie, *Faithful Performances*, 3.
52. *TH*, 114.
53. *TD* III, 207. See also §2 in chapter 4 as well as the discussion of freedom in chapter 5.

Christ's words when He says, "Truly I say to you, to the extent that you *did* it to one of these brothers of Mine, even the least of them, you *did* it to Me."

Bearing in mind, then, the pursuit of humanity's comprehension and apprehension of the enactment of the truth of *being*, Balthasar highlights that the profundity of the drama within the Bible is "God's initiative . . . And if "the Word becomes flesh" more and more profoundly, unto death on the Cross, it follows that, in the drama God enacts with mankind, not the least particle of the human and its tragic dimension will be lost."[54] Drama reflects the fullness of God's action—it is the opening up of the stage to the reality of *becoming*. In other words, the employment of drama illumines the essence of being human. Paul Harrison writes that the "quality of becoming and being human is dramatic . . . God communicates Being through the dramatic Word."[55] Through the drama of life, humanity participates in the reality of God's threefold movement as revealed through His performance in Christ through the Spirit. God's incarnational performance in Christ calls forth the movement of the Biblical script to realize its performative essence. Thus, using a model of theology that intentionally realizes the possibility and reality of life being, amongst other things, a performance, theology enters into the recognition of God's life as performance.

§3.1 The Benefits of Drama for Theology

The chapter explicitly calls for theology's recognition and use of drama. It calls for the reality as reflected in and taken up in performative studies, as well as theatrical language, to be employed in the practices of the academy and the church. The benefits of a dramatic model of theology rest within one of the fundamental characteristics of drama: action. If God is Being-in-act, the use of drama seems to be a natural step in our practices that is pregnant with possibility. Martin Esslin writes in *An Anatomy of Drama*, "what makes drama drama is precisely the element which lies outside and beyond the words and which has to be seen as action—or *acted*—to give the author's concept its full value."[56] This section seeks to emphasize the profound instrument drama can be, and is, for our theological endeavors. As humans we understand the reality of acting, role playing, character development, movement, playing a part, pretending, putting on a good performance, imagination, wearing or putting on a mask (both metaphorically and physically), dialogue, playing out a scene, the stage of life, watching the scene

---

54. *TD* II, 53
55. Harrison, "Toward a Dramaturgical Interpretation," 390.
56. Esslin, *An Anatomy of Drama*, 14.

before us; the list could go on, but the point to be taken from the aforementioned, which is a listing of common phrases, ideas or actions from drama, is the overt and familiar connection of life and theatre. Many will nod in affirmation and acceptance of Shakespeare's assertion that "All the world is a stage, and all the men and women merely players,"[57] the question remains of the impact this has or will have on today's theological endeavors.

If theology is to employ a dramatic model, there needs to be more than a simple borrowing of drama's concepts and language. Rather, there should be a full appreciation and acknowledgement of the positive influence drama and performance studies can and do have on today's theological endeavors. One such acknowledgement or recognition is the fact that the theatre's performative means engage the audience in the "expectation of a communal exercise of human faculties, intellectual and affective alike, with which to cultivate life's drama in representational form."[58] The theatre presents life through the staged action; action that draws from a text (story), plan or teaching, but gains its energy and life through its interaction and performance with the entirety of the theatre (audience, director, players, stage crew, theatre workers and author). The theatre will always survive, for as Balthasar remarks, "life manifests a fundamental urge to observe itself as an action exhibiting both meaning and mystery."[59] Humanity's continual need to see itself mirrored, writes Balthasar, "makes the theatre a legitimate instrument in the elucidation of being."[60] If, then, Balthasar is correct, the theatre has a tremendous amount of potential and power in assisting theology in its continual task of the "elucidation of being."

§3.1.1 Understanding our Humanity through a Dramatic Model

Humanity is inherently dramatic, constituted through our relations and interactions with our fellow performers on the world's stage, and thus, the interactive language and foundation of drama are natural. Furthermore, the use of drama in theological terms, concepts and dialogue encourages the embodiment of theory. In other words, rather than allowing theology to be primarily about doctrine, creeds and propositions, drama issues an explicit call towards performance. Through performance, then, theology is able to put "flesh" on its creeds, on its doctrine and on its theories, thereby avoiding

---

57. Shakespeare, *As You Like It*, II.vii.139–42.
58. Khovacs, "Divine Reckonings," 221.
59. *TD* I, 78–79.
60. *TD* I, 86.

the temptation towards an "intellectual" faith as opposed to an active and living faith.

Humanity is relational, we are social beings; and as Tracy Davis writes, "we negotiate life as social beings—sometimes but not always consciously, sometimes but not always overtly—we perform. *As we perform, we are also historical.*"[61] We are historical in the very sense that we interact with other beings (players) thereby interacting with the past through their histories while together performing in the present. Our identity, both socially and historically, encompasses the whole of who we are, that is, corporeally, individually, emotionally, etc. Identity is a complex matter, socially and historically, and drama is able to gather so much of it together, in one enactment. This social and historical aspect of life represents the social dramatic foundation of reality, and thus, in studying social dramas, which are constituted by the social events performed every day, the "anthropologist can reveal the values of a community."[62] It is from performance, then, that the understanding of our identity—our person—is expanded, for in "performance studies 'bodies' are corporeal not merely textual, and 'speech' emanates from people with corporeality as well as identities."[63]

The use of performance in theology safeguards against any platonic notions or ivory tower speculations, as performance is rooted in action and the sharing of our life experiences. As R.A. Banks notes, "drama begins with the words on the page, but it rapidly moves off the page, through the imaginations of those who 'realize' the words in performance and those who share the dramatic experience as audience and participants, into a new creation."[64] Theologically, this interactive reality of drama and life, stems from God's incarnational performance, which provides a framework of praxis and dialogue so that we might be able to present to society and the Church, God's desire for our participation in His threefold act. The theatre offers tremendous tools to further theology's endeavors through the theatre's embodiment of the central tenets of Christianity. As Johnson and Savidge write:

> The fact that live human beings embody the characters of a play speaks of the *incarnate* nature of God in Christ. The fact that the actors perform for a live audience highlights the *communal* nature of theatre and reflects the Trinity: Father, Son, and Holy

---

61. Davis, *The Cambridge Companion to Performance Studies*, 7 (hereafter cited as *TCCPS*).

62. Shepherd and Wallis, *Drama/Theatre/Performance*, 46.

63. Davis, *TCCPS*, 6.

64. Banks, *Drama and Theatre Arts*, 13.

Spirit in relationship. The fact that the relationship between audience and performer allows for interaction and influence between the two speaks of the *presence* of God transforming the world through nature and grace.[65]

Through God's *incarnational* performance, He invites humanity into His *communal* performance, which is His presence. This very invitation by God is an action that humanity cannot remain neutral towards, as it elicits a response. Likewise, the theatre itself awakens a response from the audience. This ability to elicit a response takes its direction from the Greek theatre, which intentionally involved the audience in the play. The ancient Greek spectator, writes Martha Nussbaum, "saw across the staged action the faces of fellow citizens on the other side of the orchestra. And the whole event took place during a solemn civic/religious festival, whose trappings made spectators conscious that the values of the community were being examined and communicated. To respond to these events was to acknowledge and participate in a way of life."[66] The theatre today continues much of these same sentiments, as many of its theorists, authors and playwrights intentionally script plays that not only elicit a response from the theatregoer but seek also to involve him/her in ways of life so as to examine our values. One only need to think of plays/musicals currently playing on, or have played on Broadway, shows such as *Wicked, American Idiot,* and *West Side Story*. Beyond these few examples there always remain classics such as *Rent, Les Misérables, Tobacco Road* or *The Sound of Music*. The point to be made is that the theatre has a tremendous amount of potentiality for theology's pursuit of its faithful performance.

Regarding the modern theatre and its playwrights, specifically those from the mid 1900's and onward, Banks notes that they write "in terms of man's being trapped in his own situation and his attempt to examine his relationship with it."[67] The continuing element within the theatre is the examination of humanity and its condition and situation in life. Theology's instruction from theatre and its practitioners allows for the potential movement and reality of dramatizing theology. Understanding how the theatre, playwrights, dramaturges use theatrical elements (text, language, audience, stage, performance, etc.) gives proper credence to any theological use of such terms and ideas, as it is being argued that the theatre provides a profound way for theology to explore its own dramatic being.

---

65. Johnson and Savidge, *Performing the Sacred*, 11.
66. Nussbaum, *Love's Knowledge*; quoted by Khovacs, "Divine Reckonings," 199.
67. Banks, *Drama and Theatre Arts*, 257.

Today's theological endeavors gain much depth in acknowledging the different uses of drama that we find in playwrights like Shakespeare, Calderon, Stanislavski, Beckett, Brecht, Brook, Artaud, etc. . . . Balthasar writes that the drama has much to offer through its fullness, its entirety. For example, "The actor," writes Balthasar, "puts himself and all the powers of his soul, including his emotions, at the service of the work of art, at the service of the part he is to play . . . the actor is his own sculptor, he is both conductor and orchestra."[68] Drawing then from Stanislavski's use of drama, Balthasar writes that his (Stanislavski) method "exemplifies this simultaneity with such passion" and has much to say to our theological practices and the need for them to "consist in total dedication to the role." Commenting on Stanislavski's use of drama, Balthasar writes:

> *Stanislavsky's* method consists in a total dedication—encompassing body, mind and soul—to the role, a total mobilization for its sake. *Disponibilité*: here the whole human system is made available, beginning with relaxation exercises . . . observation exercises to overcome our everyday distractedness and semiattention . . . to the total activization of the imagination . . . This training aims at enabling the actor convincingly to embody the reality of the (poetic) role, to "substantiate" its "truth" . . . There is something sacramental about *Stanislavsky's* method.[69]

Looking at the possible implications for theology from Stanislavski, we might make a connection through a sort of "theological *disponibilité*." In other words, our theological *disponibilité* would be the complete turning over of our endeavors to the leading and guidance of God, so as to "embody the reality of role." In doing this, the hope would be to substantiate not only the truth of our role, but more importantly, the truth of God's role for both the Church and the world.

The truth of life can and will allow for the continued exposure to the question of "who am I?" Drama aids in this quest to understand our personhood, as human existence, claims Balthasar, can "only be taken in complete seriousness—and that, accordingly, the Christian revelation can only appear in its full stature—if it is presented as being dramatic *at its very core*."[70] Thus, another example we could highlight, of drama assisting in moving closer to a deepened understanding of humanity's identity, might be from the work and thoughts of Peter Brook. Brook's work illumines how the theatre acts as a tool for self-exploration, as through its (theatre) evocation of

---

68. *TD* I, 287.
69. *TD* I, 288–89.
70. *TD* II, 51.

performance, we are called to participate in the past in order to understand the ontological, epistemological and teleological realities of today. Drawing from Jerzy Grotowski, Brook writes, "the theatre is a vehicle, a means for self-study, self-exploration, a possibility of salvation. The actor has himself as his field of work. This field is richer than that of the painter, richer than that of the musician, because to explore he needs to call on every aspect of himself . . . acting is a life's work—the actor is step by step extending his knowledge of himself through the painful, everchanging circumstances of rehearsal and the tremendous punctuation points of performance."[71] Using, then, Brook's theatrical understanding, we can deepen our theological understanding and performance. That is, we (theology) play an essential role in life's performance, but if we do not explore or "call on every aspect" of ourselves, and the methods by which we interact with life, the possibility remains for a poor performance. Theologically, a poor performance is the absence of theology in the Church, thereby opening up the potentiality of society, and not theology, guiding and instructing the Church body.

The richness drama has to offer theology can be further realized if theology seeks to understand the way in which playwrights intentionally construct and use the script so as to elevate the awareness and profundity of the performance. One such example is Samuel Beckett. Concerning Beckett and his understanding of language's performance, Andrews Kennedy writes:

> Here (discussing Lucky's speech in *Waiting for Godot*) there emerges, from the wreckage of syntax, the lost or potential beauty of human utterance. The speech is placed and organized in such a way that the pathological breakdown in language—the agony of lost meaning—becomes a source of creative energy in the play.
>
> It is necessary to affirm that this paradoxical experience is given as an immediate response in performance (it was what one experienced when the play was first performed in Paris and London) so as to underline that the dramatic "sense" of Lucky's speech does not depend on subsequent close reading. Even a first reading or hearing should yield at least two perceptions: the decay of rational language expresses the decay of one kind of order—that constructed by theology and other "logy" systems which turn man's hunger for *logos* into formulae; and, as the speech runs on and down . . . the deteriorating syntax releases . . . isolated word-clusters which sound like the lost "true voice" in speech.[72]

---

71. Brooks, *Empty Space*, 66.
72. Kennedy, *Six Dramatists*, 139–40; my insertion for clarification.

Understanding the careful construction and use of language in a theatrical script elevates the awareness of the stage's representation of life's reality and the presentation of life's interactions. This can prove helpful when theologians seek to elevate the awareness and presentation of life's interactive reality as presented and exposed through the Biblical script. There are many ways in which drama and theology overlap, and the hope throughout this project is to continue not only to highlight this connection, but also, to show how drama provides even more tools for our theological interpretations, exegesis and investigations of the Bible. The use and employment of dramatic tools will allow the continual theological push that intentionally seeks to move beyond a mere observation into participation.

Both the Bible and Lucky's speech interact with and draw in humanity today. In some sense, the techniques employed by Beckett and his staging of the scene mirror many of the "scenes" in the Bible. In doing so, Beckett has created a certain timelessness in his play and yet there remains a particularity, as it *is* specifically Lucky's speech. Furthermore, the speech affects the audience immediately while also having the ability to be heard, and the excitement of being heard, multiple times over. This "timelessness," or actualized recognition of temporal within the eternal, follows the dramatic nature of the creature being *in* the Creator. Concerning the reality of time for life, Balthasar writes, "there is a deep analogy between time and eternity, so eternity can always be inside time, just as time can participate in eternity."[73] The theatre's ability to maintain timelessness within every temporal performance furthers the unity between drama and theology. Such technique and practice holds tremendous potential for theology in its attempts to perform faithfully within the theatre of God's glory. Theology's acknowledgement and use of drama is the recognition of the need to remain true to the *active event* of God's revelatory performance; an event that is initially exposed through the encounter of the narrative but fully realized through the dramatic.

§3.1.2 The Expression of the Text and of Life through Performance

The use of drama provides the ability for theology not only to recognize the Biblical drama, but also to participate faithfully in its action. The theatre can help theology bring the Biblical text to its full expression, thereby bringing life to its full expression. As French actor, author, director and theorist of the theatre Antonin Artaud wrote, "instead of continuing to rely upon texts

73. *TD* V, 101.

considered definitive and sacred, it is essential to put an end to the subjugation of the theatre to the text and to recover the notion of a kind of unique language halfway between gesture and thought . . . The question for theatre, then, is to create a metaphysics of speech, gesture, and expression in order to rescue it from its servitude to psychology and human stagnation."[74] The most obvious reaction to such statements by Artaud, with relation to a theological understanding, might be the realization that the use of drama is not intended, or at least should not intend, to eradicate and remove the *sacred*—the Bible—as this *sacred* text is fundamental in our understanding and exposure to the guidance of God through His revelation. The point to be made, however, is that a dramatic model of theology employs an intentional movement that seeks to illumine the *becoming* of life, thereby moving us closer to understanding the expression and fullness of our *life*.

Recognizing this movement (becoming) allows theology to remain faithful to the enactment of our evangelical preparation, and our participation in the eternal event of God as presented in the Bible. Furthermore, theology participates in God's drama through the intentional *incarnation* of the story. That is, theology's recognition of God's call to perform is directly manifested in our own incarnational performance. Thus, the recognition that the truth of God's interaction with humanity irrupts from the story of Scripture through the drama of its *euangelion* will hopefully move today's theological endeavors to continue to seek the means of the most effective way for the enactment of our *"evangelical preparation"*?[75] Take for instance the letter to the Hebrews, where the entire community is brought on stage when the writer proclaims:

> But remember the former days, when, after being enlightened, you endured a great conflict of sufferings, partly by being made a *public spectacle* (θεατριζόμενοι) through reproaches and tribulations, and partly by becoming sharers with those who were so treated. For you showed sympathy to the prisoners and accepted joyfully the seizure of your property, knowing that you have for yourselves a better possession and a lasting one (Heb 10:32-34).

---

74. Artaud, *Theatre and Its Double*, 89–90.

75. Balthasar discusses history, with all its dramas, as the interplay between divine and human freedom. This interplay is the promise initiated by Christ in His incarnational performance. Balthasar writes of this interplay, this performance being the drama of the gospel, that "it is, then, man as a whole, with his decisions that testify to his dignity as a free creature, who stands within this *preparatio evangelica* and gives expression to himself in it" (*TH*, 61).

Two things can be highlighted, in the aforementioned Scripture references with regard to the personhood of the followers of Christ thereby shedding light on effective ways of the enactment of our *"evangelical preparation:"* (1) These Christians "shared" life, they participated in each other's "tribulations" and "sufferings." Their "enlightened" personhood—that is, their life now *in* Christ—continues to call them into a participatory reality. This is a reality and living out of what verses 23 and 24 of the same chapter call Christians to do, to "hold fast the confession of our hope without wavering, for He who promised is faithful; and let us consider how to stimulate one another to love and good deeds." (2) The dramatic *action* of the Christians (characters) takes place within the (θεατρον) *theatre* of God's glory. The depth of suffering is not hidden nor is it ignored; we see and feel the depth of their suffering as they were intentionally and willingly made a *spectacle* (θεατριζόμενοι) for the world to see. Concerning the use of θεατριζόμενοι, Balthasar remarks that "the rare Greek verb here means "publicly exhibited and exposed to the laughter of a (cruel) mob"—what *Bertolt Brecht* called the *Gestus des Zeigens*." Moving deeper into the essence of the passage, Balthasar draws on the thoughts of Thomas Aquinas, who once commented on the given section from the letter to the Hebrews that "there is nothing evil in people laughing at a clown, even if the laughter is excessive; it is a serious matter, however, if a wise man is the butt of laughter. But it is exceedingly grave if, in addition, someone torments and mocks him. Thus we see the depth of their suffering: they were made a spectacle, and no one had compassion on them but rather took pleasure, along with the tormentor, in their torturing."[76] The reality of the dramatic tension from the given scripture is elevated through theological language that encourages such text to "rapidly move off the page" into the performance of the world's stage. This recognition of the Bible's dramatic character stems from drama's ability to "concentrate on the presentation of what is essentially a sense of being, an intuition of the tragicomic absurdity and mystery of human existence."[77]

In his *Theatre of the Absurd*, Esslin discusses the ability of the theatre and of playwrights such as Beckett and Pinter to examine the human condition of man "stripped of the accidental circumstances of social position or historical context, confronted with basic choices, the basic situations of his existence."[78] This examination is the very exploration of identity being discussed by the writer of Hebrews, concerning Christ's fellow performers, when they (the Christians) intentionally choose to enact Christ's commands

---

76. *TD* I, 154.

77. Esslin, *Brief Chronicles*, quoted by Banks, *Drama and Theatre Arts*, 255.

78. Esslin, *The Theatre of the Absurd*, 391.

to "share" in one another's lives. Instead of explicitly setting out a system of rules or transposing a specific meaning to the situation, the writer highlights the openness of the stage in its confrontation of "basic choices," whereby the performers (followers of Christ) were able to "accept" and recognize the situation of their existence. Beckett, like the author of Hebrews, did not explicitly set out a systematic formula for the performance of his work, nor did he compose a set of meanings or outcomes for his plays either, irritating as it was to some actors,[79] but allowed for the enlightenment of the audience to come through their acceptance of the play's entirety.[80]

Beckett's audience has to decide what the outcome is, regarding the reality of hope, the crisis of whether or not Godot will ever come. Furthermore, just as the performers highlighted by the writer of Hebrews were made *spectacles*, so too are the characters in Beckett's plays. Take for instance the isolation and exposure of Estragon and Vladimir in *Waiting for Godot*. Calling for minimal setting (a tree, country road and a low mound), Beckett's characters are exposed, isolated from the general public yet intriguingly involved with the audience through the queries made throughout the characters' dialogue, especially in Act I. Take for instance the first encounter between the audience and the two men:

> *Estragon, sitting on a low mound, is trying to take off his boot. He pulls at it with both hands, panting. He gives up, exhausted, rests, tries again. As before.*
>
> *Enter Vladimir.*
>
> Estragon: (*giving up again*). Nothing to be done.
>
> Vladimir: (*advancing with short, stiff strides, legs wide apart*). I'm beginning to come round to that opinion. All my life I've tried to put it from me, saying Vladimir, be reasonable, you haven't yet tried everything. And I resumed the struggle. (*He broods, musing on the struggle. Turning to Estragon.*) So there you are again.
>
> Estragon: Am I?
>
> Vladimir: I'm glad to see you back. I thought you were gone forever.
>
> Estragon: Me too.

---

79. Banks recounts the fact that Ralph Richardson turned down the part of Estragon because "Beckett would not explain the meaning and significance of the play" (*Drama and Theatre Arts*, 257).

80. This draws upon the comment made by Beckett that Godot was not God, (ibid., 258).

> Vladimir: Together again at last! We'll have to celebrate this. But how? (*He reflects.*) Get up till I embrace you.
>
> *Trying to take off his boot. He pulls at it with both hands, panting.*

The dialogue is as exhausting as the boot struggle is for Vladimir, yet he continues to work through the struggle, accepting his "seizure" while revealing further the tension involved in his experience and situation. However, even amidst the exhaustion, the tension and the struggle, the performance pulls in the audience.

> Vladimir: Hand in hand from the top of the Eiffel Tower, among the first. We were respectable in those days. Now it's too late. They wouldn't even let us up. (*Estragon tears at his boot.*) What are you doing?
>
> Estragon: Taking off my boot. Did that never happen to you?
>
> Vladimir: Boots must be taken off every day, I'm tired telling you that. Why don't you
>
> listen to me?
>
> Estragon: (*feebly*). Help me!
>
> Vladimir: It hurts?
>
> Estragon: (*angrily*). Hurts! He wants to know if it hurts!
>
> Vladimir: (*angrily*). No one ever suffers but you. I don't count. I'd like to hear what you'd say if you had what I have.
>
> Estragon: It hurts?
>
> Vladimir: (*angrily*). Hurts! He wants to know if it hurts!
>
> Estragon: (*pointing*). You might button it all the same.
>
> Vladimir: (*stooping*). True. (*He buttons his fly.*) Never neglect the little things of life.
>
> Estragon: What do you expect, you always wait till the last moment.
>
> Vladimir: (*musingly*). The last moment . . . (*He meditates.*) Hope deferred maketh the something sick, who said that?
>
> Estragon: Why don't you help me?

Chapter Two—Theological Expression

Again, Beckett intentionally draws the audience in through apparent statements (questions) made by Vladimir regarding the boot struggle, while moving the audience into the inner struggle of hope deferred. The tension/struggle itself is not however with the boots, it is the waiting; and yet through the waiting, the audience is drawn into the action of the stage, which ironically is brought about through its overt inaction. The power of drama is this very aspect, the incorporating power of its text in action.[81]

Concerning the dramatic character and structure of *Waiting for Godot*, Raymond Williams notes that the "real dramatic relation is not to the morality but expressionism. The play is an usually clear example of that expressionist method in which an essentially private feeling—incommunicable in direct terms because of its very isolation—is dramatized by its projection into contrasting characters which are also contrasting modes of action."[82] The contrast of life is drawn out, understood and appreciated through the realm of the theatre and its action/enactment of the text and thus its presentation of life. The profundity of the theatre for theology comes also from its ability to transcend the limits of speech. That is, as Artaud accentuates, the "naked language of the theatre" is a "real language" that must, "permit, by its use of man's nervous magnetism, the transgression of the ordinary limits of art and speech, in order to realize actively, that is to say magically, *in real terms*, a kind of total creation in which man must reassume his place between dreams and events."[83]

---

81. The inaction is encased within the action of the dialogue (the language) and the expression of the entirety of the theatrical presentation (characters, scenery, stage, audience) thereby gaining its energy from the paradoxical tensions throughout the play. Through the reciprocity of the theatre, that is, the continued giving and receiving of lines and actions by the characters as well as the receiving of the lines and actions by the audience, who then reciprocate by returning their attention and action back to the stage, as well as towards one another, the sense of tension and anxiety in *waiting* and wondering is built up and maintained throughout the play. Furthermore, Beckett displays how drama creates and elevates energy through the performance of the mixing of the negative with the positive: "Yes yes. No no. Yes yes. No no. *Silence*," (act I); the nicknames each character gives to the other, *Gogo* and *Didi* (from French *dire*); and the absence of decision, with the play concluding with the famous exchange: "Well? Shall we go? Yes, let's go. *They do not move.*"

82. Williams, *Drama from Ibsen to Brecht*, 302.

83. Artaud, *Theatre and Its Double*, 93.

§3.2 Performative Reality of a Dramatic Model

To reiterate a previous claim, drama is action. As Kevin Vanhoozer states, "A drama is a *doing*, an enactment."[84] A drama is a sequence of action, stemming from the Greek verb drao (*drao*) which literally means "to do." It is the fundamental connection between drama's performance and the action of God that establishes the need for the Theo-drama. God is not a "static" idea nor an "Unmoved" being, but *pure action*. God's performative reality irrupts on the world's stage throughout the span of history, yet as Balthasar notes, God acts through Christ and in Christ "by giving his Only Beloved for the sake of the world. He does not do *something* for man, he does *everything*."[85] This all-encompassing act of Christ invites humanity to participate in His eternal performance, and through the dramatizing also of theology; such an invitation is brought to life in both the Church and the world.

The opening up of the world's stage through theology's continued willingness to envisage God's performance is nothing other than the recognition of life's performative reality and God's action in it. Much of what has been labelled "performance" is commonly mis-understood or under-appreciated as it is measured against the foundational elements of "the fine arts"—particularly poetry and painting. However, as Trevor Hart explains, such artistic forms as music and drama "cannot adequately be treated in such a two-dimensional manner." This two-dimensional manner tends to be textual as opposed to performative, notwithstanding the fact that poetry and painting are in their own ways extensions of a performance, and should not then be treated in a two-dimensional manner, either.

It is crucial to allow our performative reality to be exposed and understood through "the fine arts;" measured not against a two-dimensional rod but through the multi-dimensional reality of performance. Hart further explains that such "works" as music, drama, dance, "do not properly exist at all apart from some *performance* in which the relevant "text" is brought to fulfilment or completion through embodied action, and to exclude this dimension is to overlook all that is most distinctive to their art."[86] The art of performance is a necessary foundation to the growth of life, as life itself is an on-going performance. There is no better way to understand our life than through the engagement of the performative arts. For just as performance or action is essential to life, so too is it to the performing arts. Performance "is not secondary to these forms of artistic engagement with the world, but

---

84. Vanhoozer, *Drama of Doctrine*, 37.
85. *TD* I, 33.
86. Hart and Guthrie, *Faithful Performances*, 2.

essential to their artistry. It is therefore very welcome, that in recent decades, there has been a growing theological interest in music and drama precisely as performing arts, and in the performative dimensions of them in particular."[87]

What makes the reality of performance significant for theology is that performance, writes John Emigh, is "a 'model *for*' as well as a 'model *of*' not only 'religious belief,' but also social action,"[88] and of course one could add here, "religious action" and "social belief." If taken seriously, then, the performative reality of the theatre can offer theology the necessary tools to assist in our continued efforts of not only answering the question of "who am I?" but also, "what is my role in God's drama?" Remembering the first section of this chapter, as Balthasar claims, "God does not play the world drama all on his own; he makes room for man to join in," and this joining in is made possible through the performance of Christ. And from His performance, humanity is given insight into our own personhood as Christ is, according to Balthasar, "the center of the world, he is the key to the interpretation not only of creation, but of God Himself . . . God wills to maintain his relation to the world only with Jesus Christ as the center of that relationship, the content and fulfilment of the eternal Covenant."[89]

Through the incarnational performance of Christ through the Spirit, humanity is granted the freedom to perform its part and perform it well. Such freedom beckons a creaturely response to, as opposed to a formal description of, life's profundity, evolution and function. As is being argued, it is through the movement of the narrative towards the performance of the drama that theology itself moves towards the expanded understanding of the human and our interaction with and in the eternal performance of Christ.

One of the primary purposes of a theological dramatics is to raise the question, and awareness, of the location and reality of life's dramatic action. The point made through Balthasar's *Theodramatik* is not one of a revival for the Christian theatre, or its denial, but to bring into center stage "the *drama intrinsic to divine salvation.*"[90] Drawing from this perspective, one can begin to grasp how life is embodied and explored through the Theologica Dramaticas. Drama illumines and exposes the fundamental character of life *in Christ through the Holy Spirit*, thereby "presenting us with the right or perverse action of free human beings': such a presentation—a performance—of the

87. Ibid., 2.
88. Ibid., 71. Cf. Geertz, *Interpretation of Cultures*, 118.
89. *TH*, 20, 22.
90. Nichols, *No Bloodless Myth*, 23.

reality of the stage as "will no doubt challenge our personal and social sense of "ought" through its positive or negative models." The truth is, continues Balthasar, that the *"good* which God does to us can only be experienced as the *truth* if we share in *performing* it (Jn 7:17; 8:31f.); we must 'do the truth in love' (aletheuein en agape [Eph 4:15]), not only in order to perceive the truth of the good but, equally, in order to embody it increasingly in the world, thus leading the ambiguities of the world theatre beyond themselves to a singleness of meaning that can only come from God."[91]

§3.3 Framing the Action of a Dramatic Model

The framing of our theological actions occurs through God's threefold movement that opens up the stage so we might become active participants in His action. That which is illumined in and through Scripture must be "regarded as of supreme reality . . . God Himself undertakes to speak and act and give His help on earth, to be God for and with the man who lives on earth."[92] Thus, the drama of God's Word provides the framework in terms of which our theological practices are to be understood. For example, we can look at the Sermon on the Mount as a way to take theology deeper into understanding the call to action by God on His people. Jesus calls for His followers to live lives of faithful obedience to, as Samuel Wells puts it, "overaccept the gifts of creation and culture in the same way God does."[93] In the Sermon on the Mount, Jesus demonstrates how His call is one that embodies His overacceptance of creation. According to Wells, in the 5th chapter of Matthew, with the words "But I say to you," Jesus *overaccepts* the Jewish law, "saying it is not murder but anger, not adultery but lust, not unjust divorce but divorce itself, not swearing falsely but swearing at all, not measured retaliation but nonresistance, not loving the neighbor but loving the enemy that constitute the issue. Each of these is a perfect embodiment of overaccepting, none more so than the fifth: 'If anyone strikes you on the right cheek, turn the other also; and if anyone forces you to go one mile, go also the second mile.' Going the second mile epitomizes the practice of overaccepting."[94]

---

91. *TD* I, 20.

92. *CD* III/3, 434.

93. Wells, *Improvisation*, 135. God "accepts" humanity; His offer of salvation through His "overacceptance" profoundly affects the movement not only of the stage, but also of the understanding of our own performances. The idea of acceptance is discussed in chapter 4 §4.1.

94. Wells, *Improvisation*, 136.

The framing of action within the dramatic model of theology is rooted in God's Word as exposed through His threefold act of revelation, invitation and reconciliation. Followers of Christ are called to participate *in* His performance so as to secure their own faithful performances. The use of a dramatic model of theology elevates the expectation of performance through the elevation of the text being "enacted." Jesus does not stand atop the mountainside to give a sermon so that those around might simply listen to a wonderful story, and leave both warm and filled. Jesus expects His words will expose and express the active power and presence of God, with an expectation of participation. This expectation from God is ultimately recognized through the interaction of our faith in action.

The performance within the divine drama indeed results from the intimate interaction of faith and action. Thus, furthering the dramatic reality of the *Theo-Drama,* we can look at Luke 10:25-37 whereby the fullness of the dramatic content of the Bible is once again found. The intention of Jesus is made explicit through His command for His followers to "Go and do likewise." It is not (as Jesus illumines) through the simple reading or hearing of the Biblical words that the inheritance of eternal life is realized, but through such words *becoming* action.[95] For the teacher is answered by Jesus from this Biblical inheritance, but Jesus goes on to the command requiring *active* living:

> An expert in the law stood up to test Jesus. "Teacher," he asked, "what must I do to inherit eternal life?" "What is written in the Law?" he replied. "How do you read it?" He answered: "Love the Lord your God with all your heart and with all your soul and with all your strength and with all your mind;" and, "Love your neighbor as yourself." "You have answered correctly," Jesus replied. "Do this and you will live."

Jesus' insistence on an *active* faith based on one's love for God once again exposes us to the revealing of His *action* and His *being*. As Barth writes, "creaturely history is not for nothing the theatre of the great acts of God, the Father's house. In virtue of its origin and in its whole structure its occurrence is calculated to reflect and illustrate and echo these acts of God."[96] The action of the Godhead is no mere story told by the Creator, but the script given for His followers to enact and live out through the action of their own being. This action of being is explicitly drawn out and explained through the *Theo-Drama*.

---

95. The words *becoming* action is, as is being argued in this chapter, brought about through the fulfilment and movement of the narrative *becoming* the drama.

96. *CD* III/3, 50.

As noted earlier, theology must be appropriate to its matter; and if both Barth and Balthasar's assessments are correct: that God is Being-in-act (Barth), and that "if there *is* such a thing as theo-drama, and if it is fundamentally the event of God becoming man and his action on the world's behalf, there must be dramatic ways of presenting it" (Balthasar), then, the movement of the narrative to the drama seems the natural progression. Through the Theo-drama, theology is afforded ways to assist the Church and society to come to a deepened realization of what it means to be a participant in God's drama. Furthermore, from the Theo-drama, the Church's theologians, through the guidance of the Spirit, can continue to direct the Church back to her source. The Church needs this continual guidance, as the Church is the cast of characters (the actors) by which the revelation of God in Christ and through the Spirit is brought to life, so as not only to bear witness to the Christ, but also to participate in the building of the Kingdom of God on earth. In this action of God, the Church witnesses the glory of the Godhead through the immediate and incarnational power of her Bridegroom.

§4 Theological Performance

The reality presented/revealed in the Biblical texts is fully appreciated if theology remains committed not simply to revealing the story of Scripture, but also to pushing for our participation in God's drama as called for and revealed in the Scriptures. It likens to the tearing down of the fourth wall in theatre, as through such a dismantling, theology not only participates with God, but with the extended audience (society). Thus, discussing the thoughts of Brecht, Peter Brook writes, "for Brecht, a necessary theatre could never for one moment take its sights off the society it was serving. There was no fourth wall between actors and audience—the actor's unique aim was to create a precise response in an audience for whom he had total respect."[97] Theology's respect for society will assist in reminding us of our role (*mission*) in the theatre of God's glory. This role ultimately finds its performances in creating a response to the revealed action of Christ, an action that steps out from the past into the present while always moving towards tomorrow.

A dramatizing movement within theology simply recognizes that through performance the text is "brought to completion through forms of embodied action in which it is 'interpreted' faithfully for a world (and not

---

97. Brook, *Empty Space*, 81.

Chapter Two—Theological Expression 87

just a world) which looks on as it does so."[98] This embodied action is realized through the continual *becoming* (movement) of the narrative. Through the language of the drama—in dialogue and performance—theology, and thus the Church and the world, begin to apprehend and to participate in the profundity of existence through the dramatic interaction of Creator and creature. Language needs to illumine the active creation of the human, and thus, to recognize the profundity of the performance. The movement of the narrative facilitates the recognition that, as Balthasar opines, the story of the "great unwritten acts of God and Jesus are also part of the drama of world salvation."[99] The inclusion of these "unwritten acts" into the "drama of world salvation" is by no means the lessening of humanity's performance but its elevation and incorporation into the performance of Christ through the Spirit. Through such an understanding and realization of life's dramatic essence comes the recognition of humanity's performative reality.

A dramatic model of theology needs to be aware of the action (performance) of the former actors of the world's stage, thereby recognizing what Barth wrote when he stated that theology is "the continuing service to God's revelation, performed by specific men, in the form of conceptual thinking in a specific here and now."[100] What is being argued is that theology's performance should be rooted in the act and being of God that calls for a response from humanity. Balthasar speaks of how the dramatic interaction of life—that is, the life of God with the life of humanity, and human people with one another—is best captured only through the drama.

> The Apostles are witnesses of the Resurrection and of the whole life of Jesus that underlies it . . . They are not uninvolved (or even "interested') reporters, but with their lives they vouch for the testimony they give Scripture, for its part, testifies to their giving of testimony. The two coincide entirely when Paul writes a letter, and in it, testifies with his whole life to the truth of revelation, putting God's action at the center but including himself . . . he is speaking dramatically: he shows how the drama comes from God, via Christ, to him, and how he hands it on to the community, which is already involved in the action and must bring it into reality.[101]

God does not desire a simple description of who He is, but desires His creation to participate alongside Him in Christ through the Spirit.

---

98. Hart and Guthrie, *Faithful Performances*, 2.
99. *TD* II, 59
100. *T & C*, 289.
101. *TD* II, 57.

Balthasar's distinction between the epic and dramatic forms enables him to argue that the epic-narrative theology is "accredited by the distanced attitude of the reporter," such an attitude as will "quite logically assume the role of judge over the events and their actualization."[102] This assumption is prevalent in the modern forms of theology, as according to David Brown, what has been lost "is the sense that words in themselves might communicate an experience rather than necessarily only be effective, if directed entirely beyond and outside themselves."[103] What then occurs through these continued assumptions is what Balthasar claims is the forgetting of God's mystery. The theology of a distanced reporter, "continually forgets mystery—for example, in Christology and in the doctrine of the Church and the sacraments—it treats God and his grace like some component that can be manipulated by human thought."[104] Instead of "openly or secretly" making theology only about the human, our theological work should seek to draw society and the Church—through the guidance of the Spirit—into the participatory reality of God. That is, as Barth writes, if we keep this in mind, that God is act, and "if all our thoughts are always grasped by God's action, because in it we have to do with God's being, we may be sure that they cannot err, and become either openly or secretly thoughts about ourselves."[105] Thus, if God is known and grasped in action, then it follows that theology should seek to be act as well. Through this reality, theology comes closer to receiving faithfully God's grace and expectation for the world's stage. Recognition of contemporary theology's need for the dramatic will allow the move into the dynamic interaction of Creator and creature.

Looking at the entirety of the stage provides the deepened understanding that our world is indeed our shape and we are world-shaped—theological language is crucial in the continued developments and communication of the shape of life. The recognition of the need to establish the narrative within the drama, as opposed to relegating the dramatic to a secondary position, provides the crucial realization of the proper ways of apprehending and participating in truth and personhood. The active performance of life can faithfully be realized through the person-and-life-involving language of the dramatic—a language that is always active and always alive. Contemporary theology has the profound responsibility of presenting and participating in the truth of God's cosmic drama. This reality is revealed when the written word is first, inspired; and then, in use, transformed by the

---

102. *TD* II, 56.
103. Brown, *God and Mystery*, 56.
104. *TD* II, 53.
105. *CD* II/1, 272.

enfleshed word in such a way that the essence of its communication embodies the action of its object. This dramatic movement illumines the need for contemporary theology's participatory performance in the Being-in-act of God, a need we now turn to explore further.

Chapter Three—Dramatic Model of Theology

> This "theo-drama" is a "theological" undertaking; that is, it reflects upon the dramatic character of existence in the light of biblical revelation.[1]

§1 Introduction

THE INTENTION OF THIS chapter is to move the current discussion regarding the *dramatization* of theology forward. The hope of this movement is to encourage contemporary theology's continual participation in the Being-in-act of God. The argument of the chapter draws explicitly from Balthasar, who maintains that what takes place in life and in the world is simply "action."[2] Primary in this action is God's threefold movement of revelation, invitation and reconciliation, which provides the foundation not only for the world's stage, but also, for theology's action. According to Balthasar, revelation is God's action "in and upon the world, and the world can only respond . . . through action on *its* part."[3] This interaction of divine and human freedom is both active and personal; it is an overflow of grace and love from the One to the created "other." Therefore, the chapter will argue that it is through a model of dramatic theology that we are able to respond appropriately to God's action "in and upon the world."

In light of the previous two chapters, this chapter argues that through a dramatic model, theology returns to its core, that is, through the dramatizing of theology, God's interaction with His creation is realized and appreciated. God's involvement and participation with humanity through the event of revelation is enlivened through the language of the dramatic. Yet, according to Aidan Nichols, the church has "sometimes used drama to express the action-filled content of revelation, but her theologians have

1. *TD* II, 9.
2. *TD* III, 532.
3. *TD* I, 15.

Chapter Three—Dramatic Model of Theology

not in any all-embracing way (till Balthasar!) presented revelation as itself divine theatre."[4]

In this chapter I hope to show that by theology coming to understand drama and its performative focus, not only will our endeavors be significantly and positively effected, but more importantly, the fullness of the Theo-drama will be realized. Theology should attempt to emulate Christ (its object) who confronts us through His revelatory, invitational and reconciliatory performance. In accordance with this, if narrative theology remains true to its object it will continue to push for its *becoming*, or its movement towards the drama.

In section two we explore humanity's self-involved action that is effected through our incorporation into Christ's normative performance. The hope of this section is to illumine the call to participate, first, in God's performance, so as to be able, then, to participate profoundly in one another's life performances. Section three's discussion brings to light the fact that participation *in* life is made possible through the performance of Christ, who is the universal and theological focal point. Following this, we move into the discussion specifically related to the language employed within a dramatic model of theology; that is, an active language enfleshed in the performance of the Godhead. Sections five and six investigate the initial movement of theology today in our attempts of employing a dramatic model of theology. Section five highlights and discusses the state of theology today, and is then followed by two examples of theologians who employ the dramatic for theology, but, as argued in section six, could push even further into a fuller use of drama. The chapter concludes with a discussion of the profundity of a dramatic model of theology and its exposure of our personhood.

Through a dramatic model of theology, we are able to recognize the call for us to be a self-involved witness so as to begin to realize the relational essence of our personhood. As the apostle Paul writes, "we have become a spectacle to the world" (1 Cor 4:9); an on-going performance that opens up the relational reality of the creator and creature. Paul's realization of this dramatic reality results from his understanding that his writings are not themselves stories, but, as Francis Watson remarks, are the attempt to uncover "their testimony to a divine act that lies beyond the scope of human storytelling." Because of this incapability of the story, Watson continues that while Paul is "certainly a theological interpreter of scriptural narrative," it would be however, "a mistake to understand him as a 'narrative theologian.'"[5]

---

4. Nichols, *No Bloodless Myth*, 21.
5. Watson, *Narrative Dynamics in Paul*, 239.

§2 Incorporation into the Normative

God has become human for the world's sake in Jesus Christ—an act that is nothing but dramatic. What happens in the drama of salvation is God determining to be God for us in a definite way. Jesus Christ is the universal normative, the ideal of humanity, and precisely because He alone is the norm and absolute, He "remains incommensurate with the norms of this world." Thus, as Balthasar maintains, the mystery of the eternal entering the temporal is that in which all norms are subordinated to the "particular law" of "the uniqueness of Jesus Christ as the revelation, in the concrete, of the free will of God for the world."[6]

In light of Balthasar's thoughts, theology should seek to look to the normative of history—history's "world of ideas"—which is an event of dramatic proportions. "Salvation history is summed up and given its ultimate meaning by Christ, when He fulfils it and integrates it in His own human life." This dynamic performance of Christ does not "consist primarily in isolated verbal prophecies and individual legal precepts." It consists says Balthasar:

> In the whole living, and to our eyes, chaotic, series of events from Abraham to John the Baptist. That history, with all its drama, its judgments, rejections, redemptions and elections, its obduracies and its learning at long last of the lesson of prayer, its interplay between divine and human freedom, is *as such* the promise. It is, then, man as a whole, with his decisions that testify to his dignity as a free creature, who stands within this *preparatio evangelica* and gives expression to himself in it.[7]

God's Word calls for a response from humanity, seeking to incorporate humanity into the reconciliatory action of the world's stage. As argued in chapter two, a significant difference between the models of narrative and dramatic theology is that unlike narrative theology, dramatic theology does not simply recount an historical past event, but seeks to engage in the events of the past through our engagement and participation in the eternal action of the Godhead. It is the dramatic model of theology, Nichols maintains, where we come to fully realize that "God's action challenges the believer, appropriates him and makes him a witness."[8] This self-involved witness exposes the interaction of the Theo-drama, as humanity actively participates

---

6. *TH*, 19.

7. *TH*, 60–61.

8. Nichols, *No Bloodless Myth*, 51.

and engages in God's event of revelation, so as also to participate in one another's performances.

God's performance through the event and action of revelation incorporates the entirety of humanity. Revelation reveals that "within the drama of Christ, every human fate is deprivatized so that its personal range may extend to the whole universe, depending on how far it is prepared to cooperate in being inserted into the normative drama of Christ's life, death and Resurrection."[9] If, then, Christ's performance is the fullness of God's revelation that seeks to incorporate the entirety of the world's stage, what is the most effective model of theology that will illuminate such a reality? Furthermore, humanity's incorporation stems from the actuality of God's creative action; for "what is eternally present and true in God—that is, that he created all things, from before all time, with a view to Christ and actually *in* Christ—this is only in the process of coming-to-be in creation . . . The first episode to be dramatic in the real sense is the history of the Word's becoming flesh: for the Incarnation takes place in the nature of the old Adam, which is to be transformed by the entire Christ-event into what, henceforth, will be the Christ-principle operating in history."[10] Based on Balthasar's claim of humanity's *incorporation* into the drama and "norm" of Christ, the continued hope of this project is to understand best, how today's theological endeavors can promote an active desire for participation. The movement towards our embracing of a dramatic model of theology allows for the possibility of humanity finding its performative life, thereby realizing what Barth maintains, that "this participation is achieved in our own experience and activity, in that act of self-determination which we call our human existence."[11]

§2.1 Dramatic, Performative Foundation of Theology

Humanity is caught up in the perfection of Christ by our participation in His Being through the Spirit. Based, then, on Barth's account of God's Being-in-act, the *dramatizing* of theology is the product of an intentional desire, and act, to participate in God's drama. Through the dramatic reality of God, who is *act*, theology is called to participate in this action by continually guiding the Church back to her source. Through a dramatic model of theology we can come to witness our roles in life's drama, thereby making "our personal

---

9. *TD* II, 50.
10. *TD* III, 37.
11. *CD* I/2, 266.

contribution to the success of the drama as a whole."[12] Theology today has much to gain from the performative reality of the theatre. Antonin Artaud writes that theatre allows for the true spectacle of life to be realized. "To break through language" writes Artaud, "in order to touch life is to create or recreate the theatre."[13] If theology wishes to realize its own contribution to the success of the drama, the employment of theatrical language and understanding provides an opportunity to break through theological language, so as to participate in God's salvific drama.

The performative foundation of theology is the direct result of God's interaction through the role and mission of Christ. As Balthasar identifies, it is Christ that theology must gaze obediently toward, so as to realize "how he stands in time and in history as the heart and norm of all that is historical."[14] The advantage found within the drama is not a "recasting of theology into a new shape previously foreign to it." Theo-drama is the life and foundation of theology; and as Balthasar reiterates, "theology itself must call for this; it must be something implicit within it, manifested explicitly too in many places. For theology could never be anything other than an explication of the revelation of the Old and New covenants . . . this revelation in its total shape . . . is dramatic."[15]

Often times a narrative model of theology overlooks the action and direction of Christ and the Spirit, seeking simply to *describe* rather than *participate* in the action of God. For example, one the one hand, a narrative model of theology might take the parable of the Good Samaritan, analyze, discuss and observe the principles illumined through the story, all the while remaining content with the subtle separation from the story. On the other hand, a dramatic model of theology would seek to push the readers of the parable into contemplating and enacting the principles outlined in the text, so as to become faithful participants in God's drama.

God's in-breaking cannot simply be observed as it incorporates the stage's action, inviting all of the actors to participate in the Trinitarian life. Yet as William Cavanaugh notes, such participation is realized only if theology and humanity do not attempt to control such action. "We can only submit" writes Cavanaugh, for through submission we recognize that "we cannot stand back from the world and survey it; we must simply take our role in the drama that God is staging and give ourselves to it."[16] The dra-

---

12. Hart and Guthrie, *Faithful Performances*, 170.
13. Artaud, *Theatre and Its Double*, 13.
14. *TH*, 26.
15. *TD* I, 125.
16. Cavanaugh, *Being Consumed*, 81. Theology's presence in God's drama is made

matic foundation of the Theo-drama is realized through theology's belief in the truth of Christ's performance—a performance that calls for humanity's faithful participation. The truth of this performance—theology's participation—will not however, encourage society or the Church if today's theologians do not sincerely believe in God's call for participation. Drawing again from the theatre, theology must recognize that just as with the stage, so to with today's theological endeavors, if there remains a separation of truth and belief the stage's performance will lack inspiration, it will be emotionless. "Truth on the stage," writes Stanislavski, "is whatever we can believe in with sincerity, whether in ourselves or in our colleagues. Truth cannot be separated from *belief*, nor *belief* from truth. They cannot exist without each other and without both of them it is impossible to live your part, or to create anything. Everything that happens on the stage must be convincing to the actor himself, to his associates and to the spectators. It must inspire belief in the possibility, in real life."[17]

As discussed in chapter 1, God is *Being-in-act* and if theology is to encourage humanity towards an active response, today's theological practices must truthfully and sincerely believe in God's invitation so as to draw in the rest of humanity through a dramatic performance of our own. This type of belief and action, this type of acceptance of God's invitation, is the submission in which Cavanaugh speaks of as that which occurs only in Christ through the Spirit. Today's theological work can greatly benefit by: first, recognizing God's dramatic and dynamic action with humanity; and secondly, the willingness for today's theological endeavors to push towards the dramatic. The language employed today, if it fails to push for the *becoming* of the narrative, will potentially remain in the shadows of the stage rather than faithfully performing in the center. Such a possibility illumines today's sentiment that is seemingly fearful of the fullness and liveliness of a dramatic push in theology.[18]

---

possible through the act and involvement of God. It is the *kenosis* of God that creates this space and possibility for both theology and humanity. For as Cavanaugh continues, "the absolute uniqueness of Christ cannot be subsumed under any more general categories of being. If God is God, then God must always be beyond our comprehension: *si comprehendis non est Deus*. We are, nevertheless, invited to participate in the Trinitarian life through Christ and the work of the Spirit" (81).

17. Stanislavski, *An Actor Prepares*, 129–30.

18. For an insightful look into the disillusioned relationship between drama, the church, academy, and theology see Khovacs, "Divine Reckonings."

§2.2 Theological Movement: Dramatization

Being and action are essential to the foundation and movement of the Theo-drama, as through the Being and action of the Godhead the stage is created and sustained. It is being suggested that, in order to comprehend a fuller understanding of the dynamic reality of the Bible, and life, contemporary theology needs a consciousness of its foundation and a renewal of its language. However, as Colin Gunton maintains, theology, when in the middle of a theological argument/dialogue concerning its doctrines, endeavors and language, such renewal cannot begin if, "we think that all that is to be done is to shout louder or "apply" the language to new circumstances."[19] Theology must not only come to embody and respond dramatically to God's threefold movement of revelation, invitation and reconciliation, using language that is *lived in*, but it must also allow for the imaginative power of being and revelation to guide the performance of the stage.[20]

A dramatic model of theology raises the awareness of our intersecting performances, and thus, excommunicates "everything that opposes *communion* between divine and human freedom, and 'incommunicates' everything that promotes it."[21] It is God's action that sets forth the action of the world's stage, bringing it to reality. The dramatic illumines God's relational action with His creation, and upon His creation, within the temporal landscape of reality. However, the dramatic category of theology, while revealing the revelatory fullness of the Father, Son and Spirit, has tended to be overlooked within the endeavors and studies of today. Drama is not a method of analysis but an existential, living, dynamic and ontological reality. Drama is not "employed as a mere analogy; rather it is a structured reality that helps us to discover what the implications of the terms 'act' and 'person' really are."[22] Yet rather than allowing the dramatic essence of God's action to envelope its core, much of today's theology finds scholars who, as N.T. Wright notes, "not only believe in freedom to pursue their research in their own way. They also pride themselves on being detached flies-on-the-wall: observers, not participants."[23] Such a detachment has a tendency to disengage Jesus' words and actions from the world He came to transform. This disengagement breeds a theology of disconnectedness as opposed to a unified act as

---

19. Gunton, *Actuality of Atonement*, 176.
20. Theology's imaginative powers are discussed in chapter 4.
21. Nichols, *No Bloodless Myth*, 59.
22. Harrison, *Sociological Analysis*, 390.
23. Wright, *Jesus and the Victory of God*, 578.

exemplified by God.²⁴ Again, the dramatizing of theology is rooted in the action of God, an action that brings forth the interactive reality of life, the performance of the script, which is so often overshadowed through the instructional overtones of the narrative.

What is being argued is for theology to resist the tendency toward observation and a detached analysis contra participation. Our lives, and thus, our theology, are called to incarnate, to participate in, the life of the Godhead as revealed by Christ through the Spirit. God's self-revealing is the basis for His drama and the foundation of humanity's performance. To deny that this very action as the normative center of theology is to move in the direction of what Balthasar claims is an "epic-narrative theology—accredited by the distanced attitude of the reporter." Thinking back to the discussion of chapter two, it is the perspective of the distanced reporter, notes Balthasar, which inevitably assumes "the role of judge over the events of their actualization."²⁵ Through His revelatory act, God reveals His fullness while also inviting humanity into a participatory performance in His being and action on the world's stage. It is this dramatic action and interaction that is the life of God with the life of humanity—an event captured and engaged through the drama. The prophets, Abraham, Moses, the disciples, Paul, the first century church, did not live through detached accounts that simply reported God's action, but instead, through God's Being-in-act, were placed in the center of the action.²⁶

§3 Christ as the Universal and Theological Focal Point

Through revelation, humanity engages with the Trinity by being acted upon by God. Such action is the event by which active, existential and personal knowledge of God is made known by Christ through the Holy Spirit. The content of all revelation is Christ, and as T.F. Torrance writes, "the content of the Gospel is found in the Word made flesh, and in the Truth of God which is not only communicated to man but received by man and translated

---

24. The unity of the drama—the interaction of performance, time and place—has been explored and engaged throughout the scope of drama's history. Through his *Poetics*, Aristotle engaged the unifying essence of drama with his "three unities." Theologically, it is significant to recognize the foundation of the Theo-drama rests within the action of God in time (creation and incarnation) and a place (the world's stage). Such recognition actualizes a key distinction and difference between the dramatic and the narrative.

25. *TD* II, 56; cf. §5 in chapter 2.

26. Cf. *TD* II, 53–57.

into human life in Jesus Christ."[27] It is only from and through the action and revelation of the Triune God that the world's stage finds its center and clarity.

§3.1 Christ as Center, Midst and Periphery of Performance

The content and center of the drama is further illumined through the indwelling and presence of the Holy Spirit, Who, for the sake of humanity, envelopes us in the grace and love of God. Humanity's participation is through God's Being-in-act that desires and pursues an *interaction* with humanity; a relentless pursuit that is the overflow of His grace and love, and that, desires reciprocity. According to Balthasar, "there is an exchange of graces: 'God gives me the grace of baptism and I give him the grace of my return to him . . . He gives me the grace of sending me out, and I give him the grace of acting as his representative . . . For although all grace comes from God,' God still desires my response."[28] This interaction reveals the desire of God to invite humanity into His reconciliatory performance and thereby come to understand more and more, what it means to be human. Such knowledge is recognized through the event and act of God making Himself known, for as Barth writes, "the Word of God becomes knowable by making itself known."[29]

Through the action of God, humanity comes into knowledge of His Being, as God is who He is in the act of His revelation. The significance of a dramatic model of theology is that it elevates the performative reality of life. Remembering Balthasar's claim that it is action that takes place in the world, a model that draws directly from an active foundation seems to be the natural choice for today's theological acts, *if* we wish to emulate the life and being of God. The action, then, that theology is specifically concerned with is that of God's action; for in His act of revelation, "God seeks and creates fellowship between Himself and us, and therefore He loves us. But He is this loving God without us as Father, Son and Holy Spirit, in the freedom of the Lord, who has His life from Himself."[30] Thus, the Theo-drama is constituted in and by the divine act of the Triune God. Such action however, must not be understood as passivity on humanity's part, for as Barth states, "man's knowing and his being known by God is an event in the freedom of

27. Torrance, *Theology in Reconstruction*, 26.
28. *TD* IV, 108. Quoting from Adrienne von Speyr, *Johannes: The Word Becomes Flesh*, 1:125–26.
29. *CD*, I/1, 246.
30. *CD*, II/1, 257.

man," whereby humanity ultimately recognizes, by being thus recognized, "God's miracle on us."[31]

God's miracle on us is that which unveils humanity's salvation, reconciliation, and call for participation. The narrative of history is essential in exposing humanity to Christ's universal performance (God's miracle on us). However, as is being argued, the narrative *becoming* drama most effectively urges theology to engage in the interactive reality of history across the span of time. Through a perspective determined by the action of Christ, history, theology and humanity come to witness not only the profundity of life, but the significance of each individual life. The need for theology's recognition of Christ as the central figure, is as Balthasar claims, due to the fact that He (Christ) "declares himself to be "the first and the last, the beginning and the end" (Rev 22:13): he is the complete framework for that entire drama that embraces world history and the end-time."[32]

As the focal point of our theological model, Christ seeks not to dominate center stage, but to share the performance. This desire for participation and reciprocity is grace, and in it, humanity's performance is empowered by Christ through the Spirit. Christ should be our universal and theological focal point, for it is Christ who "brings us to the Father as one of us, but does so as one who, because he is God incarnate, is able to do so."[33] It is in Christ that we find Truth, for though being veiled, God unveils His hiddenness in Christ. Christ is the One to whom all creation must look in order to gain an understanding of our own particular truth. This is to say that, while Christ's performance is universal, it has specific implications for each of our own particular performances. It is in this light that Balthasar writes, "the inclusion of dramatic characters in Christ means no more than this: in Christ, God opens up that personal sphere of freedom within which the particular (individual or collective) characters are given their ultimate human face, their mission or 'role;' it is left up to them to play their part well or ill."[34] The stage's center is indeed Christ, and yet, His performance calls for and expects a response from the entire *dramatis personae*.

The responses of the actors on stage, their acceptance or blocking of God's invitation to perform, is the direct result of God's intentional interaction. Thus, the truth of the stage as well as the truth of our being, cannot be reduced to the "dimension of that general relationship between God and the world which appears to be given as inherent in creation; because God wills

---

31. *CD* I/1, 246.
32. *TD* IV, 44.
33. Gunton, *Actuality of Atonement*, 166.
34. *TD* III, 38.

to maintain his relation to the world only with Jesus Christ as the center of that relationship, the content and fulfilment of the eternal Covenant."[35] It is only through our actions *in* Christ that our faithful performances can be realized.

Christ is "the key to the interpretation not only of creation, but of God Himself. He is so not only in and through his teaching, through the particular or universal truths which he stands for, but essentially and above all by his *existence*."[36] A dramatic model of theology, in its focus on performance and action, is able to expose the *existence* of Christ to the entirety of the theatre, for as Balthasar maintains, "if the world is to come into being containing people endowed with finite freedom, requiring a drama to be played and a stage on which to play it, the Son alone can be its ground and goal; he alone can determine its entire course, irrespective, initially, of whether he himself will or will not appear in it as one of the main characters."[37] In light of Balthasar's claim, then, in order to be true to its calling, theology should remain true the action of the drama, action that is inextricably bound up and determined by Christ's performance. Drawing from a point made by Bertolt Brecht, Peter Brook writes, that "every actor has to serve the action of the play, but until the actor understands what the true action of the play is, what its true purpose is, from the author's point of view and in relation to the needs of a changing world outside (and what side he is himself on in the struggles that divide the world), he cannot possibly know what he is serving."[38] The crucial aspect and invaluable nature of the theatre and its potentiality for theology is precisely the expected identification of each character with their specific roles. This is to say that, once theology identifies with its role, and thus, its "true purpose" in the Theo-drama, it can then faithfully play its part. The aforementioned is made possible if theology, just as the actor in a community that supports the theatre, remains "as much involved in the outside world as in his own craft."[39]

§3.2 Theological Enactment

Theology's enactment of life occurs through its willingness to be a self-involved participant in God's drama. Christ's invitation is a call for performance, and God's drama speaks to the performance of life—to the reality

35. *TH*, 22.
36. Ibid., 20; italics in original.
37. *TD* II, 268.
38. Brook, *Empty Space*, 85.
39. Ibid., 86.

of living. The dramatizing of theology does not simply reveal such a reality, but pushes for involvement in it. In commenting on the profundity of *King Lear*, Brook writes that it is a play of "both question and answer. In this light, the play is directly related to the most burning themes of our time, the old and the new in relation to our society, our arts, our notions of progress, our way of living our lives. If the actors are interested, that is what we shall find. Fancy dress, then, will be left far behind. The meaning will be for the moment of performance."[40] If theology (the actors) remains interested in the action of God's drama it will continue to reveal to the world the questions and answers of our self-involved performances, and then questions and answers will be (as it were) enacted, and in doing so, reveal the essence of *being*.

The theatre of God's glory, then, is the concrete place for humanity's performance. Hence, humanity's performance in the theatre unmasks humanity's being as our performance is the manifestation of God's call on our lives. It is the answer to who we are, for, as Trevor Hart reiterates, "my life is indeed a drama . . . *This* is who I am. This is who *I* am. The answer to the question of my "hypostasis" is answered in this performance and not in abstraction from it."[41] Consequently, the stage is the place within God's theatre of glory in which we recognize ourselves in and through our performance. It is the place in which our hearts are taken hold of by the Spirit, so as to reorient ourselves within the Theo-drama. The profundity of the drama is that it captures the essence of life.

> As human beings, we already have a preliminary grasp of what drama is; we are acquainted with it from the complications, tension, catastrophes, and reconciliations which characterize our lives as individuals and in interaction with others, and we also know it in a different way from the phenomenon of the stage (which is both related to life and yet at a remove from it). The task of the stage (*and thus theology*) is to make the drama of existence explicit so that we may view it.[42]

The Theo-drama is reality; it is the *real*, concrete action and presence of the Father, Son and Spirit with the creature. Theology, if intentionally a self-interested, self-involved actor, has the ability to expose God's call for participatory performances. Such performances are elevated and enhanced by God, through the archetypal performance of Christ as directed and illumined by the Spirit.

40. Ibid., 106.
41. Hart and Guthrie, *Faithful Performances*, 171.
42. *TD* I, 17; my italicized parenthetic insertion.

Christ is the center of the Biblical drama; it is He to whom theology must turn to find its foundation and life. It is in the life of Christ that "the factual and the normative coincide not only *in fact* but *necessarily*, because the fact is both the manifestation of God and the divine-human pattern of true humanity in God's eyes. The facts are not only a phenomenal analogy for a doctrine lying behind them and abstractable from them (as Alexandrian theology still held to a certain extent); they are, grasped in their depth and totality, the meaning itself."[43] Called to participate in Christ's performance, humanity comes face to face with its *true* humanity. The dramatizing of theology helps humanity to actually *live* the scene; to be able to not only see and recognize the *facts*, but also, to *imagine* the depth of such facts. This is to say, a dramatic model of theology provides us with opportunities to realize the "divine-human pattern of true humanity." As Stanislavski writes, "there are two kinds of truth and sense of belief in what you are doing. *First, there is the one that is created automatically and on the plane of actual fact*, and second, there is the *scenic type*, which is *equally truthful but which originates on the plane of imaginative and artistic fiction*."[44] Dramatic language and the reality of theology's call to performance will push our theological endeavors towards their expected performative realities that are consistently empowered through theology's imagining the ideal *becoming* the real. Such a push or rather, a *becoming*, is needed in theology, as much of endeavors appear to be "not about the real world (*the facts*), but about human response to the structures (the logic) of our minds."[45]

§4 Characteristics of a Dramatic Model of Theology

In recognizing its role in the Theo-drama, theology (and its language) is able to realize the need for our continued exposure to God's Word as exposed through the Spirit and through the Scripture. Specifically in relation to Scripture Balthasar maintains that theological interpretation of Scripture is a "pneumatic one, that is, one which reads the (ancient) Scripture (*graphe*) with a view to the Incarnation of the entire divine Word and all subsequent Scripture in the light of the Incarnation; furthermore it will seek to interpret what it reads by the Pneuma of Christ."[46] The significance, then, for our theological endeavors and the rendering of our Biblical interpretations is that if the desire is to be true to the "active" reality of Scripture (the word

43. *TH*, 24.
44. Stanislavski, *An Actor Prepares*, 128.
45. Gunton, *Actuality of Atonement*, 41; my italics.
46. *TD* II, 114.

of God is "living and active, sharper than any two-edged sword" Heb 4:12) and its continual call for participation, a primary characteristic of the model employed should be to be active as well.

God's act in Christ elicits a response while, also calling into question the essence of our personhood. The Word-made-flesh is an action, a performance that "steps forth from the primal ground into the foreground, manifesting and displaying itself, and through self-giving, issuing a challenge to us."[47] The honesty of God in Christ's incarnational performance is at once an action, and a reminder to all of us that we are not outside of God's all-encompassing act. Through the honesty brought about by the theatre, today's theological language can find the means to bring to mind the reality of God's incarnational and confronting performance. The reality of the theatre's honesty led Artaud to propose the "theatre of cruelty." By this he means, "a theatre difficult and cruel for myself first of all. And, on the level of performance, it is not the cruelty we can exercise upon each other . . . but the much more terrible and necessary cruelty which things can exercise against us. We are not free. And the sky can still fall on our heads. And the theatre has been created to teach us that first of all."[48] There is no neutrality when it comes to God's drama. No one is outside of Christ's performance, and thus, must decide to participate with, or against His universal performance.

When one speaks of God's drama one explicitly speaks of participation. Our self-involvement in the "royal drama" of God moves beyond observation and detachment into the realm of *performance*. According to Søren Kierkegaard, we must recognize ourselves as participants in "the Drama of Dramas," for if one supposes himself to be the spectator in the theatre, "he is simply forgetting that he himself is supposed to be the actor in that little theatre and is to leave it to that royal spectator and poet how he wants to use him in that royal drama, *Drama Dramatum*." Theology is a performer; there is only one spectator, notes Kierkegaard, as "world history is the royal stage where he (God), not accidently but essentially, is the only spectator, because he is the only one who *can* do that."[49] It is our participation that Jesus calls for, not speculative observation. "Rescue us from this error" remarks Kierkegaard, "of wanting to admire or adoringly admire you instead of wanting to follow you and be like you."[50]

Our theological endeavors should push towards participation *in* God so as to *experience* His transformative performance. Our participation in

---

47. Ibid., 28.
48. Artaud, *Theatre and Its Double*, 79.
49. Kierkegaard, *Concluding Unscientific Postscript*, 1:158.
50. Kierkegaard, *Practice in Christianity*, 20:233.

the Word of God through the Word of God concretizes our reality of truth as through God's performance (and ours with His) truth—and history—become necessary and real. According to Barth, truth "felt" and "experienced" becomes "truth that is necessary and real for us, when and to the extent that it is thus felt and experienced by us, experienced in the way the paralytic experiences the beneficent shock of the electric spark."[51] Our endeavors should seek to participate in God's word so as to ignite the Church and society to the act of God, rather than attempting to do nothing more than find words that tell the story of God. Our theological model should be one that seeks to move beyond instruction and explanation, aiming to *experience* the drama of God and His Word. For example, instead of "just" teaching the "Great Banquet" parable so as to analyze and discuss it in the classroom, a dramatic model of theology would seek to enact Jesus' teaching by taking the lesson outside the classroom. In other words, this enactment might occur by the professor taking her class to a homeless shelter so as to prepare the shelter hall for a "great banquet" whereby the students would serve the attendants.

A model of theology that seeks to enact the Biblical principles allows for the possibility of "feeling" our performance. That is, theology should "feel" every moment of its performance so as to carry out its mission for the church and for the state. "The great actor" writes Stanislavski, "should be full of feeling, and especially he should feel the thing he is portraying. He must feel an emotion not only once or twice while he is studying his part, but to a greater or lesser degree every time he plays it, no matter whether it is the first or the thousandth time."[52] Drawing from the insight of Stanislavski, today's theological endeavors must be felt, they must be experienced through our real and truthful participation *in* Christ. From this, the great performance of theology will not only convince its fellow actors, but encourage their active involvement in God's drama.

Theology's performance, which is carried out by every theologian, will find its prosperity if it truly does believe in its mission. This is to say that just as every great actor must inspire the audience to *believe* in the purpose, the narrative of the play, so too must theology. The performance "must inspire belief in the possibility, in real life, of emotions analogous to those being experienced on the stage by the actor. Each and every moment must be saturated with a belief in the truthfulness of the emotion felt, and in the action carried out, by the actor."[53] The development of theology's language through the movement of the narrative to the drama allows for theology's

---

51. *CD* I/1, 146.
52. Stanislavski, *An Actor Prepares*, 13.
53. Ibid., 130.

performance to "inspire belief in the possibility in real life" that is found in our participation in Christ's incarnational performance.

§4.1 The Performance of Language in a Dramatic Model of Theology

Recognition of the Theo-drama occurs through the *becoming* of the narrative. However, much of theology today continues along the narrative trajectory while never moving into the drama. Through the performance of language, theology is able to illuminate the reality of life. This world is constituted by the narratives of both individuals and the social community, but the profundity of these narratives is best realized when they intentionally move into the realm of performance.

Narrative theology is necessary, as we identify with a story; it "enables us to make coherent sense out of our lives." Yet even Hauerwas, one of the editors of *Why Narrative?* recognizes that life must demand more than the narrative or story.[54] Followers of Christ are drawn not to the story of Jesus but into His transformative presence. The Christian belief, writes Hauerwas, "requires transformation of the self in order to see the *actuality* of our world without illusion or self-deception."[55] The actualization of belief is the performance of the Biblical script. The Biblical Word must be "appropriated" and lived-out, as it truly does place demands upon our lives. Such demands require both internal and external evidence, as Hauerwas insists, "the 'internal' evidence requires that the 'external' have a certain character, the truth of the story requires that we be truthful if we are to see rightly the way the world is."[56] In saying as much, I admit that Hauerwas' thoughts do illumine the dramatic albeit in my opinion, he locates the dramatic *within* the narrative. This is not however, the brunt of my contention. My contention rests in the finding of *truth* and its *actualization*.

Truthfulness of the story points beyond its narrative construct to the essence of truth, which as is being argued, finds its reality in our participatory performances *in* Christ. Instead of moving beyond the narrative, Hauerwas is constricted through the language of the story, referring to the narrative as that which is the "means to note the kind of actuality we believe has grasped us in Jesus of Nazareth."[57] It is agreed that our lives do contain a story, but the essence and actualization of truth moves beyond the story,

---

54. See section 6.3 for a brief discussion of the movement in Hauerwas' theological model.
55. Hauerwas, *WN*, 305; my italics.
56. Ibid.
57. Ibid., 308.

as the density of our life's performance is such that it cannot be contained within the narrative. Jesus' claim and grip upon life is the *actuality* of the dramatic—it is the ideal *becoming* the real—it is the drawing in of humanity to the action and being of the Godhead. Truth's actuality erupts through the dramatic action of God, as humanity's knowledge is contingent on God's actuality, His Being-in-act. This dramatic act and being of God is the reality Hauerwas move towards in his writings. It is a reality that is realized when the narrative *becomes* the drama, thereby elevating the essential *actuality* of our performances through the ideal *becoming* the real.

Theology, because of its object, is inherently dramatic. In recognizing, while not explicitly writing as such, that God's interaction with and revelation to humanity is the ultimate dramatic reality, Hauerwas refers to the work of Barth.[58] As Barth writes, God is "the reality through which and in which the reality of self and world is real. As preeminent reality God is *causa prima, ens relissimum* and *actus purus*, the reality of all reality."[59] The *pure act* of God exemplifies the fact that it is not the dramatic that is found *within* the narrative, but the narrative *within* the dramatic.

Today's language requires fuller development in order to reveal the dynamic interaction taking place upon the stage. The truth of the Godhead is not actualized in a story about God, but through His dramatic intra-communion that erupts in the entrance of Christ. Theology today is witnessing (slowly) the movement of the narrative to the dramatic, and even if this movement is not explicit in much of our theological writings, nonetheless, it is still present. There is no doubt that much of our exposure to Scripture is through narrative means. While this is necessary, what is being argued is that humanity's exposure needs to be pushed into participation. Thus, rather than leaving our exposure to God in the narrative, there should be a recognition that God calls for a response to His performance, and not simply the establishment of another system of instruction. According to Balthasar, the narrative is not "abolished by the dramatic but incorporated into it . . . drawn into a new, all-embracing attitude."[60] The dramatic life of the Bible stems from God's action, not humanity's construction. Theology's task is as

---

58. Hauerwas' distinction of Barth as being one to whom credit should be rendered as participating in the furthering of theology's rediscovery of narrative for theology is a bit misdirected (*WN*, 5). Barth's theology relied primarily (but not solely) on the *interactive* revelation of the Godhead with humanity as opposed to the story re-presented in the Bible. Thus, to all intents and purposes, one could claim that Barth practiced a theological dramatics in everything but name.

59. Barth, *The Way of Theology in Karl Barth*, 36–37; quoted by Hauerwas, *With the Grain of the Universe*, 187.

60. *TD* II, 59.

Vanhoozer remarks, to bring together "the diverse genres of the Bible into the tensile unity of a dialogue." Because the foundation of dialogue is active, it allows and promotes theology's participation in God's drama through a dialogue that is as, Vanhoozer continues, "not a static system so much as a dynamic equilibrium."[61] The dynamism comes through the participatory reality of the *dramatis personae* with one another, with the Bible and most importantly with God.

§4.2 Suiting the Action of the Word to the Action of the Drama

In the arena of Biblical teaching, narrative is the preferred motif. Our instructional ability to lay out the facts is less offensive, as it poses little obstruction to the reality of one's present situation. According to John Sailhamer, "historical narrative is the re-presentation of past events for the purpose of instruction." This instruction continues Sailhamer, is secured through the narrative's two dimensional make-up: (1) the presentation of the historical event itself, and (2) the viewpoint of the author who recounts the event.[62] The reading of the Bible amounts to an instructional accounting whereby its historical narrative allows for the purpose and intent of the human author to guide and instruct the reader through non-personal means and a static relationship. However, as Balthasar notes, God's "action in and upon the world" can only be understood by humanity "through action on *its* part."[63] Theology should not simply read, exegete or hear the Biblical "story" and remain unmoved. Might the purpose and intent of the Biblical author be a bit more than instructional? Might the God of all creation reveal Himself so as to invite creation into an *active* and *participatory* relationship?

Participation and invitation as called for from God's revelatory performance—revealed in Christ, as well as the Bible—pushes beyond the narrative, thus calling for theology to "suit the action to the word, the word to the action with this special observance, that you o'erstep not the modesty of nature."[64] The language of theology best suited to the action of God's Word is the dramatic. There should be a willingness to allow theological language to suit God's performance through the active call of performance on our part. It is Christ's performance that bears upon the profundity of life; for it is His performance that is a "vital nourishing source for ours, not just as we reflect on it in the narrative, but as the Spirit unites us to him, takes our

---

61. Ben Quash, "Real Enactments," in Hart and Guthrie, *Faithful Performances*, 28.
62. Sailhamer, *Pentateuch as Narrative*, 25.
63. *TD* I, 15.
64. Shakespeare, *Hamlet* III.ii.17–19.

imagination captive and makes our performance part of the same drama, the same piece."[65] Development of our theological language is strengthened through the continual remembrance that we are called into the action of the Theo-drama that is centered in, and proceeds from, Christ through the Spirit. This movement does not deny the presence and centrality of Scripture—which guides theology, through the Holy Spirit, in its involvement in the describing of the action of this drama—it simply recognizes the dramatic essence of life *in* Christ, as through God's self-giving in Christ the stage comes to *be*. Such is the case because "all encounters between man and God are included in the drama of Christ."[66]

The language of a dramatic model of theology is intentional in its elevation of God's action. As Balthasar maintains, just as God's action "takes place along with and in the words," so too should our theological language seek to be active.[67] That is, today's theological language is meant not simply for instructional purposes, but to step inside these instructional principles, stories, teachings, etc. . . . so as to embody them in our daily living. Scripture, reminds Balthasar, is indeed "part of the drama itself, moving along with it,"[68] and our theological language should move along with the drama as well.

God's *interaction* with His people is an essential aspect of the Theo-drama. It is an aspect that even Sailhamer recognizes. "God was beginning to work in their lives (the Israelites) and they were now becoming a major part (recognition of their role) of his program (His Theo-drama) to redeem the world to himself. They were being called into fellowship with a God who wanted nothing short of their perfect obedience and trust."[69] Thinking back to Cavanaugh's point in section 2.1, the Israelites were called to submit (recognize their role) to the drama God is staging and to give themselves over to it (participate in God's performance) through their obedience and trust.

Sailhamer's thoughts acknowledge God's dramatic movement and reality—albeit through an implicit acknowledgement, as dramatic language is not explicitly employed—as he recounts the purpose behind the "compositional strategy of the Pentateuch," focusing upon the *active* living of faith so to draw in the readers to this participatory life of faith in God. "The narrative strategy of the Pentateuch" writes Sailhamer, "contrasts Abraham, who kept the Law, and Moses, whose faith was weakened under the Law

---

65. Hart and Guthrie, *Faithful Performances*, 185.
66. *TD* IV, 62; cf. *TD* III, 33–40.
67. *TD* I, 17.
68. *TD* II, 112.
69. Sailhamer, *Pentateuch as Narrative*, 5; my parenthetical insertions.

... This distinction is accomplished by showing that faith and trust in God characterized the life of God's people before the giving of the Law." Sailhamer moves forward to the crux of the Biblical author's purpose, that is, the "living out of faith," by highlighting the dramatic essence of God's Word as opposed to its narrative confines. "The Pentateuch holds up the example of Abraham, a model of faith, one who did not have the tablets of stone but who nevertheless kept the Law by *living* a life of faith."[70] Again, while his language does not explicitly employ the contours of the theatre, it cannot but draw attention to the explicitly revealed dramatic reality of God's interaction and performance upon the stage. Furthermore, while Sailhamer's work primarily attempts to instruct based on a reading of God's word, the intention and meaning propagated by his exegetical work on the Biblical "narrative" ultimately reveals the dramatic.

Sailhamer explicitly discusses and contrasts a life *lived* by faith and a life *lived* lacking faith—such discussion draws not upon a re-presentation for presentation sake, but for the explicit purpose and intent to go beyond instruction to participation in a life performed (lived) by faith.[71] Participation in God's being through the act of God is the dramatic link throughout the Biblical script. God is "going to give a heart that will obey, a heart that will love the Lord and keep his commandments."[72] It is the reality and presence of God Himself through His revelation that directs and guides the Biblical script, thereby elevating God's drama, as opposed to telling a biographical story about Him. Thus, building from the argument of Walter Eichrodt, Sailhamer notes that in the Pentateuch, the "Law is presented in such a way that it is impressed on the heart and conscience."[73] Such an impression is not meant for the telling of a good story, but for the *active* performance of God's people in Christ through the Spirit.

§5 State of Theology Today

History has witnessed, writes Balthasar, the "thousands of attempts made since medieval times to present the dramatic content of Christian revelation on the stage," thereby relegating the essence of revelation to the stage

---

70. Ibid., 78; my italics.

71. The apostle Paul is explicit as to the expected participation and imitation of the believer's life with Christ when he writes that "We are taking every thought captive to the obedience of Christ . . . If anyone is confident in himself that he is Christ's, let him consider this again within his life and performance, that just as he is Christ's, so also are we" (2 Cor 10:5–7).

72. Sailhamer, *Pentateuch as Narrative*, 32.

73. Ibid., 78 n. 170.

as opposed to the classroom or academy. As Balthasar claims, theology has much to gain from drama, as "we have shown that all of today's influential theological trends . . . converge toward a theological dramatic theory yet without being able to reach it; this is in part because they are not aware of their mutual convergence."[74] The fullness of God's revelatory action is not entirely realized through the perspective of narrative theology, if it remains in story motif as opposed to moving forward into a performative motif. The state therefore of the theology today, as is being argued, is one in need of movement—the movement of the narrative *becoming* the drama.

§5.1 Explicit Belief in and Use of the Dramatic

Contemporary theology's use of a dramatic model and the employment of its language is an intentional movement beyond the story, for the sake of the performance. Through a dramatic language that reveals the performative reality of God and humanity, theology is able to reveal the relational essence of our personhood thereby performing faithfully its role for both the Church and the world. The Bible is meant not simply to be read, but to be engaged, to be entered into and performed. N.T. Wright states that "the whole point of Christianity is that it offers a story which is the story of the world," but he further realizes that this story is not simply a story, it is an active drama about the "interrelation of humans" that allows for the "actuality of knowledge . . . while also fully allowing for the involvement of the knower in the act of knowing."[75] Wright's use of the narrative language, while containing truth, overshadows the revelatory action of the Biblical drama.

God is actively involved in and with His creation, and our theological language should reflect this reality. Thus, as was the case for Sailhamer, so too for Wright, there remains an implicit belief in, and use of, the Bible as a *drama*. The Bible is not a book solely to be observed and interpreted in order to record "what actually happened," though this is obviously is not to be discounted. Rather, the Bible is God's active voice, as it reveals the dramatic presentation of God's action in Christ through the Spirit that elicits a dramatic response. Wright's own language highlights the active voice of the drama, when he insists that there are "at least three separate sorts of exercise involved when we read the gospels and epistles . . . There is listening, pure and simple; there is interaction; and there is readiness to respond appropriately (or, intent to avoid making such a response)." Furthermore,

---

74. *TD* I, 125.

75. Wright, *The New Testament and the People of God*, 41–42, 45 (hereafter *NTPG*).

Wright's reliance upon the dramatic is played out through the employment of the drama so as to secure authority for the stories of the New Testament.[76]

Wright's account of God's interaction with His people is profound, yet it seems that his own recognition of such action would benefit from an explicitly dramatic model. This is to say, an intentional use of a dramatic model would allow for the elevation of and push towards performance and participation with respect to humanity's relationship with God. He is not a God of inaction, but of *actus purus*. In fact, Wright highlights such an active and performative quality of the followers of Christ. For those who read of and heard of Jesus' life did not simply hear a story, but were consumed in the dramatic reality of the Son of Man. "Christians of all sorts in the area," writes Wright, "who would mostly not have been trained theologians, regarded it as fundamental that their allegiance to Christ cut across any allegiance to Caesar."[77] Remembering the discussion of chapter two, followers of Christ were willingly made spectacles for the sake of Christ. The reality, then, of the dramatic tension from the life of Christians is elevated through theological language that encourages such text to "rapidly move off the page" into the performance of life.

The understanding of our performance within the theatre of God's glory occurs for the same reason that the spread of Christianity continues, because humanity comes into the presence of Truth, an encounter that makes a permanent mark on the stage. Wright comments that "the characteristics and activities of Christians marked them out from the very beginning as a new sort of grouping in the ancient world . . . It was a new way of construing what it meant to be human."[78] The Truth re-created the meaning of the human, just as it should re-create the characteristics of our theological language. Language that acknowledges: first, the universality of God's drama—no one is outside of Christ's performance; secondly, that the freedom to respond negatively to God's performance is indeed a reality, but a reality that must be countered and challenged by a theological performance that seeks to elevate the freedom of God's love over-against the freedom of humanity's "no;" and finally, Christ's performance is that which gives meaning to the entirety of life, it gives the answer to "who am I?"

---

76. Cf. *NTPG*, 140–44. Wright makes the dramatic move of outlining the biblical *story* through five acts. In the description of his outline, Wright continues to remain bound to the language of the story referring consistently to the retelling of the story. This retelling relates to the story of creation, the fall, and Jesus—all of which is the entirety of the biblical story.

77. Ibid., 350.

78. Ibid., 365.

Language that continuously refers to the Biblical story in terms of dramatic language by referring to the "primary players" as such, or just by constantly drawing on "dramatic" accounts of the Bible, needs to move beyond the narrative, so as to step completely upon the stage and reveal the reality of Christ's universal performance. The authority of God's drama, that is, His Sovereign interaction and infinite freedom, is revealed through its dramatic foundation, it is a reality that, according to Wright, "is a dynamic, not a static authority."[79] God is revealed through His action which is most effectively illumined through the dramatizing of theology. Theology should risk the step into the action of God's threefold movement, so as to actualize our own faithful performance. Through the language and understanding of drama, theology is provided with further tools that can illumine the call for participation in the being of God. Life is not static, it is an active, self-involved drama that calls each of us to play our many parts, and play them well.

§5.2 Movement of Language in a Dramatic Model of Theology

Movement from the language of a story to the performative language of drama can profoundly benefit today's theological endeavors. This movement occurs through an explicit call for participation in and the enactment of God's word. Allowing the story to overshadow the drama tends to drown out our appreciation of God's Being-in-act. Theology should be careful not to place God under the microscope but instead, elevate His call for our participation in His action. According to Barth, this call to action is because the creature can "only be ready for God, or more exactly for God's action in the covenant of grace and Kingdom of Christ. It can only wait for His omnipotent mercy, acquiring its function, *telos* and character, and becoming God's servant and action, the theatre of His action and mirror and likeness of His glory."[80] The creature is called to participate in God's glory, not simply to tell of such an action.

God is Being-in-act and through His action, we are exposed to the fullness of our personhood, to our ideal. In our participation in God's Being-in-act, the reality of our relationality is opened up through an analogy of relations, which allows for a deepened understanding of ourselves, and of God. According to Barth, "the concept of analogy is in fact unavoidable," but such analogy cannot be based on one of identity whereby the essence of identity melts away leaving nothing more than a grotesque representation

---

79. Ibid., 417.
80. *CD* III/3, 52.

of being. "There is not" remarks Barth, "a correspondence and similarity of being, an *analogia entis*. The being of God cannot be compared with that of man. But it is not a question of this twofold being. It is a question of the relationship within the being of God on the one side and between the being of God and that of man on the other . . . There is an *analogia relationis*."[81]

Theology should seek to participate in the analogia relationis through the work illumining the profundity of God's dramatic interaction. The theatrical overtones of the Bible, encountered through revelation, become known through the movement and countermovement of the stage, as "God moved; he came down to earth . . . The most ancient drama, the drama that rules the world, is the drama of the meeting of God with man."[82] Such action is relational, and calls upon theology to engage and participate in this on-going action. As Dorothy Sayers remarked, "the gospel is the greatest drama ever staged." To be true to this gospel drama, today's theological language should be constituted by what Oliver Davies called the "creative rhythms of revelatory divine speech." Through such speech/language, our reading of Scripture will naturally move towards the element of performance. Such a performative reality stems from Biblical language that not only reveals the witness of God, but as Davies maintains, must affect our reading of Scripture, so that we "come to inhabit utterances that are already shaped by the divine communicative presence."[83] Only through such utterances shall there be a clear perichoretic notion of the participants on the stage; the relational reality of the faith that, as Sayers writes, is "the most exciting drama that ever staggered the imagination of man."[84]

Theology's reliance upon the narrative needs to be loosened, for, as Ben Quash maintains, "drama's appropriateness to the expression of Christian theology is demonstrated in the interaction of individual persons with one another, and with the collectively-held content of Christian faith."[85] The language of the Bible is interactive, calling for a participation in the Being and action of God. The Bible is essential to our understanding of God's revealing; and although it can never "contain the 'breadth and length and height and depth' of the incarnate Word," it is essential to humanity's performance, because, as Balthasar continues, "this testimony, since it is inspired by the Spirit, is always more than itself: what seems on the surface to be a

---

81. *CD* III/2, 220. Cf. II/1, 204–54. See §4 in chapter 4 of this thesis for further development of *analogia relationis*.

82. Leeuw, *Sacred and Profane Beauty: The Holy in Art*, 111; quoted by Vanhoozer, *Drama of Doctrine*, 38.

83. Davies, *Creativity of God*, 75.

84. Sayers, *The Greatest Drama Ever Staged*, 1.

85. Ben Quash, "Real Enactments," in Hart and Guthrie, *Faithful Performances*, 23.

book is inwardly 'spirit and life.'"[86] The Bible must not be reduced to a static collection of stories and other kind of writings to be read, nor investigated as by an "uninvolved spectator and reporter." It must be recognized as part of the drama itself as it is "one aspect of the Word's total Incarnation event that shares in the theodramatic character of this totality."[87]

When the narrative is not developed into a performative realm, that is, the dramatic, the possibility of humanity's fullness is potentially lost. According to Balthasar, "If 'the Word becomes flesh' more and more profoundly, unto death on the Cross, it follows that, in the drama God enacts with mankind, not the least particle of the human and its tragic dimension will be lost."[88] Humanity's distanced observation and study, etc., of the Biblical narrative tends to elevate the written word above and beyond the *enfleshed Word*.[89] The text of Scripture does guide the performance; a guidance that while assisting, never detracts from or overtakes the primal direction of the Holy Spirit. Scripture is meant to reveal the transformation of history, the reality of God's acts of grace as performed through the Word becoming flesh. As Balthasar maintains, "the drama that begins with Christ and attains its culmination in him is continually showing us more of its prehistory, to which it belongs, which renders it intelligible and gives it its whole range and ultimate motivation."[90] The movement of the drama is the transformation bound up in the communion (*analogia relationis*) of Creator and creation. Its truth is the whole of history such that, as Balthasar insists, "the New Testament turns back and takes in the Old; it goes back as far as creation, (Adam-Eve and Christ-Church throw a light on each other: Eph 5), right back to God's plan 'before the foundation of the world,' which is revealed and unfolded, at the end of the ages, in the Church, to the amazement of the 'principalities and powers in the heavenly places' (Eph 3:10)."[91] The drama of life is the reality and truth of God Himself, a reality that exposes the truth that, God is "eternally involved in Christ crucified for my sake and for the sake of the whole world." And thus, "I myself cannot, in the face of this, stand by as a mere spectator."[92]

God's Word and action revealed through Scripture stand above yet never beyond the written word. This revealed Word is the Godhead's

---

86. *TD* II, 108.
87. Ibid., 114.
88. Ibid., 53.
89. For further discussion, see *TD* II, 53–62.
90. *TD* II, 58.
91. Ibid.
92. *EG*, 46.

interaction with humanity; it is, as Barth insists, "the action of the Lord... When and where Jesus Christ becomes contemporaneous through Scripture and proclamation, when and where the "God with us" is said to us by God Himself, we come under a lordship... In Jesus Christ we understand the Word of God as the epitome of God's grace."[93] Yet much of today's theological paradigm tends to pay attention "only to the medium of the written word." Through such a limited perspective, those who pay little attention to the action of God and "resist imaginative reconstruction of the very palpable events to which it (the Bible) claims to bear witness will miss much of the fully sensual and even theatrical nature of God's self-revelation."[94]

§6 Development and Movement of Theological Language

Revelation does not reveal Scripture per se, but the God who speaks and reveals truth in and through Scripture. As Barth maintains, "It is hard to see how in relation to Holy Scripture we can say what is distinctive for the holiness of this Scripture if first we do not make it clear (naturally from Holy Scripture itself) who the God is whose revelation makes Scripture holy."[95] The God of Christian revelation is He who reveals Himself through the incarnational performance of Christ. Through a dramatic model of theology, and its enfleshed language, this relational and incarnational reality is not only illumined but properly revealed as being a call for humanity's own relational and incarnational performance. The narrative is significant, and while it is true that the meaning of the Biblical narrative is Christ, such meaning points beyond the narrative to the living Christ.[96] The narrative is incapable of the density of action that permeates from the living Christ. Christ is not only the "authentic human response to God but also provides for us the pattern for true human existence,"[97] as He (Jesus) is humanity's original and truthful performance. Through our self-involvement in the act of God we (humanity), enter into profound participation within the theatre of God's glory. Thus as Hart reveals, "When God speaks his Word into the realm of flesh it results not in an echo, but precisely in a reply, a response for the side of the creature to the Creature's call."[98]

93. *CD* I/1, 149-50.
94. Harris, *Theatre and Incarnation*, 7.
95. *CD* I/1, 300.
96. This idea was raised by Oliver Davies, in his paper highlighting the primacy of Christ (Davies, "The Lordship of Christ.").
97. Clark, *Divine Revelation*, 75.
98. Hart, *Regarding Karl Barth*, 22.

Contemporary theological language's inchoate stage of its development in a model of dramatic theology is moving toward the arena of performance and the dramatic. However, there is still a tendency to allow the narrative to remain outside the realm of performance and even overshadow Christ's performance. Let us look first at two examples that present the overshadowing of Christ's performance before moving to two brief examples of dramatic models of theology that elevate and center the action of theology in God's Being-in-act.

§6.1 Vanhoozer and the Drama of Doctrine

Looking first at Kevin Vanhoozer's *The Drama of Doctrine*, my argument is that his reliance on the narrative in reference to Christ when discussing the aspect of the Canon, Christ, and Scripture, leads to a subtle stripping away of the dramatic action of Christ. Christ's life, writes Vanhoozer, was copied down in a "commissioned transmission of events" that comprise the "mission of Christ."[99] Through Vanhoozer's use of the narrative to present the dramatic, Christ becomes a figure from history as opposed to the dramatic transfiguration of history. This is to say that Vanhoozer's elevation of the canon as the "normative specification of the identity of the divine *dramatis personae* and of the shape of the divine action," rather than Christ, inserts an un-dramatic sense to God's drama.[100] According to Vanhoozer, centralizing the drama of the Bible in Christ creates a situation in which "doctrine thus appears parasitic; it lives on the second story, over the store as it were."[101] It is true that Vanhoozer recognizes the need for the performance of scripture, but his insistence on its (Scripture) priority overshadows the incarnational performance of Christ and the direction and guidance of the Spirit.

Vanhoozer writes that it is the canon, not Christ, that remains the "supreme norm and measure of dramatic consistency," the "rule and criterion, then, not apart from but precisely because of its place in the divine economy of redemption," giving the "form and content of the theo-drama."[102] Admittedly, Vanhoozer's account of God's drama does promote the performative element of Scripture, however, in its presentation there seems to be a slight elevation of the canon above Christ for it is the canon which seemingly gives the dramatic final shape to our talk of Scripture and thus, salvation

---

99. Vanhoozer, *Drama of Doctrine*, 146.
100. Ibid., 236.
101. Ibid., 7.
102. Ibid., 146–47.

in Christ.[103] It is not that the canon is not necessary, but rather, that we need constantly to remind ourselves that the primary or "supreme norm" of our faith is Christ, the Word of God expressed and revealed through the word of God (Scripture). Vanhoozer does not dismiss God's revelatory act in Christ, but does what I believe subtly occurs on a consistent basis within the evangelical movement, he moves away from revelation pointing first and foremost to its meaning in Christ by focusing on the supremacy of Scripture. Such theological movements and understandings of revelation that move away from the primacy of a Christological perspective, whether subtly or blatantly, end up presenting revelation as being directly given into the hands of humanity. Such understanding sets aside the revelation of God—the Word-made-flesh—which is, writes Balthasar, an "incarnated language of being and of concrete existence."[104]

The call for the dramatizing of theology is the return back to the core of our theological foundation. It is the Lord who builds the house, not Scripture, theology or the Church. Thus, as Barth indicates, "our talking, speaking, or arguing in theology can only be an appeal to God's speaking to men which happened and is continually happening in Christ. To complete that speaking does not in any sense lie within our competence and capacity. What we have to do is to conform ourselves to it."[105]

§6.2 The Drama of the Biblical Story in Bartholomew and Goheen

The second example I wish to look at is the book called *The Drama of Scripture: Finding our place in the Biblical Story* by Craig Bartholomew and Michael Goheen.[106] In this book we witness some of the features of a dramatic model of theology. However, the model at times oscillates between the narrative and dramatic as is initially apparent from the title. The essence of life is, as Bartholomew and Goheen present it, to be understood from "within some narrative," not from the dramatic. The "biblical story opens with the words 'In the beginning God,' so to unfold the Genesis story of creation" which finds its highpoint in the "making of humankind." Bartholomew and Green look to the "story of Jesus" as the "climactic episode of the great story of the Bible." The Bible is the "grand story . . . the one true story told in the Bible . . . At the very center of this story is the man called Jesus." While

---

103. For Vanhoozer's argument, see especially his section on the rule of Canon, *Drama of Doctrine*, 146–50.

104. *TD* II, 28.

105. *TC*, 302.

106. Bartholomew and Goheen, *Drama of Scripture*.

Bartholomew and Goheen recognize and acknowledge Christ as the center of the Biblical story, His dramatic performance is often overshadowed by the epic-telling of *His story*. "The world of the Bible is our world and its story of redemption is also our story." This narrative format detracts from the Biblical drama, elevating the story and humanity's place within the story, as we need to "know the biblical story," as opposed to the One from whom the script came. "Where we are in the story" engulfs the action and performance of Jesus.[107] Humanity's place upon the stage is significant and essential, but such is the case only because of the Son and Spirit. Our performance stems from our creation in the image of God, not of the script. We find our "true humanity in perichoretic unity with God and one another,"[108] as through the performance of Christ the stage is rooted in the eternal action of the Godhead.

The need for the dramatic is essential, and today's need within theology is indeed beginning to play out through the likes of Vanhoozer, Horton, Hauerwas, Johnson and Savidge and Harris.[109] Theology's acknowledgement of God's interaction through His interactive Word simply recognizes the conviction, as noted by Hart, that "all life is lived in terms of a "performative" aspect from beginning to end."[110] This conviction is the realization moving today's theological language into the fullness of the drama.

§6.3 Performing the Faith: Stanley Hauerwas

While it can be said that Hauerwas' early theological language promoted a narrative model of theology, the claim remains that his theology has gradually moved beyond the narrative into the dramatic. Through the dramatic we are able to recognize the profundity of our performance in Christ. It is the dramatic that actualizes our recognition of God's action. Hauerwas writes that "Christians worship a God, who is pure act, an eternally performing God . . . Our God is a performing God who has invited us to join in the performance that is God's life."[111] Hauerwas' theological language has

---

107. For development and use of the narrative in Bartholomew and Goheen, see ibid., 1–7, 13, 103, 151.

108. Torrance, *Worship, Community*, 38.

109. Hauerwas for instance, edited and contributed to *Why Narrative?* in 1997. *Performing the Faith*, written in 2004 shows what I believe to be the movement from a narrative theology toward the more dramatic and performative based theology within Hauerwas' own work.

110. Hart and Guthrie, *Faithful Performances*, 3.

111. Hauerwas, *Performing the Faith*, 77.

continually moved toward revealing the dramatic essence of his theological reflections.

Writing in *Performing the Faith*, Hauerwas says that "creation and redemption name the great drama in which we become participants, performers, in God's care of all that is."[112] Chapter 5 of the same book might be thrust forward by some as defense for Hauerwas' narrative roots, but even Hauerwas states that he has "increasingly become convinced that rather than talking about narrative as a category in itself, we are better advised to do theology in a manner that displays what we have learned."[113] This active display of theology that constitutes the foundation of our theological performance and dialogue is manifested in the essence of the dramatic—the living out of the enfleshed Word. Hauerwas' theological model continues to embrace the dramatic through its continual push and elevation of Christ's incarnational act that draws humanity in to its reconciliatory performance. Hauerwas writes that Christians can do nothing more important than to "live the story we believe makes us participants in God's life."[114] Such participation and living illumines the foundation of the "lived-in story," or rather, the narrative *becoming* drama, also illumines our performance in Christ through the Spirit, upon creation's stage

§6.4 Incarnational Performance of Theology through a Dramatic Model

In his *Theatre and Incarnation*, Max Harris offers an encounter between the theatre and life that provides an effective way that theology can draw on the theatre for our theological endeavors. Theology misses out on some of the Bible's dramatic and relational content when it does not realize that the events described in the Bible are "inherently theatrical." Theatrical precisely because, as Harris maintains, at the "heart of the *narrative* is the transformation of the Word into flesh."[115] A dramatic model not only illumines this transformation, but encourages our participation in this act, as through this act, we (humanity) come into the presence of our "true humanity." According to Balthasar, in Christ, "true humanity is revealed, not only the humanity of man but also the humanity of God."[116]

The recognition of God's active revelation and thus, His transformation of the human, as presented through the incarnation, leads Harris to

---

112. Ibid., 16.
113. Ibid., 140.
114. Ibid., 149.
115. Harris, *Theology and Incarnation*, 8; my italics.
116. *TD* II, 406.

center the drama in Christ, thereby moving the stage always toward the incarnational performance of the Trinity. Such a move and recognition by Harris further allows him to remain faithful to the dramatic performance of God with humanity, as it is played out in the "transformation effected when word becomes performance." The "Christian concept" claims Harris, "of God's mode of self-revelation is theatrical."[117] Theology should continue to move toward the incarnational and relational performance of Christ. According to Harris, "The proclamation that 'all the fullness of God' became flesh once for all in Christ and continues to be incarnate in the members of his body, the Church, sets limits, for the Christian, to the theatrical evocation of spirits."[118]

§7 Performance and Person as Exposed through a Dramatic Model of Theology

A dramatic model of theology attempts to elevate our awareness of God's call towards performance thereby raising awareness to our personhood as it is through our relationship with Christ that we come to apprehend the fullness of our identity. Humanity's performance and person are realized and recognized from the reality that as Barth writes, "God is the Lord of the covenant of grace," and it is this covenant of grace that "characterizes (positively or negatively) man's being and action as also the creature and the future heir of God, not the reverse."[119] It is in light of this relational reality that a dramatic model of theology seeks to be intentional in its desire to participate in, and express the action of God.

Through the drama, theology comes to witness, understand, and know the relation to the Creator, Reconciler and Redeemer—a relationship overwhelmed and consumed in love and grace that penetrates to the core of our humanity. The depth of this relational reality opens up through a model of dramatic theology that reveals the centrality and profundity of Christ, "who is not only the ontic but also the noetic basis of the whole of Christian truth and the Christian message."[120] If taken seriously, then, and under the direction of the Holy Spirit, a dramatic model of theology can help to produce a theological performance that continues to seek answers to humanity's relational identity. The underlining premise of the drama rests within the identity of the Father, Son and Holy Spirit, thereby reminding once again of

117. Hart, *Theology and Incarnation*, 12
118. Ibid., 128.
119. *CD* IV/4, *Lecture Fragments*, 9.
120. Ibid.

the importance of the analogia relationis. As Balthasar claims, the analogy, "which is essential to a theory of Theo-drama, is absorbed in identity."[121]

§7.1 Performance and Personhood Rooted in Christ

Our theological endeavors should seek to be rooted in the performance and person of Christ, so as to elevate the profundity and possibility of humanity's performance and personhood. Rather than constructing a system of principles or a set of stories theology's move into a dramatic model opens up the possibilities of today's performances. Trevor Hart writes that there are "no historical preconditions for the resurrection of Jesus to be sure; yet Christian experience is now filled with happenings which are analogous to it in the sense that they too introduce the lustre of the new into the old order. That they too derive not from potentialities latent within nature, but from the creative power of God calling forth life out of death." There is an analogy to be recognized here, but it is, concludes Hart, "always in one direction, *from* the paradigm event of the resurrection *to* those subsequent partial and dependent anticipations of the new creation which arise out of its power at work in the world."[122] Thus, a model of dramatic theology insists upon an interaction (the *becoming* of the real) between the revealer (Jesus Christ) and the hearer (humanity).

The relationship between the revealer and the hearer—Christ's performance through the Spirit—is rooted in the active and *real* love of God. It is this love that overcomes the chasm of difference between Creator and creature. As Moltmann writes, "the deity of God is revealed in the paradox of the cross." This revealing, in the person of Christ through the Spirit, is the contradiction of the cross, the performance of God that brings forth the reality of humanity's perfection in the midst of humanity's imperfection. Moltmann continues his thought on this contradiction and relational reality, as he writes, that the deity of God revealed through the cross makes it easier to understand what Jesus did: "it was not the devout, but the sinners, not the righteous but the unrighteous who recognized him, because in them he revealed the divine righteousness of grace, and the kingdom. He revealed his identity amongst those who had lost their identity . . . and was recognized as the Son of Man amongst those who had been deprived of their humanity."[123] It is the *ideal* and concrete performance of Christ that has reconciled man to Himself thereby graciously granting humanity the

121. *TD* I, 67.
122. Hart, "Imagination," 72.
123. Moltmann, *Crucified God*, 27.

possibility of the ideal *becoming* the real. This is the drama of salvation and it is the gracious gift of participation, or what Barth calls, "the freedom of obedience."

The movement of the stage is the freedom made real and possible from the command of God; a God who relentlessly pursues us amidst our continual turning away. Barth comments that:

> The freedom to call upon God is authentic freedom, not one of the inauthentic freedoms that man usually arrogates to himself and grasps and steals in his rebellion against God. It is not contrived or achieved by Christians. It is given to them as freedom for obedience to the command received by them, the command of God from which they have turned aside but which turns to them with the order to pray "Thy kingdom come," and in so doing awakens them and keeps them awake to know this kingdom even in the midst of the kingdom of disorder, to look toward it and to call for it. As they use the freedom for this prayer this is given them with the command, they already stand on a rock even here and now, when everything around them and everything in their own hearts and lives and consciences is tottering and falling.[124]

The freedom found in Christ makes concrete any and all analogical attempts of theology. Analogy is made concrete—*real*—through the reality of Christ. Christ's reality and His act towards humanity are concretized through His incarnational performance and the relational action of Creator to creature is that which solidifies both our performance and our personhood in and through the eternal action of love. In the incarnational, crucified, resurrected and ascended performance of Christ, God has re-humanized the human. Here, writes Moltmann, "God has not just acted externally, in his unattainable glory and eternity. Here he has acted in himself and has gone on to suffer in himself. Here he himself is love with all his being."[125]

The recognition of Christ's central role and action concretizes our theological endeavors. Any analogous performance, maintains Balthasar, must recognize that "analogy is an ultimate relational term" that is the absoluteness of love through Christ.[126] To illumine the actuality of the simple analogy overcome through the analogia relationis is to insist upon a determinate focal point. Through our relational reality *in* Christ, we are granted the ability to participate in God's threefold movement of revelation, invitation

---

124. *CD* IV/4, 234.
125. Moltmann, *Crucified God*, 205.
126. *TKB*, 109.

and reconciliation. This is made possible because of Christ; for as Balthasar claims, it is Christ who opens up the acting area, *der Spielraum*—the playing room or space—in which all other characters of the Theo-drama are to receive their role.[127] Only in Christ, through the Spirit, does theology—and more importantly, the Church, and thus, humanity—find its perspective, purpose and direction.

§7.2 From Our *Analogia Relationis* towards the Ideal Becoming the Real

Christ is the fullness of our reconciliation, the one-and-only analogy needed, as He is our salvation; He is revelation, and through the Spirit, offers the invitation into the glory of the theatre in which we perform. The point here is that the drama of the divine, the inner-working and outpouring of God are revealed concretely in Christ through the Spirit. In Christ, the concrete analogy of being becomes the interactive reality of the analogia relationis. Only through the drama is the great expression of our need, to surrender ourselves to something that transcends, and gives meaning to, the limited horizon, brought to fruition. Such dramatic interaction "sheds light upon a reality in which we glimpse something of the ultimate horizon of existence and our own truest selves."[128] Ultimately, the drama of Jesus can or must be understood to 'create ways both of speaking of God and of realizing His action in the world."[129] Through His action, theology is granted the possibility of imagining the real. This is to say, through the performance of Christ, humanity witnesses the *ideal* of humanity that invites us to imagine the *becoming* of our own performances.

It is being argued that through a dramatic model of theology we are afforded ways of re-shaping our theological endeavors so as to be faithful to the revelation of God exposed through the Biblical script, as well as its elicitation of performance. The profundity of a dramatic model of theology stems from the fact that God is *Being-in-act* and His action is not meant simply for narration, as God's action takes place along, with, in, and beyond the words, but is meant for an active response and engagement.[130]

It is the action of God that sets in motion the possibility of our participation, in His threefold movement. Aidan Nichols writes:

---

127. *TD* III, 41–43.
128. *TD* I, 308.
129. Gunton, *Actuality of Atonement*, 52
130. *TD* I, 17–19.

> What else is this beauty-inspired confrontation in language and action where human freedom is set in motion, for good or evil, than the dramatic itself—that quality of existence which the theatre brings out, with its many voices, its plots, and *dénouements*, its dramatizations of choice and freedom, whether against the grain of reality or in harmony with it, all for the sake of enabling us the better to understand our lives and the world in which those lives are set?[131]

Contemporary theology's move into the action of God gives meaning to our mission, and purpose to our performance. In this light, Balthasar writes, that the implication of God's performance is "something that can only be accepted and pondered in a faith that precedes all personal initiative . . . Following Christ, which has become possible through his self-surrender, will not consist in doing *some right thing* but in fundamentally surrendering everything, and surrendering it to the God who has totally emptied himself, so that he can use [that right thing] for the world, according to his own purposes."[132] From our relational reality *in* Christ through the Spirit (analogia relationis), humanity is granted the ability to imagine the real, which is to realize the essence of its identity while recognizing the profundity of our own performances.

A dramatic model of theology opens humanity up to the profundity of personhood through the reality of performance. That is, through our analogia relationis, we are granted the ability to imagine the real through our performance in Christ. The performance of God's Word reveals His invitation and desire for reconciliation. This threefold movement is what makes real the ideal of humanity. We now move to chapter four so as to move deeper into understanding what is the *becoming* of the ideal into the real. The hope is to understand the ability of a dramatic model to awaken the imaginative powers of theology so as to imagine the real.

---

131. Nichols, *No Bloodless Myth*, 5; italics in original.

132. *TD* I, 33–34.

Chapter Four—Imagining the Real

> How is the creature's *ideal* envisaged? Two factors present themselves, the second dependent on the first. The first is this: Since the world is designed and created in Christ, our Idea is also "in Christ": He has taken on the task of showing us our nature as heaven planned it; we have our nature *in him* . . . The second factor has to be the Idea of our mission (of our charisma) within the economy of Christ's universal redemptive Body.[1]

§1 Into the Real

THE REALITY OF TOMORROW gains its beauty and glory through the performance of today. To entertain the hope encompassed within the movement of the world's stage, theology's endeavors must continue to risk moving deeper into the action of the ideal becoming the real. We find that the movement of the ideal into the real helps to shed light upon the ultimate meaning of life. Balthasar maintains that it is through the perspective of the Absolute that meaning is determined and through this perspective, "we find not only the ultimate meaning of reality as such, but also, beyond that, the *ideality* that provides the meaning, or determines "what *ought* to be", which is the ultimate measure of the truth of reality."[2] God's ideal of us becomes concrete through our faithful performances. In other words, from a Christian standpoint, our faithful performances can only occur when we realize God's particular idea of me that is revealed in Christ through the Spirit. As Balthasar writes, God's Idea is "the realized Idea of the world," which means the concrete world, is the "unity of the ideal and the real." Realization of this unity, as will be argued, occurs through the ideal becoming the real.

This movement—the *ideal* becoming the *real*—is a movement poised between memory and eschatology, while enlivened through the power of hope. It is through imagination that our recognition of such movement is

---

1. *TD* V, 391–92.
2. *TL*, I, 61.

apprehended, as from our imagination we make "sense of this hopeful living towards God's future."[3] If appreciated, the power of the imagination can propel humanity deeper into recognizing the ideal of our mission.[4] This is to say that God's ideal of the human plays out in our real mission upon the world's stage. It is the answer to the query of "who am I?" It is an understanding made possible through the power of imagination; a power stemming from the willingness to look towards the realization of what can be.

Through our imaginative powers, humanity is given the possibility of imagining what can be or can happen with regards to our being through our *becoming*. Imagination, writes Stanislavski, "creates things that can be or can happen, whereas fantasy invents things that are not in existence, which never have been or will be . . . In this creative process imagination leads the actor."[5] It is a movement that directly connects the creature to the Creator as it is the realization by the creature of God's idea of what the human is meant to be. According to Balthasar, "In thus showing us what our nature is meant to be, he (God) causes our idea in him to move (in Erigena's sense) toward us, in a sense that is both universal or Catholic (as in the case of the Platonic Idea) but equally in an individual and personal sense that cannot be overtaken by any reditus to God."[6] Inherent in God's future and His interaction with the stage is the truth of Christ's reconciliatory performance. This action, as being argued throughout this book, is best recognized and realized through the dramatizing theology.

The intent of this chapter is to raise awareness of our imaginative powers and the once active use of them. Movement of the ideal into the real reveals the hope of tomorrow so as to encourage its performance today. The trajectory of this theological project moves along the lines of being and action in the hopes of ascertaining a deeper knowledge of what our faithful performances involve. In this chapter I hope to highlight some of the pejorative misunderstandings that accompany the imaginative. It is not a query anymore of whether or not we are imaginative beings. Instead, the chapter will proceed along the understanding offered by Trevor Hart:

> Imagination is better thought of as *a way of thinking, responding and acting* across the whole spread of our experience, not some arcane "thing" with a carefully specified and limited remit. And

---

3. Hart, "Imagination," 54.

4. Our mission is the recognition of our identity and our movement in Christ and upon His stage. This concept and understanding is developed in section 4 of this chapter.

5. Stanislavski, *An Actor Prepares*, 55–56.

6. *TD* V, 391.

an "imaginatomy" would render us incapable, therefore, not just of certain "artsy" activities we might (or might not) manage or be better without, but of much (possibly most) of what makes us human at all. The imaginative is the psychical equivalent not of our appendix (which, when it becomes troublesome or painful, we can simply cut out and flush away without loss) but the blood supply which circulate the things (both good and bad) around our entire body.[7]

We are imaginative beings and must begin to embrace this reality if we hope to understand the performative possibilities of our existence.

First, the chapter seeks to understand what it means to *become*. That is, what is the reality of the human being "embedded in God" and how is this reality made real for the creature? Section two seeks to introduce us to what it means to recognize God's action thereby exposing us to His hope and idea of the human. Finally, section two looks at God's threefold movement of revelation, invitation and reconciliation. It is a movement utterly profound in its imagining of the stage's eschatological future so as to elevate the real of today's performance.

Section three seeks to understand better the imaginative powers of theology by discussing the reality and foundation of imagination. "Imagination is the means by which we are able to represent anything not directly accessible, including *both* the world of the imaginary *and* recalcitrant aspects of the real world; it is the medium of fiction as well as fact."[8] Furthermore, the section will look at some of the negative sentiments towards our theological imagination. Even amidst these sentiments, the section argues that through the employment of our imagination, we are given further tools that provide deeper possibilities in comprehending the fullness of Christ's actualization of the real from the ideal. The discussion of today's re-imagining is thus followed by a discussion of the meaning and use of imagination for this project.

In section 4, we move into a discussion of what it means to imagine the real. What does it mean to state that the ideal is *becoming* the real? Through the incarnational performance of Christ, God enacts His most imaginative action so as to reveal, invite and reconcile. The last two sections of the chapter move into the elevation of the real, so as to begin our imaginative movement into our faithful performances (which is taken up fully in chapter 5).

---

7. Hart, "A Suspicion Observed," 5.
8. Green, *Imagining God*, 66.

§2 Embedded in God

§2.1 Imagining the Real: Our Performance in Christ

The world's stage is inclusive of the entirety of humanity through Christ's salvific performance as illumined across history by the action of the Holy Spirit. Our perfection remains real for humanity due to the possibility of being incorporated in Christ's ideal performance as revealed through His incarnational action. Christ is the universal performance while also being the particular performance of God. This apparent paradox is the foundational truth and reality that establishes and sustains the possibility of humanity's perfection. According to Richard Bauckham, Christ "is of universal significance because he stood in a unique relation to God and in a unique relation to humanity. The only way any individual can transcend his particularity without losing it, is in his relationships."[9] Through God's relational reality, ad intra and ad extra, humanity witnesses the possibility of its perfection. In other words, the achievement of humanity's perfection as witnessed in Christ is the ideal become the real. From Christ "(T)he possibilities of God's open future, are, then, genuinely anticipated in the midst of this present age, with a resultant transformation of present ways of being and doing and thinking in the world on the part of God's people."[10] This act and its transformative result, finds its roots in its "leaving" and "returning" to God, which is found "uniquely in Christ." Balthasar claims, the Son, "on behalf of himself and those who are his, is always doing nothing but his Father's work of creation; his Father cooperates in this fulfilment by giving gifts and 'rewards:' both, however, together with those who are the recipients of these gifts, allow themselves to be filled with the overflowing bounty of the Holy Spirit."[11] Again, if Balthasar is correct, then, humanity's realization of its identity comes through the willingness to receive the "gifts" of the Godhead, but also our willingness to participate in the overabundance of life's performance as directed through the Holy Spirit.

Today, however, the drama still witnesses humanity's contradiction to God due to our continued desire to displace Christ; that is, to remove Him from the central action of the stage, thereby narrowing the acting area of world history. God, on the other hand, is not in contradiction to the creature, precisely because of His revelation, invitation and reconciliation. Through *His* performance, God envelops the stage with His grace and mercy, thereby closing the chasm once present on the world's stage. God is

---

9. Bauckham, "Christology Today," 20 (hereafter cited as "CT").
10. Hart, "Imagination," 63.
11. *TD* V, 380–81.

the "Father of mercies (2 Cor 1:3)" that "comforteth those that are cast down (2 Cor 7:6)." Furthermore, and most significantly, He (God) is the "Father of Jesus Christ, the One who in Him reconciles the world to Himself. And as this God He is the Law-giver and Himself the law for those who know Him in Jesus Christ, who can rejoice in their own atonement made in Jesus Christ: those who can recognize themselves as the children of God in Jesus Christ (exalted in Him and by Him)."[12]

God's divine plan is accomplished in Christ who is the very "something" that every event, every being, points towards. This, claims Balthasar, is true because "in reality, every being, every event, has significance, is laden with meaning, and is an expression and a sign pointing to something else."[13] Theology can bear witness to this sign pointing to something else, through its attempts to express God's desire for humanity's participation. For in Christ, God's covenantal plan and performance is not only complete, but revealed to the entirety of the acting area. Balthasar points out that "God's plan for the world is to unite all cosmic reality, in heaven and on earth, in Christ, who is the Head (Eph 1:10)."[14] Through the action of God, theology is incorporated (embedded) in His transformative performance. This incorporation is the basis of hope and transformation. That is, through humanity's incorporation into God's actions, hope is gained from tomorrow's glory transforming today's reality. Picking up from points made by Jürgen Moltmann, Trevor Hart writes that "the nature of hope is to force a radical interpretation (reimagining or reimaging) of the real seeking a meaning for the present which is historical in the sense that it is teleologically determined."[15] Those *in* Christ are specifically confronted with a performance that seeks to incorporate us into today's hope. As Hart continues, "the *Gestalt* shift has to do not with the future alone, but with the present which that future informs and shapes. Our view of what *is* the case as well as what *will be* is transfigured."[16]

Christ's performative reality enables theology to imagine the ideal becoming the real, for it is this becoming that gives significance to our theological performances. Theology's becoming—its participation in Christ's performance—is the necessary action needed to guide the church and society, to point them once again to the "something else." Taking a cue from Antonin Artaud, theology might be able to recognition the currents of the

12. *CD* IV/1, 191.
13. *TL*, I, 103.
14. *TD* III, 15.
15. Hart, "Imagination," 63.
16. Ibid.

day, and respond. Artaud writes, "but there are too many signs that everything that used to sustain our lives no longer does so, that we are all mad, desperate, and sick. And I call for *us* to react."[17] The reaction by theology occurs when theology moves against the current flow of the world stage's movement—a movement into self-aggrandizement and selfishness—so as to accept Christ's invitation to participate in His redemptive performance. Theology must awaken humanity once again to that which transcends us. If, writes Artaud, "in Shakespeare, a man is sometimes preoccupied with what transcends him, it is always in order to determine the ultimate consequences of this preoccupation within him."[18]

Our theological performances are not in and of themselves the proprietors of their own significance as it is only *from above* that the actions *of below* gain validity and significance. This is to say that when theology acknowledges its imaginative powers and allows them to guide its endeavors, the reality of Christ's performance becoming ours will not only be realized, but will elevate our own performances as well. The ideal becoming the real is an action performed through the guidance and leading of the Godhead, it is an action made possible to humanity. Balthasar notes that "Christ has been sent down 'from above,' lowered to earth by God's free action; by nature he is not composite, rather he is the single capstone of the entire vault of creation built up 'from below.' Both aspects belong together: Christ is determined from below by the whole world drama, and, on the other hand, he is *not* determined by it since he alone is 'from above' (John 8:23)."[19] If, then, theology intentionally employs our theological imaginative powers to *imagine* our participation in Christ's action, the "vault of creation," we can participate in this action specifically by illumining to the Church and the world, God's threefold movement.

§2.2 The Threefold Movement of Revelation, Invitation and Reconciliation

Understanding God's action gives us access to His hope and idea of the human. Unpacking our understanding of God's action exposes the reality of God's action, that is, the threefold movement of revelation, invitation and reconciliation. This movement, while involving distinct actions, is a unified movement bound up in the performance of Christ as revealed through the interaction of the Spirit. The unity of the movement reveals the truth of

---

17. Artaud, *Theater and Its Double*, 77.
18. Ibid., 77.
19. *TD* III, 15.

Chapter Four—Imagining the Real

being, while inviting the creature to appreciation and understanding of the beauty and goodness of God's eternal performance.

§2.2.1 Revelation of Being

The first act in the threefold movement of God is the rendering of person through the revelation of Being. That is, God's action discloses the diverse, active, particular "essence" of personhood through the opening up of Being by His in-breaking in Christ through the Spirit. It is through the action of Christ that we gain access to the truth of our personhood, both of our own "particular" personhood, and of what we share with others. According to Balthasar, the fullness of the human is brought to truth because, "to the extent that creatures are, were or will be in God, they participate more in being and are more true there than in themselves."[20] This participation in God illumines the earlier point made by Bauckham that the essence of both universality and particularity within humanity is realized through relations, first and foremost, our relation with God, and secondly, our relations with one another. This ordering of relationality is the needed recognition that "in Jesus Christ a Christian has already come into being, but in himself and his time he is always in the process of becoming."[21] Going further in this thought, Barth later writes of the believer of Christ, "How could they be what they are in Christ if they did not continually become it?"[22] The eschatological tension illumines the continued reality of humanity's *becoming*, a becoming that is rooted in the hope of tomorrow enacted today. Such hope is a hope that refuses to "buckle under the weight of actuality . . . insisting upon living as if it were not thus, living in the light not of the way things are, but of the way things will be in God's future."[23]

Our living towards tomorrow through our performance today is the realized movement and becoming of role to mission. It is the mission of the person that recognizes her identity in Christ, who is the model for all other actors, so as to realize her role in His normative performance. Being in Christ is the only way to close any gaps created by our turning away (exiting) from God, an action that perpetuates the continued division between identity and role. In other words, our *mission* is the recognition of our identity and our role (participation) in Christ. As Nichols maintains, "it is only

---

20. *TD* I, 546.
21. *CD* IV/2, 307.
22. *CD* IV/3, 547. By contrast, Jesus Christ is the "One who is to-day and will be tomorrow in the then completed *operatio* of His being as God and man" (*CD* IV/2, 112).
23. Hart, "Imagination," 51.

the identity of character and mission in Jesus Christ which makes the *world*-drama a *theo*-drama. For *this* identity derives from the fact that the agent concerned has been given a mission not accidentally but as a modality of his eternal personal being."[24] The entrance into Christ's transformative action is the opening up of personhood, as the core of our being was and is exposed through the revelatory act of Christ. This exposure is the essence, the reality of our person: "It is when God addresses a conscious subject, tells him who he is and what he means to the eternal God of truth and shows him the purpose of his existence—that is, *imparts a distinctive and divinely authorized mission*—that we can say of a conscious subject that he is a 'person.'"[25]

§2.2.2 Invitation to Humanity

The second act of God's threefold movement is that of an invitation. This invitation, however, is not any general or ordinary invitation, as through revelation humanity is invited to step into the action of Christ so as to participate in His eternal performance. God makes and shakes the foundation of His drama through His self-involvement. His invitation to humanity is the opening of the infinite to the finite; it is the offering of potentiality to us through our participatory reality, actualized by our participation in Christ's action. Through such a reality, we are embedded in the action of God thus realizing our *imago Trinitatis*. It is through our *imago Trinitatis* that we come to find ourselves, as through our relational reality both with God and with the "other" we recognize the stamp of God, and thus are able to embrace the meaning of what it means to be human. According to Balthasar, "The finite person bears the stamp of the *imago trinitatis*, which means that it can only be and become a person by relating to the other persons it encounters on its way through life."[26] Through the on-going dialogue and performance of the stage, humanity realizes its potential and its place within history (past, present and future) in Christ through the Spirit. Furthermore, through His invitation, God enables the individual to "have contact with the absoluteness of God," exposing and incorporating the person into Christ who is the "Firstborn of creatures in their return to the Idea and hence to God."[27] God's invitation leads to the opening up of the ideal into the real; it is the endowment of freedom from God to humanity that relies on nothing other than the truth of freedom itself. As Balthasar maintains, through "the Father's

24. Nichols, *No Bloodless Myth*, 103.
25. *TD* III, 207; my italics.
26. *TD* V, 302.
27. *TD* V, 388.

self-surrender to the Son and their relationship in the Spirit (which grounds everything)—human freedom participates in the divine autonomy, both when it says Yes and when it says No."[28] Thus, the reality of humanity's "freedom of obedience" insists there must remain the freedom to exit, or move away from Christ's ultimate performance of obedience. Nichols writes, "The trajectory (*die Kurve*) of human life which starts in God and with death begins like a boomerang to return to him, is only possible because of the more foundational space-time track of the incarnate Son in his *exitus* from and *reditus* to the Father."[29] Regarding such movement and freedom, the attempt of a person to exclude themselves from life in Christ so to be their "own private hell" is still "embraced by the curve of Christ." Balthasar writes:

> The created person must one day be confronted with this Word that is "laid up" in God and that is fundamental to its creaturely being. Furthermore, since this Word has always been bent on reconciling the world, and since all things are created with a view to the Cross, it is Christ himself who is our essential freedom. The curve of man's life which begins in God, sweeps away from God and returns to God in death, is enclosed within the curve of the word made man, which runs its pure course in God, from the birth of the Lord to his death . . . Attachment to Christ, and it alone, leads us into "the perfect law, the law of liberty"(Jas 1:25), just as "Jesus being bound to the Cross was at the same time the highest realization of his freedom." To be bound to him, therefore, means to let freedom rule in us.[30]

Through the freedom of choice, that is, the creature's ability to say no, humanity witnesses God's absolute love. The drama of God's self-surrender is comprehended by theology's willingness to participate in Christ's loving performance rather than to simply observe, analyze and describe it. God's love "reaches out to and identifies with all humanity, not by some mere doctrinal statement of the fact nor by some mere religious symbol of it, but concretely in the form of Jesus' particular human life. This particular life history is not simply an illustration of God's loving identification with all humanity, it is actually the way in which God brings his love for all humanity into actual human lives."[31] Through its imaginative powers, theology can awaken humanity to the limitless possibilities that are actualized through our response to participate in the self-surrendering, "other" elevating,

28. *TD* IV, 328.
29. Nichols, *No Bloodless Myth*, 215.
30. *TD* V, 303–4.
31. Bauckham, "CT," 22.

invitation of Christ. This action of self-surrender comes to fruition through our imaginative powers, that allow us to comprehend the ideal becoming the real while also recognizing the possibilities and power of God's love. Commenting on imagination's capacity and power of illumination, Hart writes:

> It is precisely imagination, the capacity which is able to take the known and to modify it in striking and unexpected ways, which offers us the opportunity to think beyond the limits of the given, to explore states of affairs which, while they are radical and surprising modifications of the known, are so striking and surprising as to transcend the latent possibilities and potentialities of the known.
>
> If, therefore, the promise of God is the source of hope, it may be that we must pursue the suggestion that it is the *imagination* of men and women to which that promise appeals, which it seizes and expands, and which is the primary locus of God's sanctifying activity in human life.[32]

The promise and hope of God's invitational action in Christ is illumined through the imagination. The dramatic tension of Christ's action, promise and eschatological hope is actualized into theology's "reality"—its *ideal* becoming *real*—through an imaginative modification of the "known." Apart from its imagination, theology stands the possibility of missing out on Christ's transformative performance. Through Christ, humanity gains its concrete purity, that is, the envisaged idea of the human which ultimately gives humanity the hope for today's transformative performance of Christ. We can, through our imagination, envisage the beautiful possibilities—the potentiality—that await the enactment of our creative performances. As Hart avers, "The capacity to construct futurity, we might rather say, which is a central function of the imagination, is essential to our humanity and to its movement forward in the creative purposes of God."[33]

§2.2.3 Reconciliatory Performance

Finally, the third act of God's threefold movement is reconciliation. Humanity's invitation exposed through God's revelation is worked out in its perfection through the reconciliatory action of Christ. As Balthasar maintains,

---

32. Hart, "Imagination," 76.
33. Ibid., 58.

Chapter Four—Imagining the Real

"In Christ, the life of the Trinity is bent on reconciling the world to God."[34] Such action is not only the re-establishment of the once broken relationship between God and humanity, but the betterment of this relationship. It (reconciliation) is the re-humanizing of humanity that answers completely the query: "Who am I?" How is it that the human can attempt to construct an answer to the questions of truth, of goodness and of beauty if she does not even understand who she is? No one can respond to the aforementioned queries without first understanding what it means to "know thyself." It is the inquiry of who I am that pushes beyond a simple knowledge of what is the human; it is this question—Who am I?—that stands before each and every one of us. The question of personhood has percolated throughout the annals of history with the hopes of attaining a deepening understanding of what it actually means to "know thyself." Building from the argument once made by Klaus Kremer, Balthasar remarks that the query of the goodness of being "crops up all the time in scholasticism; the view that, in God, existents possess 'not only true and genuine being but . . . a far higher, more noble, more sublime, more eminent and more excellent being than they possess in themselves' is 'one of the standard teachings of ancient and medieval philosophy.'"[35] The movement towards the betterment of humanity amidst the efforts to answer the aforementioned questions points towards the attempted desires to realize and procure the goodness of being. Such attainment however, does not come from any Promethean performances but through the performance—the faithfulness—of Christ.

Christ's performance confronts theology, and through it "we are confronted with the fundamental theodramatic law of world history: the greater the revelation of divine (ground-less) love, the more it elicits a groundless hatred from man."[36] The action of the Cross closes the gap between the ideal and the real through its transformative and reconciliatory love act. When humanity lives not in what it "seems" to be or can be, but what it truly *is*, it will realize the purity of its performance. It is in Christ that "once and for all, the duality of 'being' and 'seeming,' which goes through man's entire structure, is absolutely overcome in the identity of person and mission in Christ." The world's stage, which witnesses such a performance, is, continues Balthasar, "always occupied by an ensemble of fellow actors; he (Christ) is inserted into the ensemble."[37]

---

34. *TD* V, 303.
35. *TD* I, 547.
36. *TD* IV, 338.
37. *TD* I, 647.

The insertion of Christ is the normative action of God that beckons each of us to imagine the reality of the *ideal*. It is when we intentionally step into Christ's normative performance that our faithful performances come to life. The reality of such performances is that which must embody an eschatological vision that plays out its hopes and outcomes today. Tomorrow's reality cannot be but performed through today; it is a performance that embarks upon the real by understanding the ideal. And then further, to understand the real, we must first imagine it, as that which cannot be imagined cannot become, and thus, the ideal will not be realized as the real apart from our imaginative powers. Theology's faithful performance in God's drama is revealed through its imaginative powers enacted on the world's stage. Theology can only assist society and the church through its action. As Stanislavski once wrote, "activity in imagination is of utmost importance. First comes internal, and afterwards, external action."[38]

§3 Theology's Use and Recognition of Its Imaginative Powers

What does it mean to state that theology must use its imaginative powers? Instead of being comfortable with discussion concerning the imagination or the call for a recognition of our imaginative powers, much of theology is suspicious at such suggestions. Imagination, instead of being equated with the intellect or a stronghold for our interpretive powers, is deemed, by some, to be irrational and the antithesis to the logical formation of doctrine. As John McIntyre writes, "by some imagination is seen as the medium which diminishes the real character of religion; it distorts the relation in which religion stands to reality."[39] However, if properly understood and employed, imagination has the ability to enlarge theology's perspective so as to reinterpret the performance of today in light of tomorrow's hope, thereby coming to witness the fullness of reality.

Through theology's imaginative thinking, the future hopes indwell the present reality, thus grounding them in the truth of today, rather than leaving them as abstract concepts. As Hart posits, "(E)ternity, indeed, is not some abstract and timeless simultaneity but 'the power of the future over every historical time.'"[40] It is through the concreteness of Christ's performance that tomorrow's hopes are enacted today. The relational reality of Creator and creature directs the stage towards its final scene whereby the

---

38. Stanislavski, *An Actor Prepares*, 58.
39. McIntyre, *Faith, Theology and Imagination*, 12.
40. Moltmann, *Crucified God*, 23; quoted by Hart, "Imagination," 64.

ontological reality of Christ's incarnated performance illumines the *ideal* of humanity. It is the immediacy of our imaginative capabilities that continues to draw us into the participatory reality of Christ's revelation, invitation and reconciliation, all of which point us toward the meaning of the human. We step into the fullness of life through our imagination. This movement is not an attempt to escape reality by living in our own created fantasy worlds, but a movement towards an "imaginative vision in which the dominant way of seeing things (both present and future)" is "fundamentally challenged and an alternative picture painted of the potentialities and possibilities inherent in God's future."[41]

Every movement made on creation's stage stems from our ability to envisage God's will and purpose for us. Thus, theology can draw from Stanislavski when he writes, "every movement you make on the stage, every word you speak, is the result of the right life of your imagination."[42] Theologically speaking, then, the "right life of imagination" is determined by our participation *in* Christ's transformative performance. Through the imagination, theology does not seek to fantasize about an ethereal reality, but quite the opposite, to imagine heaven's hope played out through the concrete performances of today. However, this type of theological performance will not come to fruition if entered into half-heartedly. Theology must fully commit itself to participate in the self-surrendering performance of Christ. This compete self-commitment is what is demanded of theology, as no performance is authentic if not in some sense, self-surrendering. "A conscious, reasoned approach to the imagination," writes Stanislavski, "often produces a bloodless, counterfeit presentment of life." What is required, continues Stanislavski, is that an "actor's whole nature be actively involved, that he gives himself up, both mind and body, to his part. *He must feel the challenge to action physically as well as intellectually* because the imagination, which has no substance or body, can reflexively affect our physical nature and make it act."[43] Through the willingness to enact its imaginative powers, theology is allotted the possibility to meet the challenge of today, and guide the Church, and society, towards the betterment of the human, thus illumining the ideal *becoming* the real.

The becoming of the real is the realization of reality; it is not only the acknowledgment of the original performance of Christ, but the active participation in this performance. This is to say that, through the willingness to imagine *what can be*, theology moves beyond what *seems to be*, so

---

41. Hart, "Imagination," 54.
42. Stanislavski, *An Actor Prepares*, 71.
43. Ibid., 70.

as to realize the revelation and invitation of God. The imagination, writes Green, is "not the opposite of reality but rather the means by which manifold forms of both reality and illusion are mediated to us."[44] We are able to access that which is transcendent through the imaginative powers granted in creation. As Paul Avis points out, "it is primarily through the imagination and the genres typically generated by the imagination (metaphor, symbol and myth) that we are brought into living contact with our object (the sacred, the divine, revelation, God), both in living religion and in theological reflection."[45] Rather than diminishing our theological endeavors, the imagination elevates them through its ability to draw us deeper into the being of God. Avis continues in his assessment of our imagination, saying that "the creative human imagination is one of the closest analogies to the being of God. The mystery of imagination points to and reflects the mystery of God. As Coleridge (among others) suggested, human imaginative creativity is "an echo, a spark, of the divine creativity that is poured out in the plenitude of creation."[46]

Even amidst the possibilities offered through our imagination, today's hesitation towards the imagination is rooted, ironically, in illusory logic that has created the false dichotomy of a separation between the imaginative and the world of facts. Such direction, that claims inquiry is about the facts of this world, and should be left to the sciences. Yet as George MacDonald maintained, while it is true our investigations are limited to the world that God has made, it is the main function of the imagination to investigate God's world. MacDonald continues his argument stating, that the imagination "seeks understanding," as it (the imagination) "is aroused by facts, is nourished by facts, seeks for higher and yet higher laws in those facts; but refuses to regard science as the sole interpreter of nature, or the laws of science as the only region of discovery . . . There were no imagination without intellect, however much it may appear that intellect can exist without imagination."[47] What is more, contemporary theology's negative sentiments towards imagination are many of the same sentiments it has held against the dramatic.

The reluctance to move into a fully dramatic theology stems from a misunderstanding of what it means to be both dramatic and imaginative. What is needed is the simple reminder from Keith Johnstone, who writes that the "imagination will not destroy you." However, most theological

---

44. Green, *Imagining God*, 83.
45. Avis, *God and the Creative Imagination*, vii.
46. Ibid., ix.
47. MacDonald, *A Dish of Orts*, 11: quoted by Dearborn, *Baptized Imagination*, 92

endeavors have neglected this, and thus continue as the student who does not heed Johnstone's reminder concerning the imagination, and thus they "go on *pretending* to be dull."[48] The dullness, or suspicion towards the imagination and the theatre today, returns us back to the initial Christian response, which was, writes David Brown, "uniformly hostile."[49]

In his thesis work, Ivan Khovacs highlights the historical disenchantment of the church towards the theatre through his look into why theologically the church has "held the theatre in contempt." Such a perspective has subtly concealed much of today's theology from the imaginative and dramatic interaction of Creator and creation. Khovacs notes how this historical mis-cue has been "a detriment to theology's own understanding of life under God" and thus, a detriment to understanding and recognizing humanity's participation upon God's stage of creation.[50] The lack of awareness concerning the powers of imagination quietly turns today's theological endeavors towards an "observatory perspective," as opposed to encouraging a participatory reality. Instead of stepping into the power of the imagination and the dramatic, much of theology continues to maintain a negativity that seeks to disengage from any types of imaginative or dramatic endeavors.

The work done by Balthasar, as well as others interested in theology's dramatic essence and imaginative powers, exposes the health of theology today to our mind's eye. Balthasar's dramatic theology, and its recognition of the world's theatre, is an attempt to "break through Christian antipathy, disinterest and ambiguity historically shown to the theatre and its notion of the dramatic."[51] While the idea of dramatizing theology is beginning to enliven our imagination, many aspects of theology today still remain suspicious towards the dramatic, imagination, and the arts. It is in light of such suspicion that this project seeks to offer a counter-argument, that the arts do have a serious theological tradition in the Church, which through its faithful imagination, has continuously participated in the dynamic dialogue between the arts and theology.

Through the imagination, theology witnesses the performative reality opened up to it through God's revelation, invitation and reconciliation. Speaking specifically about the theodramatic and its imaginative undertones that give a fuller meaning to the action of truth known through the Word made flesh, Khovacs writes, "The dynamics of words given life in action, marking out for this purpose a light and sound environment, the

---

48. Johnstone, *Impro*, 84.
49. Brown, *God and Mystery*, 158.
50. Khovacs, "Divine Reckonings," 10.
51. Ibid., 18.

actor's embodied personification of character, these are all manifestations of the dramatic moment which, apprehended by the senses and projected on the backdrop of the imagination, becomes the event we call the theatre."[52] Yet through the lasting effects of the neo-scholastic trend of "rationalism," theology has remained distant from any type of dramatic or imaginative employment in theology. It is this distance that has caused theology to re-imagine and re-create its role. In other words, instead of propelling the notion of participation in Christ's salvific performance, much of theology today has "re-imagined" God's revelation as representing a thing only to be observed and discussed. Discussing his discontent with such a perspective, Balthasar writes that this trend within theology is the result of a "rationalistic theology" that "treats God and his grace like some component that can be manipulated by human thought."[53]

§3.1 The Result of a Rationalistic Theology: The Re-Imagining of Theology

The continued negative sentiment towards the imagination can be well traced throughout the strands of time, both inside and outside of theology. Reluctance towards an imagined theological perspective is slowly diminishing through some of today's current projects concerning the imagination. However, a full investigation into this issue would warrant not simply a chapter but a whole other book. For the purposes of this chapter and our discussion of the imagination, I will take a brief look first at some of the sentiments towards drama sustained through the work of Augustine, and then move to four further factors identified by Trevor Hart that have contributed to the sometimes negative reception of the imagination within theology.

§3.1.1 Imaginative Products: A Look at Augustine

Augustine is arguably one of the most influential minds of theology. Thus, in looking at today's theological understanding of the imagination the benefit of a brief investigation into Augustine is valuable.[54] Augustine's own critique of the theatre affected his views and understanding of the imagination, all of which stemmed from the "supposed" ability to point people away from

---

52. Ibid., 13.

53. *TD* II, 53.

54. For a fuller development of Augustine and his thoughts towards the theatre and the imagination, see chapter 3 of Khovacs, "Divine Reckonings."

CHAPTER FOUR—IMAGINING THE REAL

God and towards a self-seeking pleasure. Self-indulgence stems from what Augustine considered to be the result of our longing to "gratify the senses and our pleasures," which leads to our becoming a slave to this ungodly pursuit. What occurs through these imaginative pursuits—what Augustine refers to as our inquisitiveness—is a form of idolatry whereby the pleasures replace our worship of God.[55] More specifically, for Augustine, the imagination is bound up with memory. In her article concerning the role of the imagination in Augustine's work, Marianne Djuth writes that for Augustine, the imagination is "inextricably bound up with his understanding of memory and the role that memory plays in storing, reproducing, and arranging the images generated in it on the basis of sense experience."[56] Djuth points out that Augustine's thinking in regard to the imagination grounds it in an empirical origin rendering an understanding of the imagination associated with Aristotelian, Stoic and Neo-Platonist habits of thought. Furthermore, for Augustine, "the memory refers to the mind's ability to retain information gathered on the basis of sense experience and to restore it to consciousness if need be, not to the process of recollecting the eternal, incorporeal notions of logic, number, and goodness essential to the pursuit of wisdom."[57] The memory is responsible for collecting the images taken in through the senses, gathering them and then making a connection to their meaning. As for those things not taken in through the senses, those which we "intuit within ourselves without images," the memory gathers together the understanding of such images that the "memory already contains" but has not yet discovered.[58] This apparent unknowingness—the meaning within that, which remains veiled—leads Augustine later to write of the questionable status of the meaning presented through the imagination which tends towards the creation of one's mind, that is, a human conjecture. Things which we suppose, the presentation of the imagination, are "in every point wholly unreal; and the things which we perceive by sight and the other senses, are, as you see, far more near to the truth than these products of imagination."[59]

Augustine's apparent negativity towards the imagination has continued to influence the historical trends of theology; however, a closer look

---

55. See Augustine, *Confessions*, book 10.35.55; it is also interesting to note Augustine's rendering of Romans 1:21–22 in 7.9.14 where he writes "Thus, though they know God, yet they do not glorify him as God, nor are they thankful. Therefore, they 'become vain in their imaginations; their foolish heart is darkened, and professing themselves to be wise they become fools.'"

56. Djuth, "Veiled and Unveiled Beauty," 79.

57. Ibid.; cf. Augustine's *Confessions* 10.8–10.26.

58. Augustine, *Confessions*, 10.9.

59. Augustine, *Letters of St. Augustine*, Letter VII.2.4

into his work actually illumines an imaginative undertone that is essentially the dramatic presentation of his faith. One clear example highlighted by Khovacs of Augustine's dramatic presentation comes from Augustine's *Christian Doctrine* where Augustine writes:

> Now of all who can with us enjoy God, [. . . w]e ought to desire . . . that [unbelievers] should all join with us in loving God, and all [believers] . . . should tend to that one end. For in the theatres, . . . if a man is fond of a particular actor, and enjoys his art[,] . . . he is fond of all who join with him in admiration of his favorite [thespian], not for their own sakes, but for the sake of him whom they admire in common; and the more fervent he is in his admiration, the more he works in every way he can to secure new admirers for him; and if he finds any one comparatively indifferent, he does all he can to excite his interest by urging his favorite [actor's] merits . . . . Now, if this be so, what does it become us to do who live in the fellowship of the love of God, the enjoyment of whom is true happiness of life, to whom all who love Him owe both their own existence and the love they bear Him, concerning whom we have no fear that anyone who comes to know Him will be disappointed in Him, and who desires our love, not for any gain to Himself, but that those who love Him may obtain an eternal reward, even Himself whom they love? And hence it is that we love even our enemies [. . . for they are] separated from Him whom we love. For if they would turn to Him, they [would] love Him . . . and love us too as partakers with them in so great a blessing.[60]

With regards to Augustine, Khovacs writes that while the aforementioned is not sufficient to attribute a dramatic foundation to Augustine, it does however indicate that "drama is in fact central to how Augustine conceives of salvation and its outworking in the act of conversion."[61]

Historically, though, the relationship between Augustine's thought and Platonism has rendered a negative sentiment towards the imagination. This is due in large part to the Platonic picture of the proper way of acquiring knowledge. Thus, drawing from Plato's *Phaedrus*, James Smith notes, "true knowledge (is) visible only to intelligence, (247d)." Smith goes on to illumine a Platonic understanding of "true knowledge" that did have influence on Augustine's own understanding of the soul and thus, the imagination. Highlighting the Platonic thought that influenced Augustine, Smith

---

60. Augustine, *Christian Doctrine*, I.29.30; quoted by Khovacs, "Divine Reckonings," 87.

61. Khovacs, "Divine Reckonings," 87–88.

Chapter Four—Imagining the Real

writes, the soul "'that is concerned to take in what is appropriate to it" finds its delight and pleasure, not in the sensuous feast of words and images offered up by the rhetor or actor, but rather is delighted by "seeing what is real and watching what is true'(247d)."[62] When viewed in this Platonic light, "the imagination and the senses on which it depends for its memory images clearly occupy an inferior position in the hierarchy of the sensible and intelligible realms. Given its close ties with the senses, the imagination remains confined to the sensible realm because it lacks reason's capacity to comprehend the truth independently of the senses."[63] The reaction against the imagination is due to the belief that because of the fall, the imagination is prone to error and must be "rescued" by reason. However, returning back to the example raised by Khovacs from *Christian Doctrine*, the belief that Augustine lacked an imaginative and dramatic undertone is slowly beginning to fade. This is to say that through a closer reading of Augustine, we can see that there does persist in him the acknowledgement and use of the imagination.

Recognizing that the imagination is "at the crossroads of salvation," Augustine does acknowledge how both "admonitions of truth and memory images . . . enter the mind through the senses." As Djuth continues, in regards to Augustine and the role of the imaginative, "when used responsibly, both the imagination and the senses are instrumental in the acquisition of a true understanding of the Christian faith."[64] Indeed, reason is also needed and thus, this separation of imagination and reason is a false dichotomy. The fact remains that through the Incarnation, God sought explicitly to appeal to human senses.

The hope here is to show while it is thought that Augustine was seemingly anti-drama and skeptical of the imagination, he nonetheless uses both in order to expose his theological and spiritual confessions. Khovacs points out that "(for) however much Augustine may have opposed theatrical representations and the images they project, to say nothing of the emotive pull they have for the proselyte writer, he nonetheless affectively engages his readers through a most dramatic and vividly imaged account of his struggles in the faith."[65]

---

62. Smith, *Literature and Theology*, 125.
63. Djuth, "Veiled and Unveiled Beauty," 90.
64. Ibid., 91.
65. Khovacs, "Divine Reckonings," 51.

§3.1.2 Negative Reception of the Imagination

Concerning the negative reception of the imagination inherited in the modern or contemporary theological atmosphere, Trevor Hart highlights four prominent factors: first, Hart points to the negative spin given to the imagination in the 1611 translation of the King James Bible. Such influence has had and continues to have a lasting effect on the minds (imaginations) of those who engage this text. A word search regarding "imagination" will lead one into the realm of an active plot against God's will. For example, using *Young's Analytical Concordance*, Hart illumines the fact that instances where the human "inclination" or "stubbornness" of heart are elevated as that which motivates against God's will in the NRSV or NIV, in the KJV they are translated as "imagination."[66] Secondly, Hart details the prejudices tacitly against the imagination implicit in the language often attributed to our imagination. If something appears to be incorrect or not "real," it is said to be a figment of one's imagination, or a creation of an "overactive imagination." All of which—the pejorative use of "imagination"—continues to project negative sentiment or a reluctance to acknowledge the power and need of the imagination within theology.

Hart moves forward from the way in which the imagination is connected to our language to his third point or factor of the continued negative sentiment towards the imagination, the historical distaste Protestantism has had with art and artistry. The mistaken understanding, and lack of clarity in theology's understanding, of the arts has led many to look at the artist and their "creative imagination" as being nothing more than an attempt to displace God. These "creative attempts" are thought to lead the artist and theology *ipso facto* towards the "re-imagining" of God in light of the human. However, the historically "dubious reputation" of the imagination needs not to be "anathematized" or "excommunicated" but precisely to be "reclaimed and redeemed." The responsibility of this task lies precisely at the feet of today's theologians, who must move beyond the known, so as to gain access to the potentialities that await such movement. Finally, Hart's fourth factor draws attention to the work done within Christian theology, that while attempting to extol the imagination succeeded instead in strengthening the fears already active against the imagination. Hart points to the likes of Feuerbach and Kaufman whose theological constructivism simply "re-imagines" the foundation of the Christian faith, once again displacing the

---

66. In this word study, Hart highlights Genesis 6.5 for the aspect of "inclination" and Jer 3:17 for the "stubbornness" of the heart. Hart further shows this negative translation preference by looking at Rom 1:21, Luke 1:51 and 2 Cor 10:5, all of which indicate a translation other than the KJV preference of "imagination."

centrality of God for sake of humanity's "creative imagination, "while also seeing "imagination" and "revelation" as alternatives. Once again, this form of "re-imagining" ultimately produces a human product, thereby distorting humanity's perspective, and blinding theology to the most imaginative events of history, the full revelation of God Himself.[67]

§3.2 Today's Theological Imagining

When imagination is separated from the intellect it is understandable that many will ask why we should be interested in our supposed imaginative powers. Thus, through such a dichotomous perspective, the fullness of the imagination is lost amongst the speculations of the uninformed or shall we dare say, the unimaginative. This false dichotomy lacks the depth of awareness concerning both the imagination as well as our being. Revelation and imagination are not contentious terms that one must choose from. As Hart argues, "if the things that the church has traditionally believed about God and the ways in which God makes himself known to us are true, then revelation looks like a highly imaginative sort of thing, and our appropriation of and response to it similarly so."[68] Our theological imaginative uses are ways in which we become empowered by the perichoretic relationship between the imagination and the intellect. To separate the two is almost like trying to separate the body and the mind—it leads toward a Gnostic foundation of religion that continues to separate the body and the mind. Humans are thinking and creative beings who can only be understood when rooted within the relational reality of the imagination and intellect. Imagination, writes Hart, is "essential to Christian believing and living, and to Christian theology."[69]

The need of the imagination rests within its ability to allow theology to see simultaneously what is and what might yet be for the best. Furthermore,

---

67. In his discussion of the negative reception of the imagination, Hart notes that while there are lots of different factors involved in the "nervous mood detectable when the word imagination is put on the agenda for discussion in Christian circles," the discernable association of the nervousness between the multitude of factors, in Hart's estimate, has to do with "an unwarranted association of the imagination in particular with human fallenness and sin." However, it must be conceded that sin has indeed affected our imagination (and our reason). The ways in which we as humans have historically found to enact evil upon one another presents how the imagination can and is used for evil, for example, as Hart indicates, the torture chamber is quite imaginative. For the full account of Hart's discussion concerning the factors involved in our anxiety of the imagination, see Hart, "A Suspicion Observed," 7–12.

68. Ibid., 12.

69. Ibid., 15.

the imaginative powers of theology are not limited by the world, but instead, meant to investigate, and to participate in, the on-going creative reality of God. The imagination "is that faculty which gives form to thought—not necessarily uttered form, but form capable of being uttered in shape or in sound, or in any mode upon which the senses can lay hold."[70] This formation of form or fashioning of thought is the discovery of our imaginative powers. Discovery is crucial to theology, as through our theological studies the depth of life's meaning becomes more and more unveiled. This is to say that through the willingness to explore as well as imagine the depth of personhood, theology opens the potentiality of exposing humanity to the core of what it means to be a faithful participant in God's drama. Drawing upon George Macdonald, McIntyre notes how the "function of the imagination to enquire into what God has made, as well as following out the divine function of putting thought into form" is the human opportunity to participate in the "God's creative activity."[71] Through the imagination humanity participates in the re-creation of Christ's continual transformative performance, as it is only through a "*Christological recreation*" that creation comes to terms with "all that we are."[72] Humanity's potential is through participation in God's continual activity on the world's stage, and it is this that causes Balthasar to write "everything that, in the created world, appears shot through with *potentiality* is found *positively* in God."[73] Through its participation, humanity's imagination is opened to the potentiality deposited in and through the shaping of the world. William Dyrness points out that humanity's imagination gives shape to the world's stage and this shape comes through "the images and practices that express this shape."[74]

The foundation of the imagination is not merely a psychological or fantastic element of our thought, but precisely a fundamental element in our ways of figuring the world. To imagine the future and envisage the hope of today illumined "in the light of God's promise is thereby also at once to force a reevaluation of the present and its significance."[75] This radical and imaginative reinterpretation re-figures the world through the incarnational performances of the players. Such performances occur through the intentional imagining of what *can be* in light of what *is*. This is to say that participation in Christ's performance is the recklessness of an imagined, but still

70. McIntyre, *Faith, Theology and Imagination*, 13.
71. Ibid., 14–15.
72. Nichols, *No Bloodless Myth*, 227.
73. *TD* V, 389.
74. Dyrness, *Reformed Theology*, 6.
75. Hart, "Imagination," 63.

disciplined performance, as the discipline of our performances comes from our taking in and following Christ's performance.

Participation *in* Christ brings about the fullness of who we are so that if criticism does occur, it is at least directed at our *real* performance. Through our imagining the real, we begin to recognize that Christ calls for a participatory performance that stems from the truth of who we are, the covenant partner of God. Again, as been noted throughout this book, this is where the theatre has much to offer. That is, in the attempt to imagine the faithfulness of our performances, to imagine the real so as to realize the gift of God's covenant, we have to seek the truth of who we are, which can result in, the inner understanding of self, guiding the external performance. Stanislavski writes that what is significant in understanding the truth of our performance is "the inner life of a human spirit in a part and a belief in that reality." He goes on to write that "what we mean by *truth* in the theatre is the scenic truth which an actor must make use of in his moments of creativeness. Try always to begin by working from the inside, both on the factual and imaginary parts of a play and its setting. Put life into all the imagined circumstances and actions until you have completely satisfied your *sense of truth*, and until you have awakened a *sense of faith* in the reality of your sensations. This process is what we call *justification* of a part."[76] Theology's performance, if it is to gain its *sense of truth* and *sense of faith*, must rest within the action of God as from His action we come into contact with "the way, the truth, and the life" which invites us to participate in the fullness of His "way, truth and life" so as to realize our "way, truth and life." This is a performance that imagines all circumstances so as to illumine the ideal of humanity, incorporating us into His performance, thereby igniting the becoming of our *real* performances.

Through theology's imaginative powers, then, humanity is exposed to the shape of the world—to the shape of life. Imagination constitutes "all the resources of man, all his faculties, his whole history, his whole life, and his whole heritage, all brought to bear upon the concrete world inside and outside of himself, to form images of the world, and thus to find it, cope with it, shape it, and even make it."[77] Through the imagination humanity embarks not on an abstract path of fantastical hopes and illusions, but enters into the performance of life. As Michael Murphy notes, "It is an imagination, theologically speaking, that sees Christ as the revelatory key to the cosmos and figures aesthetics in terms of the Incarnation as axial miracle of history, as existential, as continually Eucharistic, and as locus of (and reason for)

---

76. Stanislavski, *An Actor Prepares*, 129.
77. Lynch, *Christ and Prometheus*, 23.

community."[78] A return to the imagination is a return to the root of what it means to be human. Imagination is not simply a small part of who we are, but it "lies at the heart of our existence." To imagine is to "understand what it is to be."[79]

Theology's imaginative powers, as guided by the Holy Spirit, provide a means to truly see reality as it *can be*, so as to participate in and propel its *becoming*. The ability to imaginatively view the world allows the human, and thus theology, the possibility to participate in—to enact—the good while closing out the negative. Each participant within God's drama participates in the creation of the good through their constructive acts in Christ's truth. Balthasar maintains that the person "disposes of a constructive unmindfulness, which by rejecting some things, helps bring the essential cognitive elements to the fore and, in this way, fashions the world of truth into a vivid relief."[80] Fashioning the word of truth occurs through the imagination. By imagining the real, that is, what can be in light of what Christ has done, the participant acts with the Spirit to fashion the word of truth so as to enact such truth within the world.

Only in recent times has the imagination been shifted to the background, placed behind logic and reason. However, the imagination has had a significant influence throughout history. Far from being the "magical faculty of the soul," the imagination provides the way in which humanity interacts with and connects our ideas of reality. Connection comes about through the imagination's ability to draw together the multiple facets of human action. Iser claims that the power of the imagination is revealed directly from this ability. "By bringing different abilities to work on each other, the imagination reveals itself to be a power of fusion that extends human beings beyond themselves."[81] If understood properly, this extension of the self will allow for theology to faithfully perform as it continues to imagine the real of life.

§4 Imagining the Real

§4.1 Overcoming the Unimaginative

God's incarnational performance is the imaginative action that seeks to overcome the chasm between He and His creation. This overcoming action

---

78. Murphy, *Theology of Criticism*, 7.
79. Kearney, *Poetics of Imagining*, 1.
80. *TL* I, 110.
81. Iser, *Fictive and the Imaginary*, 180.

is necessary due to man's weakness. Regarding God's action through Christ, Balthasar writes that "because of man's weakness and the difficulty in making the creation, involved as it is in Christ's humanity, participate in this supreme relationship, the vertical dimension is presented horizontally, as extended in time."[82] The elevation of the human to the beauty of its *imago Trinitatis* is accomplished through the performative expression of God in Christ. Thus, the beauty and profundity of God's descent to humanity is witnessed in His elevation of the human through the ascension of the Son. As Balthasar notes, "Christ, God's greatest work of art, is in the unity of God and man the expression both of God's absolute divinity and sovereignty and of the perfect creature."[83] Through the person of Christ humanity is able to imagine the perfection of creation, as the reality of Christ is the reality of the human.

The universal significance of Christ establishes and solidifies both the universality of humanity as well as its particularity. In other words, on the one hand, I universally find meaning to who I am because of the life and work of Christ, which have universal significance, while on the other hand, Christ's particularity illumines the meaning of my own particularity as He knows me as a being who is distinctly imaged—that is, existing as my own particular *imago*—yet inseparably linked to the whole of humanity because of Christ's universal significance. Richard Bauckham writes that "the proper function of the incarnation is not to abstract Jesus from his human history. Its point is quite the opposite: to point to God's utter involvement in Jesus' human history. It means: that particular history is God's own human history. It means: in Jesus God particularizes himself. In Jesus the universal God particularizes himself as a concrete human reality in the midst of this world."[84] It is from Christ's actions that the paradox of the God-human relationship is transformed into the theatre of His Glory. The realness of the world's stage is recognizable only through the uniform purity of the Godhead. God's unified action is inescapably through Christ. Balthasar claims that, "We can never attain to the living God in any way except through His Son become man, but in this Son we can really attain to God in himself, so, too, we ought never to speak of God's beauty without reference to the form and manner of appearing which he exhibits in salvation-history."[85] Humanity cannot attain the beautiful life through its individual, autonomous and disconnected performance; pure and unified beauty is absent

---

82. *ET* I, 117.
83. Ibid.
84. Bauckham, "CT," 23.
85. *GL* I: *Seeing the Form*, 124.

from humanity, apart from the performance of Christ. Again, the significance of Christ's universal performance is that it makes real each of our own particular performances. Bauckham notes that while we know who Jesus is through the Biblical script, His life's actions become "relevant to us as they meet or intersect our own stories, as we find the points of connection where God's loving identification becomes loving identification with us."[86] The importance of this identification is understood if the proper meaning of Bauckham's use of "our own stories" is apprehended. Thus, in order to further clarify, Bauckham explains:

> By "our own stories" I mean both our individual life stories and also the wider stories in which they belong: the stories of our society, our culture, even the story of our contemporary world to the extent that it now has a single story. The term story here should not be understood in too narrowly literary a way: it does not, for example, exclude social and political analysis of our situation. But in talking in narrative terms has the value of preserving both the particularity of the incarnation—it is the actual history Jesus lived that matters—and the particularity of our own stories—for times, places, cultures, individuals have their own rather different human stories. The universality of his story is found at points where it meets all other human stories.[87]

The intersection of our "own stories," with God and with one another, comes about with the movement of narrative to the drama, it comes with the call of God towards a participatory performance in Christ's reconciliatory mission.

The human paradox, then, is due to humanity's inability to solve its own problems. Theology should continuously seek to guide the Church back to her source so as to re-capture the beauty of her performance. The Church and thus, humanity, cannot re-create the intended beauty of creation's relational reality. God, in His creation, intends for a relational foundation to the world's stage—this cannot be re-created by human attempts to circumvent God's action. The human paradox is based upon an anthropological perspective that cannot move beyond the krisis, as it continually seeks to establish its own way as opposed to The Way. "Who am I?" is unanswerable if left to the "arbitrariness of a 'role.'" Through the imagination, theology is able to move beyond its role, so as to apprehend its mission. Furthermore, through the leading of the Holy Spirit, the imagination unveils the realization of the *ideal* becoming the *real*. Balthasar writes that we need to move away from the "arbitrariness of a 'role' that was simply

---

86. Bauckham, "CT," 25.
87. Ibid., 25.

thrown over a 'colorless I' like some coat that happened to be to hand and could at any time be exchanged for another, and to arrive at an 'I' that was irreplaceable as such and thus could be enabled to take on a genuinely dramatic role in the realm, not of the theatre, but of life."[88] This dramatic role is the realization of the entirety of the person; it is our *mission*, the idea of the particular human that comes from the concrete love of God. From this outpouring of love, humanity is engulfed in the knowledge of its potential; yet such knowledge can never be separated from God's Being, as the becoming of the ideal into the real is a movement that can never be divorced from God. As Balthasar maintains, the human ideal is found "in Christ," as it is Christ who has "taken on the task of showing us our nature as heaven planned it; we have our nature *in him*."[89]

§4.2 Realizing Our Mission: The Becoming of the Real

It is from God's movement toward us that we are able to explore the understanding and knowledge of the self. In other words, it is that we (humanity), "cannot find the ultimate solution to the paradox of being *simul justus et peccator* in ourselves; we must look to Christ for it."[90] In Christ we encounter our ideal. It is an encounter with one's own uncreated idea, which writes Balthasar, is an encounter that "can take place only at the point where the Father eternally generates both the Son and, simultaneously, that Idea of the world which is to be implemented in the Son."[91] The ideal becoming the real is the very movement of our mission in Christ, which is both an *egressus a Deo* and the *reditus a Deo*. The freedom of the creature, that is, our ability to exit and return ensures the distinction of Creator and creature while maintaining our inseparable relationship and mission that occurs by our being in Christ.

Our becoming is maintained through the eternal performance of Christ—through His revelation, invitation and reconciliation—all of which summons a participatory response from the creature. According to Balthasar, "Everything that is in process of becoming, within the world's total becoming, has a somehow indefinite profile until it attains its definitive shape, ultimately, in full participation in the life of the Trinity."[92] Full participation in the life of the Trinity, if Balthasar is correct, is our mission

88. *TD* I, 645.
89. *TD* V, 391; italics in original.
90. *TKB*, 377.
91. *TD* V, 390.
92. *TD* V, 101.

that is manifested through a life transformed through God's revelation, invitation and reconciliation. The fullness of such action is the foundation of our participatory mission within God's theatre of Glory.

Christian theology, in its continued movement of faith, needs to seek participation in Christ's reconciliatory performance. Through our being in Christ, we gain the confidence to open ourselves up to an intentional interaction with the entirety of the stage. When we imagine what *can be* we are open to the possibility of an improvised performance because we are willing to accept the unknown. Theology's performance, if intentionally participatory, comes closer to the understanding of personhood, to what it means to be a human. A theological performance that allows its imaginative powers to guide its endeavors opens the stage area, thereby participating in God's desire and hope for reconciliation. Our improvised performances are a sign of our confidence to act faithfully because of our faith in Christ. Thus, if theology realizes its role in God's drama, it can assist humanity in not only realizing God's offer, but move closer towards the realization of our being. Again, Johnstone lends insight to our theological endeavors when he writes, "when you learn to accept offers, then accidents can no longer interrupt the action . . . This attitude makes for something really amazing in the theatre. The actor who will accept anything that happens seems supernatural; it's the most marvelous thing about improvisation: you are suddenly in contact with people who are unbounded, whose imagination seems to function without limit."[93] Understood theologically, the theatre elevates the invitation of God in Christ's incarnational performance. This offer, if "accepted" or "blocked" profoundly effects the movement not only of the stage, but also of the understanding of our own performances.

Understood Theo-dramatically, then, the understanding of our performances results from the realization of our role, which is ultimately our personal *mission*. Thus, our engagement and interaction with God can be nothing other than a "participation in the once-for-all, all embracing mission of Christ."[94] Humanity's hope is not created but given through the action of Christ. Centered on the crucified and resurrected person of Jesus of Nazareth, "the fullness of divine life (Trinity) is bound up with man's perfectibility (resurrection)," and it is here, in this interaction that "theology and anthropology interact to produce a dimension that can be claimed

---

93. Johnstone, *Impro*, 100. Johnstone calls anything an actor does an "offer." An offer is opposed by what Johnstone calls a block. "A block is anything that prevents the action from developing" (97). For a fuller account of "blocking" and "accepting," see Johnstone *Impro*, 94–108.

94. *TD* IV, 406.

to be unsurpassable."⁹⁵ Today, however, there remains a subtle tendency to observe, analyze and explain God's Being-in-act instead of seeking to participate in His act.

Being true to oneself ultimately finds its meaning in the truth and transformation of Christ's in-breaking performance. It is this performance that calls theology to imagine the fullness of what can be so as to participate in the ideal *becoming* the real. Neglect of imagination's capacity to expose truth lends towards a "real" that "may well prove to be other than what appears to be actual."⁹⁶ Theology should continue to move beyond observation into the reality of an interactive performance. Involvement in the continued performance of Christ can occur through many forms, but what is essential is that it is an on-going dialogue and participation with the Church and society. Theology is called to present the "offer" of God to humanity so as to illumine humanity's need of "accepting" this offer.

§4.3 Realization of Our Participatory Mission

Through its imaginative powers, theology is able to imagine the real, that is, to imagine the depth of meaning and truth of our personhood to be gained through our participation in God's drama. Chapter 1 discussed the event of Truth, its reconciliatory reality, as well as its incorporation of humanity through the incarnational act of Christ. Moving this trajectory further, our imaginative powers can unveil the fullness of God's drama that is brought to life through the truthfulness of faith. And it is the movement into this truthfulness that continues to illumine the fact that the action of the stage in the midst of its *becoming*, that is, its performance of the ideal into the real, is spiritual, personal, physical, and biblical. There is no room for neutrality in this process of the ideal becoming the real, as humanity's performance is only recognizable through the real actions of God; actions that are inclusive of the entirety of humanity's actions across the span of time. Through the event of revelation humanity not only comes to the forefront of personal knowledge of God—His self-revelation—but, of self-knowledge, of its very own performance in the whole of history. Barth comments:

> We cannot impress upon ourselves too strongly that in the language of the Bible knowledge (*yada, gignwskein*) does not mean the acquisition of neutral information, which can be expressed in statements, principles and systems, concerning a being which

---

95. *TD* II, 121.
96. Hart, "Imagination," 54.

> confronts man ... What it really means is the process or history in which man, certainly observing and thinking, using his senses, intelligence and imagination, but also his will, action and "heart," and therefore the whole man, becomes aware of another history ... that he cannot be neutral towards it, but finds himself summoned to disclose and give himself to it in return.[97]

Theology's knowledge of this self-involved performance is the result of God's irruption which denies the possibility of remaining neutral—all participate upon God's stage. The realness of faith is the movement beyond the attempt to rely on reason alone, through our self-involved participation in God's eternal performance.

Building from the realness of faith and its movement beyond gnosis, Barth writes that "*Pistis* says more than *gnosis*, but in all circumstances it says *gnosis* too."[98] Yet what is exposed in our faith seeking understanding is not so much an absence of certain kinds of knowledge but an expansion of being human—that is, to know God is to know thyself. Thus, only through the willingness to imagine the real does theology recognize the point made by Barth, as noted by Hunsinger, that "knowledge of faith always meant fundamentally the *union* of the knower with God and only secondarily the *rational content* of that knowledge."[99] The relational reality and truthfulness of God's interaction with His creature rules out any possibility of neutrality, as a neutral understanding of God's performance is "impossible for faith, precisely because faith by definition was self-involving—a living response to personal encounter with the living God."[100] God does not act alone. He not only invites humanity to participate in His reconciliatory performance, but through this incorporation, gives humanity the essence of its truthfulness, its life. As Balthasar writes:

> In a Christian theodramatic theory we have the right to assert that no other, mythical or religio-philosophical anthropology can attain a satisfactory idea of man ... It alone can release man from the impossible task of trying to, on the basis of his brokenness, to envisage himself as not broken without forgetting some essential aspect of himself in the process. It releases him from the burden by inserting him, right from the start, into

---

97. *CD* IV/3.1, 183–84.
98. *CD* I/1, 229.
99. Hunsinger, *How To Read Karl Barth*, 50.
100. Ibid.

the dramatic dialogue with God, so that God himself may cause him to experience *his* ultimate definition of man.[101]

This incorporation into God's drama is realized through the imagination of theology, that encourages and elevates humanity's thinking, to envisage the ideal *becoming* the real. What is important about the movement of the ideal to the real is not simply the transcendent reality of its movement, but what this means for humanity. This dramatic potential is the foundation of seeing the "original form" or "God's idea" of the human. When the "Logos becomes incarnate and begins his work of addressing individuals (not only in speech but by his whole being), I am assured that the notion of access to the idea God has of me is no illusion."[102] The importance of the idea God has for me relates directly to the universal and particular implications of Christ's incarnational performance. God has a particular idea of me—He has a particular role for me to play in His drama. God's personal involvement with humanity rules out neutrality, as it calls for a self-involved participation in the Theodrama. It does not mean however, that humanity is "dispensed from the effort of planning and fashioning himself, but he is shown the way to do it and the ultimate destination he should have in mind."[103] This is the essence of the ideal *becoming* the real, it is the movement of the human by the Spirit so as to apprehend the ultimate destination of life: being *in* Jesus Christ.

§4.4 Realizing the Possibilities through Our Interactions

God's integration of humanity into His revelation occurs through the absoluteness of His love, which ultimately exposes to the participants what it means to be a person. The truth of our performance in life comes through our recognition and acceptance of what it means to be an actor in God's drama. Life is constituted by our continual interaction, interaction that continues to invigorate the action of the stage. Stanislavski once wrote that communication between persons is invaluable on the stage, that "this truth derives from the nature of the theatre, which is based on the inter-communication of the *dramatis personae*."[104] However, Stanislavski reminds us that such inter-communication will only be real if each actor accepts his role, if he will "give himself up wholly to his part" and when he does, "he becomes completely identified with it and is transformed. But the moment he

---

101. *TD* II, 343.
102. Nichols, *No Bloodless Myth*, 226–27.
103. *TD* II, 343.
104. Stanislavski, *An Actor Prepares*, 196.

becomes distracted and falls under the sway of his own personal life, he will be transported across the footlights into the audience or beyond the walls of the theatre, wherever the object is that maintains a bond of relationship with him. Meanwhile he plays his part in a purely mechanical way."[105] In order to remain engaged in a real performance of truthful inter-communication and interaction, theology cannot be distracted from the central figure of the play (the universal normative), Jesus Christ. This perspective is illumined through the interaction of God in Christ with humanity. Through this action, light is shed upon personhood, while empowered through the imaginative powers of theology's self-involved performance upon God's stage. Through our participation in God's performance, we come to recognize how the theatre and its dramatic essence cannot be "dispensed from the task of indicating that which gives meaning in concrete reality."[106]

The realness of life is ascertained when the imaginative powers of theology guide our explorations beyond mere analysis and dissection. It is the ability of participation that makes the dramatic necessary for our theological endeavors. The ideal *becoming* the real occurs through a participatory expectation and gradual fulfilment illumined through the elevation of the imagination within the drama as opening out and forming the drama's reference to life, which "arises of necessity from the reality of performance, keeps drama from the temptation of being art for art's sake."[107]

It is the ability of the imagination to raise our theological endeavors to the truth of participation that makes it not only necessary, but infinitely profound. Imagination's participatory ability and reality is what allowed Coleridge to identify imagination as the "living Power and prime agent of all human perception." As Coleridge noted:

> The IMAGINATION then, I consider either as primary, or secondary. The primary IMAGINATION I hold to be the living Power and prime Agent of all human Perception, and as a repetition in the finite mind of the eternal act of creation in the infinite I am. The secondary Imagination I consider as an echo of the former, co-existing with the conscious will, yet still identical with the primary in the *kind* of its agency, and differing only in *degree*, and in the *mode* of it operation. It dissolves, diffuses, dissipates, in order to recreate; or where this process is rendered impossible, yet still at all events it struggles to idealize and to unify. It

---

105. Ibid.
106. *TD* I, 266.
107. Ibid.

is essentially *vital*, even as all objects (*as* objects) are essentially fixed and dead.[108]

The importance of the imagination is its creative power to illumine the realness, the originality of life. Through imagination theology becomes more aware not only of the movement of the stage, but of its essence, its being. Such action or *becoming* dramatizes the profound interaction that takes place within the theatre of God's glory.

Through its imaginative actions, theology participates in the action of meaning, thereby unveiling the depth of meaning to be found and experienced in life. This participatory reality is the freedom of existence made possible and available by the work and action of God. And through God's action we are constantly made aware of the truth of our being. A truth that, according to Balthasar, realizes that the "infinite Creator has equipped it (the created being) with the grace of participate in the inexhaustibility of its origin."[109]

The movement of revelation, invitation and reconciliation discloses the unrelenting realness of God's movement toward creation. This reality of love is not simply exposed through its in-breaking, but profoundly elevates the relational move of the ideal into the real, through the relational reality of the Creator and His creature. This relationality—the analogia relationis—is dramatically rooted through its reciprocity, that is, its continual inter-communication and interaction. Through the *analogia relationis*, then, theology is made aware of the unmistakable and undeniable movement of the ideal into the real—a movement illumined through theology's imaginative powers.

§5 Relational Reality

§5.1 Identity of Mission

The identity and realization of our mission arises through the movement and apprehension of "Who am I?" This movement is the ideal becoming the real, which occurs through the *analogia relationis*. In Christ is the entrance into the real as the incarnational performance of Christ brings forth the ideal reality of humanity, the eschatological "not yet," into the real, the eschatological "here and now," truthfulness of our existence. Truthfulness of existence includes the recognition of our mission; it is the comprehension

---

108. Coleridge, *Biographia Literaria*, 202.
109. Ibid., 107.

of our created image and likeness, for in it, "God reflects Himself and all things." Moving further in this understanding and portrayal of our relational reality, Balthasar quotes John of Ruysbroeck:

> In this Divine Image all creatures have an eternal life, outside themselves, as in their eternal Archetype; and after this eternal Image and in this Likeness, we have been made by the Holy Trinity. And therefore God wills that we shall go forth from ourselves in this Divine Light, and shall reunite ourselves in a supernatural way with *this Image, which is our proper life, and shall possess it with Him, in action and in fruition, in eternal bliss.*[110]

This reality is recognized by humanity solely because of God's creative and imaginative performance. The incarnation is God's most imaginative action, as through it, He reveals, invites and reconciles. Christ's incarnational performance is realized through the imaginative powers that illumine the ground-breaking reality of the ideal actually becoming the real. All missions exist within Christ's very mission of revelation, invitation and reconciliation.

> If the mission is the real core of the personality, it opens up the latter—because it comes from eternity and is destined for eternity—far beyond the dimensions of which it is conscious in the world or which others allot to it. This is why a mission that is begun on earth, if it really originates in Christ's mission, does not cease with death but comes to perfection in eternal life.[111]

The role of the actor finds its ultimate mission when she enters into a participatory performance made possible through the invitation of Christ. Acceptance of Christ's invitation is the reality of *in Christo*. Being in Christo means that "every man can cherish the hope of not remaining a merely individual conscious subject but of receiving personhood from God, becoming a person, with a mission that is likewise defined *in Christo*."[112] Identity, then, while invested in role, ultimately recognizes the ideal of the person, through the binding of role and identity. In other words, our mission is the recognition of our identity and its movement (role) in Christ and upon His stage.

When humanity is addressed by the ideal of the Godhead, it is not only exposed to the faithful performance of Christ, but more importantly, invited to enter into and participate in this movement. Concerning such participation, Balthasar writes that "to the extent that creatures are, were

---

110. John of Ruysbroeck, *The Adornment of the Spiritual Marriage*, quoted by Balthasar, *TD* V, 390–91.

111. *TD* V, 393–94.

112. *TD* III, 220.

or will be in God, they participate more in being and are more true there than in themselves."[113] Through the person of Christ humanity is offered the opportunity to close the chasm between what I represent and what I am in reality. The query given notice at the onset of this chapter—"Who am I?"- is only answerable in the *mission* (person) of Christ. Balthasar's use of mission allows for theology to take into account the entirety of the person, and in so doing, we avoid allowing a dichotomy to emerge between who we are and what our role is, that is, a division between identity and role. As Balthasar maintains, "(W)hen the Logos-made-man addresses the individual—and this takes place through the words and the whole being of Christ—I am granted an insight into and access to that Idea God has of me."[114] This is an access and insight into the entirety of who I am—the knowledge of the whole of my mission, for it is in mission where I find myself. "Who am I" gains its realization in the idea God has for me, an idea that flows forth from the mission of Christ.

> Christ calls man to a mission "at the point where he has accepted his own from the Father. It is like a flowing fountain of missions: a constantly new gushing forth from the central source. And because the Son desires that every mission should serve the glorification of the Father, he does not have the missions link up with his in a peripheral way but, rather, lets them arise centrally, out of his own center." The mission embraces life, for it comes from eternity.[115]

That mission embraces life cannot but illumine the fundamental relational reality of life. *In Christ* is a statement that accentuates the fullness of the ideal as the real. Thus, the foundation of God's drama is established and sustained through the presence, direction and indwelling of the Spirit whereby Christ's performance calls forth the human to imagine the becoming of the real. Through such an imagined reality, humanity glimpses how His (Christ's) incarnational performance re-humanizes humanity thereby elevating humanity to its rightful place upon the stage.

Through its incorporation into Christ's action humanity not only participates in the real, but in doing so, meets the demand to "know thyself." Because of our relational reality, we cannot be understood apart from God, and apart from one another. Understanding anthropology through Christology is the only way to secure our explorations into the query of "who am I?" Apart from its Creator, the creature becomes nothing more than an

---

113. *TD* I, 546.
114. *TD* V, 391.
115. *TD* V, 393; quoting Adrienne von Speyr, *The Birth of the Church*, 398.

abstraction that is unable to comprehend its concrete form and thus, its concrete meaning. Knowledge of self is through the relational reality determined and made possible by God.

§5.2 Relation of Being

The creature's participation with God, through grace, occurs in the concreteness of our relational reality, made available only by the action of Christ as expressed and revealed by the Spirit. And while it is by the power of faith that humanity begins to recognize the movement of the ideal becoming the real, it is through our relationship with God that we come to realize the essence and existence of our being. The analogia relationis is not subsumed in the analogia fidei as some might argue, nor is the analogia relationis nothing more than scholastic talk that "expresses nothing but a relation of being."[116] Rather, it is within the relational reality with the Creator that the creature is even able to recognize the aspects of faith and of being. The human does not have the capability to first create his own faithfulness so as to enter into relationship with some transcendent being. Instead, humanity is graciously confronted by faith through the interactive in-breaking of The Word. According to Barth, the human exists because of the Word and because of this, "he (the human) has not created his own faith; the Word has created it. He has not come to faith; faith has come to him through the Word."[117] Humanity does indeed recognize the acts of God through the reality of faith, thus, the analogia relationis by no means denotes the absence of the analogia fidei or even the analogia entis. In fact, it is because of the analogia relationis that each of the other analogical understandings find their meaning. That is, because the human is the subject of faith, and the creature or being of Being, she cannot recognize God firstly through these as she must first be in relation to God in order to begin comprehending His reality. However, because of her relational standing with God, she is opened to the possibility of faith as well as the deepening understanding of her being. It is explicitly due to the work of Christ that humanity is able to fulfil its covenantal role of partner with God.

The understanding of relationality acknowledges the constitutive nature of the human who is a social being (relational being) created in the image of a relational God. Thus, while some might point to the primacy of faith in light of the belief that Barth did not build upon an explicit use of the analogia relationis, his realization of the God-human relationship

---

116. *TKB*, 163.
117. *CD* I/1, 244.

never diverted from the fact that there is "a correspondence and similarity between the two relationships. This is not a correspondence and similarity of being, *analogia entis* . . . It is a question of the relationship within the being of God on the one side and between the being of God and that of man on the other. Between these two relationships as such—and it is in this sense that the second is the image of the first—there is correspondence and similarity."[118] The correspondence and similarity revealed through the *analogia relationis* provides the necessary means to recognize first: the relational reality of the Trinity; second, the relational reality of the human; and third, it is through our relations that we come to understand the profundity of faith and the truth of being. It is ultimately because of this relational reality, the fact that humanity is "a social being who lives by intersubjective relationships," that we are capable, continues Balthasar, "in the first place of entering into a covenant with God, as God has intended. And *this* natural order is for its part only possible on the basis of God's own interpersonal nature, his triune nature, of which the human being is a true image."[119]

Again, the movement of the ideal becoming the real is made clear through the person and actions of Christ—through His mission. Yet the profundity of the performance cannot be understood properly if there exists a separation between role and identity. The dramatic dimension of life is that the creature participates in and with the Creator, through the established relationship made real by the Creator. God's covenantal relationship with humanity establishes and secures the performance on the stage. This relational reality is the embrace of the creature by the Creator and, as Barth writes, it is a reality through "a covenant that God made with him and brought to its goal for him: a covenant which God did not just establish between himself and man but in which man was called and impelled to play his free and active part."[120] This ability to play one's part—to realize his mission—is made real through the analogia relationis. From the foundation of relation, established in Christ through the Spirit, humanity is invited to participate in the faithful performance of Christ, thereby coming closer to the originality of its identity. Balthasar claims that, "The closer man comes to this identity, the more perfectly does he play his part."[121] If Balthasar is correct, it is from our relational reality that we are made aware of our mission, thereby providing the potentiality of our perfected performances.

---

118. *CD* III/2, 220.
119. *TKB*, 163.
120. *CD* IV/4, 74.
121. *TD* II, 14.

The redemption of the human comes through the relational reality of humanity with its Creator. This, writes Balthasar, occurs because "(S)omething in man must be identical to his original state, (*status naturae integrae*), something must be identical to his fall from it (*status naturae lapsae*); something in him must correspond to the historical phase of his preparation for redemption in Christ, (*status naturae reparandae*), and, finally, something in him must correspond to the effect in him of this transformation wrought by Christ, (*status naturae reparatae*)."[122] Humanity's real performance in Christ through the Spirit is the elevation of humanity, through its "present actuality" of becoming. The elevation of the real occurs when theology imagines and enacts its entrance into God's Being-in-act thereby insisting upon a "participatory actuality." God's event of revelation, invitation and reconciliation beckons theology to live as a real witness to the truth of this on-going act.

§6 Elevation of the Real

Through the person of the Holy Spirit humanity is exposed to the real. Through this exposure, humanity experiences firsthand, "what the 'glory' of absolute freedom can be, and they experience it more and more deeply, the more they are initiated, through God's "Word," into the divine nature."[123] It is from this experience that humanity gains its identity and role as our mission is not found within the confines of society but from Jesus Christ through the Holy Spirit. Again, Balthasar points out that humanity only comes into understanding of the real through the movement and action of the Godhead. "It is when," writes Balthasar, "creatures are thus lifted above their own creaturely nature to one that transcends them absolutely that they become aware of the yawning gulf between them and experience their own creatureliness for the first time."[124]

The elevation of humanity into the absolute "otherness" of God occurs through the revelation of Christ through the Spirit. This act should be understood as the ideal taking to itself the non-ideal so as to manifest the real. That is, God takes to Himself the creature that has turned his back on Him so as to incorporate him into the divine performance. Such movement however, must not be allowed to annihilate the distinction between that which is infinitely real and that which is becoming real, for as Aidan Nichols reminds, "the Incarnation does not, of course, abolish the difference

---

122. *TD* II, 12–13.
123. *TD* II, 399.
124. Ibid., 399–400.

between Creator and creature, but it *unifies the two in a common accord*. We are to move ever more towards the idea that God has of us, thus finding our measure at one and the same time both in God and in the creature that we are."[125] If taken seriously, theology's imaginative powers open up the possibilities of coming to know the world, to know one another, and to know God, as each are meant to be known. We step into the self-revelation of God to the extent that we allow ourselves to imagine the ideal becoming actualized as the real. In other words, through a deepening of our understanding of God's in-breaking, we gain a deepening understanding of our personhood, thereby securing our faithful performances in God's drama.

The plea to take imagination seriously is, as Hart maintains, "nothing less than a summons to reckon with something lying close to the core of *what it means to be human*, a feature of our humanity that shapes our essentially human response to others, to the world and to God."[126] Such recognition of the imaginative powers that lie at the core of the human does not simply awaken us to the generalized understanding of the human but to the specific realization of what it means for me, for you, for each of us to be a particular person living and acting on the stage of creation. In fact, through the imagination theology can come to comprehend the depth of being. Thus, as discussed in the introduction, the query to be made transcends the general question of what it means to be human, pushing us towards the specific understanding illumined through the question of "who am I?" The essence of being is that which reveals the depth of the meaning of life, both for the whole of society and for the specific person. Humanity's importance, its significance, is because the Word became flesh. He did not incarnate a "general" body, but was and is the distinct person Jesus Christ. Balthasar writes:

> The fact that Being in its totality can be present and reveal itself in individual beings; that—in Augustinian terms—the individual being is illuminated by an absolute light and can be read and interpreted in that light; and that the very uniqueness of the individual being causes the indivisible uniqueness of Being in its totality to shine forth with peculiar clarity—all of this, as H.J. Verweyen has shown, provides the basis for God's revelation in the individual form and figure of Christ and for man's transcendental ability to apprehend it.[127]

---

125. Nichols, *No Bloodless Myth*, 226.
126. Hart, "A Suspicion Observed," 5.
127. *TD* II, 22.

Through the truth revealed in God's revelatory action, we become aware of our freedom. Furthermore, through our apprehension of truth and awareness of our freedom, we move further and further into the *real* of our humanness. That is, we step deeper into the becoming of the ideal into the real. This movement of the being into the reality of truth spawns understanding of self. Being "coincides with consciousness of self-consciousness, thus becoming its own object. This is the true meaning of the *cogito ergo sum*."[128] However, attempts to "know thyself," to explore "who am I," through the rationalistic powers of reason and analysis will render the human incapable of the fullness of truth and the fullness of life. When theology guides the explorations into knowledge of self through its given powers of the imagination, the answers to self-understanding become apparent. As Hart remarks, "it seems that God has made us imaginative beings, and placed us in a world which calls forth from us responses of an imaginative sort if we are to indwell it meaningfully and well. Life itself, let alone 'life in all its fullness' is from top to bottom, from beginning to end, a highly *imaginative* affair."[129]

§7 Imaginative Movement towards the Actuality of Our Faithful Performances

When the movement into understanding our imaginative need occurs, theology begins to realize the potentiality involved with its performance. This is to say that, through the willingness to allow for our imaginative powers to guide our theological endeavors, the ideal becomes the real, thereby entering into the *actuality* of our faithful performances. However, such performances can only occur when the perspective of theology begins by the imagining of, and working out from, the luminosity of faith. Faith is the seal of the "vision of God'; it is, writes Balthasar, the "dark *inchoatio visionis*. Together with love and hope, faith constitutes the conscious side of grace in so far as grace is the ontological assimilation to God's being."[130] Balthasar further maintains that the certainty of faith is through the action, (the performance), of the Spirit. It is the Spirit's action on us that actualizes the ideal becoming the real through faith in Christ. Through the imagination, theology can witness, and does witness, the certainty of our explorations, if done through the guidance of faith through the Spirit.

The Spirit is the "seal of the good thing for which we hope (2 Cor 1:22; 5:5; Eph 1:14)—a deliberately realistic expression implying that faith brings

---

128. *TL* I, 93.
129. Hart, "A Suspicion Observed," 5.
130. *GL* I, 162.

with it something of the substance and quality of its object; thus faith itself is the seal of the vision of God: *inchoatio visionis*."[131] The seal of God's vision is the actualization within our relational reality that continues through and by the movement of faith. This constant action of the stage, the moving from the ideal into the real, occurs through the "present actuality" of theology's faithful performances, led and directed by the Spirit. Such guidance is recognizable however, only through the realization brought about through our relational reality of faith. Our relationship in Christ and through Christ is the imaginative movement towards our faithful performance. As Balthasar maintains, "in God we shall see how man was intended to be, and in man we shall see how God reveals himself to him. In heaven the mystery of Christ . . . that accompanies us on our earthly path of faith will continue to be the center that illuminates everything."[132]

The actuality, then, of our faithful performances is not only promulgated by the Spirit's action, but also through our response to God's action, which is manifested through our deliberate and obedient focus on Christ. Theology must "with its gaze obediently turned toward Jesus Christ, simply and directly describe how he stands in time and in history as the heart and norm of all that is historical."[133] Our theological endeavors are not meant to disengage from the relational reality of Christ with creation; a reality that steps into history and cannot be separated from the historical. However, while Christ performed within the historical, His action continues for all eternity. Christ's performance invites humanity into this eternal mission, for He (the Son), "grants to each who follows him participation in the same substance, in the same directedness and limitlessness of his eternal mission."[134]

In order for theology to understand the narrative of humanity better, allowing for and entering into the movement of the narrative toward the dramatic holds the potentiality of exposing us to the core of being, through the insistence of our participation in God's Being-in-act. Through the becoming of the narrative, we can come to realize the magnitude of interaction throughout creation's history, beginning with Adam and Eve, extending through the Israelites, the first century Christians, the Reformation, and so on, culminating with Christ's second coming. It cannot be denied that the narrative does in some sense offer clarity to the complexity of historical events by proposing the story form with a "beginning, middle, and end, a story with a recognizable plot, a story whose participants can

131. *TD* V, 148
132. *TD* V, 392.
133. *TH*, 27.
134. *TD* V, 393.

be identified and their respective roles characterized."[135] Yet it is when the story transcends characterization and identification, and moves into participation in Christ's performance, that the fullness of reality is exposed. Through the *mission* of Christ and His incarnational performance, we gain the ability to enter into His faithful performance, thereby coming to realize our own faithful performance. We now turn the discussion to chapter 5 that seeks to move deeper into understanding and enacting the reality of our faithful performances.

---

135. Dunn, *Narrative Dynamics in Paul*, 217.

Chapter Five—Performative Reality

> The action itself will reveal who each individual is; and it will not reveal, through successive unveilings, primarily who the individual *always was*, but rather who he *is to become* through the action, through his encounter with others and through the decisions he makes.[1]

§1 The Opening Movement

THROUGH THE ACTION OF God humanity enters into the *becoming* of personhood. Our personhood is revealed through our performative reality; both our personhood and performative reality are rooted in God's Being-in-act. From the performative reality of Christ we are opened up to the image of perfected humanity. In Christ humanity not only encounters the image and likeness of our perfected humanity, but we are drawn in to the becoming of the ideal into the real. This final chapter seeks to further the given proposal that through our participation in Christ our ideal becomes the real, thereby resulting in our faithful performances. The becoming of our performances is the reality of our own personhood in its *becoming*.

The chapter first discusses the recognition of the performative reality of life—a reality best understood and expressed in action. The performance of the Theo-drama summons a performative response from theology. Thus, the ensuing discussion concerns the on-going push of the dramatizing of theology. What does it mean to dramatize theology? If, as so many have deduced, life and death are enveloped within the drama of everyday, then, might it be possible that, because all the world's a stage, life is best understood dramatically? If this is, theology should contend with the implications for its practices, which, as is being argued, are benefited most through a full embrace of the dramatizing of theology. Section 3 first attests to the identity of the *theologica dramaticas* before moving into common mis-conceptions of the relationship between theology and the theatre. Section three is followed

1. *TD* II, 11.

by a theological interlude that takes a brief look at the role and performance of the Spirit in Balthasar's *Theo-Drama*. Next, section 4 attempts to unveil some of the thoughts and influences that continue to mis-inform today's performances. The core of who we are comes into fullness through the performance of Christ. Theology needs to step into His action so as to unmask our own performance. Upon the unmasking, the chapter takes "the meaning of life *is* drama," and fleshes this out through a deepening understanding of humanity's own faithful performances. Through the apprehension of performative truth, our theological performances enter into the transformation of history, so as to participate faithfully in the eternal performance of Christ. The chapter concludes with the final sections looking into our theological performances that are Eucharistic and eschatological.

§2 Dramatic Movement

Being or personhood is undoubtedly relational, but beyond this, the human is a thinking, spiritual, and performative being. Thus, there remains a tremendous need to acknowledge the breadth of meaning that comes from understanding the creation of the human, which, claims Barth, "sets the stage for the story of the covenant of grace. The story requires a stage corresponding to it; the existence of man and his whole world. Creation provides this."[2] If theology is to apprehend the meaning of life and the call to participate in this "story of the covenant of grace," it needs to be faithful to its object, for it is the object that founds our understanding of the creature. Barth continues his thought, writing, "in the Christian concept of the creation of all things the question is concretely one of man and his whole universe as the theatre of the history of the covenant of grace; of the totality of earthly and heavenly things as they are to be comprehended in Christ (Eph 1:10)."[3] If Barth is correct, then, the movement of theology into the dramatic seems most natural, as through action (performance) the drama of life continues to be exposed.

§2.1 Performance within the *Theologica Dramaticas*

It is through God's action that humanity is confronted by the performance of grace and salvation thereby being exposed to the potentiality of life's meaning, its *mission*. The world is the place for God's salvific performance, it is His theatre, and as Barth maintains:

2. *CD*, III/1, 44.
3. Ibid.

> this theatre of the great acts of God in grace and salvation . . . Even as God's creatures, and within the world of other creatures, caught up in the great drama of being, we are not in an empty or alien place . . . If we take this seriously, our eyes are open to the fact that the created world including our own existence fulfils that purpose and constitutes that *theatrum gloriae Dei*.[4]

Through the richness of our performances, and ultimately through the performance of God in Christ through the Spirit, humanity comes to recognize not only its role upon the stage, but its mission. Balthasar continues to draw our attention to the fact that the mission of humanity is not as much as an observer, an analyzer, a theorizer, etc.—the tendency of a "rationalistic theology"—but as a participant. Through its performative foundation, the movement of the stage resonates from the totality of the Church's history—a history, it is argued, that in allowing the narrative to become the drama, receives its fullness of expression, thereby ensuring our faithful performances. This assurance is nothing more than the recognition that those coming before us did not simply attempt to tell or recount their own stories, but sought to encourage participation in the very drama of Jesus Christ. Balthasar writes:

> What Paul and the other writers do in the Letters, the evangelists do in their own way: they do not recount stories in which they are not involved; in fact, they know that their only chance of being objective is by being profoundly involved in the event they are describing. They exercise objectivity by giving their witness before the Church and the world, handing on the drama of Jesus' life, the life of the incarnate Word of God, to the catechesis of the primitive Church, a catechesis designed to incorporate the lives of the young Christians into the mystery of Christ's life.[5]

Insofar as we act or recognize our performance, we recognize our humanity. In other words, instead of observing, analyzing or describing one another's performances, we should intentionally seek to share in these performances. Through our sharing of particular performances, we come to a deepened realization of our own meaning, our *imago Trinitatis*. This image comes to us through God's gracious covenant, His free gift of life granted to the entirety of the dramatis personae. Two things to note though: this image and potentiality of participation does originate from outside of God, and it is realized only through our analogia relationis. It is this relational reality

---

4. *CD*, III/3, 48.
5. *TD* II, 57–58.

that leads Barth to write "it is the true *humanum* and therefore the true creaturely image of God."[6]

The movement of God evokes a reciprocal movement on humanity's behalf. History demands participation, as it has not simply been entered into by the Son of God and left unchanged; history has been transformed, it has been re-humanized through the performance of Christ through the Spirit. Through Christ the "empty area between infinite and finite becomes a place 'inhabited by God.'"[7] Through this dynamic closing and opening up of the space on the stage, humanity is enveloped in God's eternal action. Through this action Balthasar writes, "The entire acting area is an atmosphere of reciprocal indwelling and interpenetration on the part of God and man/world, but it is not something static."[8]

Dramatizing theology is not the attempt to commandeer a "new" linguistic system borrowed from the language of the theatre, but is the recognition of the dramatic essence of theology—the drama *is* the reality of God's interaction with His creation. Jesus did not simply speak of hearing the message εἶπεν δὲ αὐτῷ ὁ Ἰησοῦς· πορεύου καὶ σὺ ποίει ὁμοίως. (Jesus told him, "Go and do likewise," Luke 10:37). Jesus insisted—the verbs here are in the imperative (πορεύου and ποίει)—that His followers *go* and *do* likewise, thereby drawing upon the intimacy of one's faith and their actions. That their response to His words was and is manifested in performance— ὅτι θέατρον ἐγενήθημεν τῷ κόσμῳ (spectacle unto the world—1 Cor 4:9) is the message and expectation of the Christian faith.

Nothing stands outside of the performative reality of God's drama; as Balthasar maintains, "there is no standpoint external to theo-drama."[9] Failure to realize this foundational understanding can lead towards a theology built solely on propositions and principles, rather than the fullness of performance and interaction, as embodied and encouraged through God's gracious acts of revelation, invitation and reconciliation. From the act (performance) of God, humanity is not only made witness to the relational reality of the real, but invited into and encouraged to become an active participant of the *communio sanctorum*. Theology should continue its move into faith thinking, as opposed to creating systems of thought intent on determining faith. In order to apprehend God's movement, it is being argued that it is beneficial for theology to avoid giving priority to a systematic dissection of God's continual performance and interaction with humanity,

---

6. *CD* III/1, 186.
7. *TD* III, 54.
8. Ibid.
9. *TD* II, 62

in lieu of becoming attendant to the active reality of faith as it seeks to guide and encourage our theological endeavors. Balthasar writes:

> We have tried to erect theology on the articles of faith (and not vice versa): on the Trinity, the Incarnation of the Son, his Cross and Resurrection on our behalf, and his sending of the Spirit to us in the apostolic Church and in the *communio sanctorum*. It is only on the basis of such a theology, today and in the future, that men can give witness in their lives and in their deaths to that "highest gift of God" which is "irreversible and unsurpassable".[10]

Theology today does indeed recognize God's drama, through our recognition of such action as Christ's reconciliatory action, the "highest gift of God." However, much of this recognition is only an acknowledgement of the principle of such action as opposed to the intentional sharing in, of Christ's action. That is, the incarnation, cross, resurrection and ascension are not merely to be observed, analyzed or discussed, they are the life events of Christ that call for a response from the ones He came to save. It is through theological inquiries that move beyond the initial investigations, so as to encourage action from her theologians—participation in life—that the Church and society will come closer and closer to the truthfulness of Christ's performance, and are thus, opened to the event of truth.

It is in light of the event of truth that theology must continually seek to give performance to truth, for in doing so it will participate in the continuous act of God. As was discussed in chapter 1, truth is "always conceived as an event," such an event rooted in God's Being-in-act. This event of truth is "always therefore in essence identical with God's being itself."[11] The event of truth is an ontological reality that undergirds theology's faithful performance. By this it is understood that theology's performance is only faithful if its essence—its being—is in the truth of the Godhead as expressed through the Theo-drama and manifested through Christ's Eucharistic performance. Hunsinger writes that "a truth cannot be had in abstraction from an encounter with the person of the living God."[12] Christ is the foundational truth of God's revelation to humanity. Theology can only be faithful to this truth if it seeks to participate—to share—by its word and deed in Christ through the Spirit.

A faithful performance insists on the Theo-praxis illumined through the action of God. It is then, through participation in this action as opposed

10. *TD* V, 14.
11. Hunsinger, *How To Read Karl Barth*, 67.
12. Ibid.

to an attempted mirroring of such action that the Christian understands herself. The disciple or follower of Christ is actively to be *en Christōi*. Sharing in Christ's performance is the full recognition of our relational reality of being in Christ. Through our sharing in Christ's action—participation in His Being-in-act—the criterion of personhood is further revealed as its criterion of quality is in "both the act itself and the character of the agent."[13]

Who we are is ultimately found only in Christ. Bauckham maintains that it is this fact, Christ's concrete identification with each of the stage's participants, that "Jesus concretized God's solidarity with people not only in the common human conditions, but with people in all varieties of the human condition, people divided by all the differences . . . Jesus intended God's loving solidarity with all people to create loving solidarity among all people."[14] Thus, it is argued that the character of the saints is rooted in the action of the Godhead—such action that moves beyond the simple reading of the narrative, into its dramatic performance. In other words, by the narrative becoming the drama, the world's stage finds its strength and its character in the dramatic event and in-breaking of Christ. This action is exposed and illumined through the "plays" within *The Play*. In Christ through the Spirit, our lives participate in the dramatic act of God's sovereign initiative, and in so doing, we find and realize our own faithful performances.

§2.2 Dramatizing Theology

The opening up of the Godhead, through revelation, invitation and reconciliation, establishes and encourages an interactional reality that allows our theological endeavors to be receptive to the *regnum Christi* which is continually manifested through the *regnum gratiae*. The power received through God's grace stems from the fact that "man is no longer left to himself but is given into the hand of God."[15] Because of the concrete way in which Christ incorporates and transforms humanity through His performance, there is left no ambiguity to God's interactive desire concerning His creature. In fact, the reception of such power is not an arbitrary encounter but the "transposing of man into a wholly new state of one who has accepted and appropriated the promise, so that irrespective of his attitude to it he no longer lives without this promise but with it." The significance of such an understanding is that this new state is "the claim of the Word of God," which is not as such, "a wish or command which remains outside

---

13. Hütter, *Suffering Divine Things*, 32.
14. Bauckham, "CT," 27–28.
15. *CD* I/1, 150.

the hearer without impinging on his existence. It is the claiming and commandeering of man . . . man as a hearer of His Word now finds himself in the sphere of the divine claim; he is claimed by God."[16] God's claim on humanity is elevated in its comprehension, through language and action that seeks to expose God's revelation through a dramatic reality. Such a reality—the dramatizing of theology—opens humanity up to its participatory *mission* in the active knowledge of redemption and the reality of salvation. Drawing from Rowan Williams, Ben Quash maintains that the truth of the world is apprehended through a participatory mission upon life's stage. This occurs because, "knowledge is essentially participatory . . . (as recognition of a place within a network of relations), [that] it is inseparable from history and *praxis*."[17] Thus, the participation in life is participation in the act of becoming, an act that encompasses that whole of creation through its incorporation into the performance of Christ.

Incorporation into Christ's performance is the epitome of dramatizing theology as it is the recognition of Him being *pro me*, that is, just for me. Through His relational performance Christ reveals to me, the truth of being which answers "Who am I?" For in Christ through the Spirit, the realization is exposed that I am the creation of the God of all creation; and not simply an insignificant creature, but His covenantal partner created in His image. It is the realization that my very existence is taken up in the performance of Christ, thereby finding the essence of my performance and my personhood.

> Jesus Christ is, in fact, just for me, that I myself am just the subject for whom He is. That is the point. That is the newness of being, the new creation, the new birth of the Christian. Everything else follows from this, especially the fact that, whatever may be the force of the basis and validity of the *pro me*, it can never be a *pro me* in the abstract, but includes in itself and is enclosed by the communal *pro nobis* and the even wider *propter nos homines* . . . Without the *pro me* of the individual Christian there is no legitimate *pro nobis* of the faith of the Christian community and no legitimate *propter nos homines* of its representative faith for the non-believing world.[18]

Through revelation, God's claim, and interaction with creation, is made apparent; He desires our covenantal partnership. This action on humanity by God is an event able to be recognized, when its dramatic essence is brought

---

16. *CD* I/1, 152.

17. Rowan Williams, "Balthasar and Rahner," quoted by Quash, *Theology and the Drama of History*, 28.

18. *CD* IV/I, 755.

to life through theology's risk of stepping out from behind the observance wall and into the action. Again, such movement occurs through the dramatizing of theology, a movement that recognizes that all the world's a stage and we all participate together in the quest for an active, participatory knowledge of self.

Theology is inherently dramatic because of its object; and because, writes Balthasar, "life manifests a fundamental urge to observe itself as an action exhibiting both meaning and mystery,"[19] so too must theology. This is to say that it is through drama, and thus, the dramatizing of theology, that humanity not only recognizes but actively comprehends its performance and participation in life, thereby reminding that participation is essential not only in our theological endeavors, but in life as well. Drama enables "existence to attain understanding of itself" as it, the dramatic, is a "legitimate instrument in the elucidation of being."[20] Dramatizing theology, first, recognizes the absence of "external positions" as we do not stand outside, above or beyond God's drama. Secondly, "we do not simply 'arrive' at our experience like spectators. We are *invested* in our experience, and it is invested in us."[21] Dramatizing theology is the recognition of our sharing or participation in the reality of life because of the reality presented by our being *in Christ*. Third, and most importantly, dramatizing theology returns us back to the proper perspective, foundation and trajectory of theology—God's revelation, invitation and reconciliation performed by Christ through the Spirit. Such a return to our proper perspective sheds light upon the answer to existence and our interaction with God and one another.

Interaction with the "other" occurs multiple times on a daily basis; there is no denying of this fact. Through the dramatic we come not only to recognize, but to realize the profundity and truth of our humanness through its relational and performative reality. Balthasar maintains that "the *good* which God does to us can only be experienced as the *truth* if we share in *performing* it (John 7:17; 8:13f)."[22] If left unattended, the performance of the stage will continue to move towards the *krisis*, as opposed to sharing in Christ's performance. As discussed in chapter 4, humanity remains stagnant in the construction of its own *paradox* when it attempts to re-construct the image of humanity in the likeness of itself. Such re-construction occurs when theology is absent from the stage, as there remains no measure or guide to keep the stage aware of its mis-steps. Focus upon drama simply

---

19. *TD* I, 78–79.
20. Nichols, *No Bloodless Myth*, 19.
21. Quash, *Theology and the Drama of History*, 27.
22. *TD* I, 20.

for drama's sake would miss the mis-steps, instead calling them "creative expressions" that allow for the human to establish its own way as opposed to *The Way*. The great achievement of drama is to "strip externals away and put in their place . . . the self-conscious and active individual as the living embodiment of truth." Drama allows for the apprehension of truth and thus, of being, as it rests in the performance of life, which finds its root in the "dramatic movement within the Trinity to us."[23]

§3 Beyond Theatre into *Theologica Dramaticas*

§3.1 Discovery of Identity

The call now being slowly heard within the walls of theology is the need to recognize the theatrical within theology, while not getting caught-up in the dramatic motif, but instead, through it, realizing the reality of performance within theology. Performance is the root of our theological endeavors. According to Vanhoozer, performance suggests that "we are in the realm not of propositions only but of action. And to speak of action is to emphasize the role of the actor."[24] The biblical and theological understanding of performance transcends the theatrical device of performance for a show, or for the sake of an audience. Theological performances are meant primarily for the One audience (God) and secondarily for the dramatis personae, yet in saying as much, it should be recognized that in this performance, we participate in something that is far more than a mere role. As Vanhoozer points out, "(T)o put on Christ's righteousness is to do far more than to play a role; it is to recover one's deepest and truest identity."[25] The discovery or rediscovery of identity is the movement of role becoming mission. As argued in chapter 4, humanity's mission is secured once the person recognizes his identity in Christ, and this is why it is crucial for the Church to realize and understand her own mission so as to apprehend her faithful performance in God's drama.

Today's theological direction, and thus, our ecclesial direction, should stem from the dynamic interaction of the Creator and the creature. It is through the action of God that humanity has its meaning; dramatizing theology opens up the acting area to such dynamic movements. Concerning this relationship, Barth writes:

---

23. Quash, *Theology and the Drama of History*, 37, 50.
24. Vanhoozer, *Drama of Doctrine*, 361.
25. Ibid., 362.

> The act of creation as such is the revelation of the glory of God by which He gives to the creature meaning and necessity . . . Giving it being and existence, He makes it the exponent of His intention, plan and order . . . The meaning and necessity which the creature reveals, which as such it denotes and attests, is God's free love, i.e., the love of God in which He wills and posits another by Himself and is Himself for it—the free love in which He accomplishes this willing and this positing in His own power and by His own independent resolve. It is in the same free love that He Himself is God, i.e., the Father in the Son and the Son in the Father by the Holy Spirit. Again, it is in the same free love that He has resolved in Himself from all eternity on His fellowship with man in the person of His own Son.[26]

This is to say that life and creation's stage are the external work of the internal love and being of the Trinity. Theology is the dramatic, and should not be absorbed into a "system of drama," or a "system of doctrine," but allowed to give life and meaning to the movements of creation's stage and its exposure to the work of God. The recognition of the *theologica dramaticas* enhances, while enriching, today's theological performances, because through such recognition the reality of our interaction and participation *in* Christ's reconciliatory performance moves further and further into *becoming* the real. Theology should remember that "the process of reconciliation, at the center of which stands Christ (and hence Christology), is dramatic, both within the Godhead and in the relationship between God and man."[27]

Theology is performative in its nature directly due to its being rooted in God's action that is dramatic in "the light of biblical revelation."[28] The drama of the theatre does not give life to theology, but quite the opposite, theology sheds light upon the drama, upon the whole of existence as it continues to expose humanity to the eternal performance of the Triune God. Theology's profundity stems from its inherently dramatic reality that continues to expose humanity to the free offering of God. This action is that which is able to provide the life and performance of the theatre; a provision based on the self-revealing, self-involving act of the Triune God. The dramatizing of theology is not the removal of the theatre, but the intentional recognition of theology's inherent dramatic essence, so as then to be able to realize how the theatre can help further theology's understanding of the world drama. All of which is the case because "our view of God, the world and man will not be developed primarily from below, out of man's 'understanding of himself:'

26. *CD* III/1, 230.
27. *TD* III, 121.
28. *TD* II, 9.

it will be drawn from that drama which God has already 'staged' with the world and with man, in which we find ourselves players."[29]

§3.2 Driving the Dramatic

It is true that in order to understand the dramatizing of theology, we have to recognize the relational reality between drama and theology. Yet even amidst such recognition, theology should be mindful that in a dramatic model of theology, our endeavors need to be driven by our theology. However, today, critique has been made that Balthasar's *Theo-Drama*, while seeking to illumine a dramatic model, does not give due recognition to the performative foundation of drama. Ivan Khovacs claims that Balthasar's dramatic model of theology, "freezes the action," thereby lacking the fullness of a dramatic model. In looking at Khovacs' claim, I believe it is important to maintain that theology is dramatic, and thus, there can be no separation of the two. Furthermore, this project also claims that humanity is able to realize its dramatic essence preciously because of its interaction with Christ through the Spirit. What should be recognized primarily, is that life and its *Theo-logic* is enlivened by its *Theo-drama*. Secondarily, then, through the use and employment of the performative reality of drama, theology can witness the potentiality of our faithful performances. To use Balthasar's words, "The drama introduces the spiritual being with his finite progress in all its proportions—albeit 'in a mirror, dimly'"—to the norm that will judge it."[30] By no means is this an attempt to discount the essential importance of drama—instead, what is being argued is that while the drama "introduces," it is dramatic theology that exposes the fullness of our interaction with God. Thus, what is needed is a realization of the inherent "drama" within our theology. The recognition of theology's inherent "drama"—the dramatizing of theology—provides further opportunities that strengthen our understanding of what it means to be a human participant in God's drama.[31]

According to Khovacs, however, Balthasar underestimates the theatrical orientation in and through the Theo-drama, tending to "foreground a dramatic structure in theology at the expense of the performance act inherent to the theatre."[32] Such an assertion is a subtle accusation against

---

29. Ibid.

30. *TD* IV, 88.

31. In the dramatizing of theology, we must be mindful, writes Johnson, "to note where theatre stops and the Christian faith begins; theatre doesn't replace the Church" (*Performing the Sacred*, 141).

32. Ivan Khovacs, "A Cautionary Note on the Use of Theatre in Theology," in Hart and Guthrie, *Faithful Performances*, 38.

Balthasar's argument invoking a separation of act and identity over-against a more existential or even spiritual nature. However, as will hopefully be shown, through Balthasar's rooting God's drama in God's Being-in-act, he (Balthasar) highlights and exposes the performative reality of a dramatic model of theology.

§3.2.1 In Perspective: Investigating Balthasar's Approach

According to Khovacs, Balthasar "undermines the drama of theatre as art in performance; he 'freezes' the action of the play into an ideal picture of its literal script untouched by the messy business of performance interpretation." Furthering this critique, Khovacs maintains that although Balthasar adopts a dramatic style and form, he does not adopt its content. "Balthasar accepts the essence of what makes the dramatic yet pays scant attention to performance as the medium in which theatre achieves the dramatic movement."[33]

In critiquing Balthasar's approach to the Theo-drama, Khovacs assumes that the primary focus for Balthasar was and is the restoration of the theatre in theology. However, the mistake made here, with this perspective, is two-fold: First, Khovacs' assumption projects upon Balthasar a focus that is seemingly unpronounced in Balthasar's work. Indeed, Balthasar does wish to re-introduce the importance and depth of availability found in drama and literature, an aspect that has been absent as "no theological textbook has found it worthwhile to refer to the names of Shakespeare or Calderon."[34] However, Balthasar's primary perspective and focus, while incorporating the profundity of the drama, is not the theatre for theatre's sake, but theology for theology's sake. Only through the Theo-drama is humanity exposed to the essence of its humanness—the answer to "Who am I?" Yet in recognizing the dramatizing of theology, it should be remembered that the primary focus is not upon the theatre, but upon the dramatic essence of God's interaction through His revelatory performance. Thus, in our dramatizing of theology, the interactive performance of one's mission upon the stage opens up the understanding and apprehension of our personhood. Such an opening and realization is the becoming of the real.

In Khovacs' critique of Balthasar's use of the dramatic, he (Khovacs) overlooks the fundamental focus of Balthasar in and through the *Theo-Drama*, that is, the interaction of the Creator and His creature. As Balthasar writes, while the revelation of God is the "prelude to the central event: the encounter, in creation and in history, between infinite divine freedom

---

33. Khovacs, "Divine Reckonings," 34–36.
34. *TD* I, 125.

and finite human freedom,"[35] God has manifested Himself (Christ) so as to draw in His creature (reconciliation) in order to fulfil His desire to see *all* of humanity faithfully participating in His Christological performance. Drama does indeed elevate our theological understanding of the reality of such interaction as Balthasar writes, "God does not want to be just 'contemplated' and 'perceived' by us, like a solitary actor by his public; no, from the beginning he has provided for a play in which we must all share."[36] However, the primary focus is not drama for drama's sake, but the realities on and in which life rests and acts, realities which we try to express through our theological practices, which, because they are rooted in God's Being-in-act, are dramatic. Thus, what is needed is not a study of drama or an attempt to subsume theology into drama, but quite the opposite, the fullness of theology being illumined through our dramatizing of theology.

Khovacs claims that Balthasar's use of drama results in the "freezing" of the action, into "an ideal picture of its literal script," yet Khovacs' estimate overlooks the eschatological reality of the Biblical drama, as scripted in the Bible and revealed through Christ. It is through God's revelation—the opening up of God's Being-in-act—that the Bible becomes God's word and, as Barth claims, "in the statement that the Bible is God's Word the little word "is" refers to its being in this becoming."[37] The Bible indeed presents the "ideal picture," in the midst of much darkness, an action that beckons a real response, that is, an intentional act of participation in Christ's incarnational performance. Yet this response is not elevated through its dramatic movement, its movement is dramatic because of the undertakings of God to call upon and act with His creature.

Take for instance two examples that provide clear pictures of not only the ideal, but the real: 1) Rev 19:6-7, "Then I heard something like the voice of a great multitude and like the sound of many waters and like the sound of mighty peals of thunder, saying, 'Hallelujah! For the Lord our God, the Almighty, reigns. Let us rejoice and be glad and give the glory to Him, for the marriage of the Lamb has come and His bride has made herself ready;'" 2) Rev 21:3-4, "And I heard a loud voice from the throne, saying, 'Behold, the tabernacle of God is among men, and He will dwell among them, and they shall be His people, and God Himself will be among them, and He will wipe away every tear from their eyes; and there will no longer be any death; there will no longer be any mourning, or crying, or pain; the first things have passed away.'" Both of these examples present God's revelation of the

35. *MWR*, 97.
36. Ibid.
37. *CD* I/1, 110.

ideal picture that should guide the performances of humanity so that life is lived as the becoming of the ideal into the real. This eschatological hope is not something the Church, nor her theologians, can simply overlook. Today's theology, according to Balthasar, "must remember that all hope yearns for happiness or, at a deeper level, for salvation or the fulfillment of human wholeness; and as a result it experiences the abyss of the 'not yet.'"[38] Through the dramatic recognition and push towards an interactive performance from the entirety of the stage, theology will truly find its faithful performance.

Balthasar recognizes the essential need of the "ideal picture" as such a picture presents to the dramatis personae the reality of what is to become so as to allow each performer the opportunity to envisage the real. Drama apart from theology does not allow for this realization, as its attempts to answer the questions of the essence of life and personhood apart from theology, will produce nothing more than feeble attempts at finding the real, that is, the improvised attempts at creating a performance outside of Christ. Instead, what needs to be realized is the oneness of theology and drama. From this unity, humanity comes to witness the profundity of being in Christ.

The path forged from the theological reality of drama not only elevates theology's and the Church's understanding of personhood, providing the escape from the ambiguity of the person to the concrete understanding of performance, but furthermore, safeguards all such performances. Within the Theo-drama we witness how, at any time in the world's drama that action that seeks to separate itself from the direction of the Holy Spirit enables the reality that our "role" could be "exchanged for another." However, with the Theo-drama, such misdirection of role, or better yet, *mission*, is safeguarded, through the Theo-drama, which, according to Balthasar, "enables humanity to take on a genuinely dramatic role in the realm, not of the theatre, but of life."[39] This very security occurs through our being in Christ by which we come to share in His performance that seeks to return the darkened and stained performers, to our proper place of glory in God's drama. However, with our continual attempts to step beyond the performance of Christ, or simply say "no" to His invitation, we lose sight of God's threefold act. But this is not the last word, the final act, as through our incorporation into Christ's performance, we encounter our salvation, and this should be theology's continual encouragement to participate in God's Being-in-act; dare we hope that all are saved?

---

38. *TD* V, 150.
39. *TD* I, 645.

§3.2.2 Performative Foundation

My second objection to Khovacs' critique of Balthasar rests on his (Khovacs) assertion that, while accepting the essence of the dramatic, Balthasar pays "scant attention to performance as the medium in which theatre achieves the dramatic movement."[40] However, as stated earlier, Balthasar's *Theo-drama* centers on the action of God through His revelation, invitation and reconciliation, such action that is all performance. For theology, it is God's Being-in-act that must (and in my belief, does) propel its performance, not anything else. Thus, while the performative essence of the theatre offers tremendous insight into our theological endeavors, the primary focus is the performance of God, not the theatre. The Theo-drama by nature cannot but help recognize the medium of performance if it wishes to be true to its object—God—who is *act*. The foundation of Christianity is scandalous and, as Balthasar points out, this scandal cannot "be removed by further theoretical discussion but only by *praxis* . . . God shows his truth to us through *acting*, and the Christian (including the anonymous Christian, the Samaritan) likewise shows that he is following in Christ's footsteps by acting in love towards his fellow men."[41] Theology is inherently inter-active—it is dramatic and all of theology's movements naturally "converge toward a theological dramatic theory."[42] Through the inherently active foundation of theology, it cannot but be a performance.

While it is my claim that Balthasar does maintain the proper performative perspective, it could be argued that such perspective does not find its intensity until the second or third volume of the *Theo-Drama*. Even Balthasar admits as much when he writes that the "truth of revelation should not be watered down in a 'lyrical' direction—'spirituality'—or dissolved in an 'epic' direction—'theology' (*Theo-Drama*, II, 55), as is shown in the tendencies toward the dramatic in modern theological thought, tendencies we twice examined."[43] All of which was examined in the first volume, thus leaving much of the *Prolegomena* at a level of discussion/dialogue, which is essential in revealing the profound reality of theology's performative nature. Thus, while I concur that the first volume of the *Theo-Drama* might be a bit lacking in its exposure of theology's performative reality, I cannot agree entirely with Khovacs' claim that Balthasar's initial lack of performative recognition warrants enough emphasis to detract from the overarching point revealed

40. Khovacs, "Divine Reckonings," 36.
41. *TD* I, 32.
42. Ibid., 125.
43. *TD* IV, 62.

through the *Theo-Drama*: God's performative interaction with His creature through His revelation, invitation and reconciliation. The entirety of the *Theo-Drama* must be taken into consideration, such that, as Balthasar notes, "our starting point was the interplay of infinite and finite freedom (vol. II) . . . then (vol. III) we discerned the figure of the God-man, making possible and embracing all that is creaturely; this revealed (in "Christology") an initial glimpse of the divine Trinity." This confrontation of course is embedded within the interaction and thus, performance of the entirety of the world's stage, and in order to be discerned, theology can do nothing but recognize its performative reality. Finally, as Balthasar continues, "Confronted with the world's alienation from God (in vol. IV), Christology changed into 'soteriology' . . . All the same it is clear that the Trinity, and not Christology, is the last horizon of the revelation of God in himself and in his dramatic relationship with the world."[44] From the performative reality set out by the *Theo-Drama*, theology, and thus, ecclesiology, cannot but help to be performative. Through such a performance, theology and the Church are both allotted the ability, the privilege, to "echo" and participate in God's salvific act. As Balthasar notes, the Church's entire action "is nothing but an echo of the Lord's prior action of grace; it is the action, through the Son, of the triune God."[45]

The Theo-drama is, as Balthasar insists, "the drama of the Trinity." It is a drama, he continues, that "lasts forever: the Father was never without the Son, nor were Father and Son ever without the Spirit. Everything temporal takes place within the embrace of the eternal action and as its consequence (hence *opera trinitatis ad extra communia*)."[46] It is only through performance that the essence of personhood is revealed, as Balthasar claims, the actor has revealed "who he *is to become* through the action, through his encounter with others and through the decisions he makes."[47]

Khovacs' critiques of Balthasar do indeed illumine the continued necessity of our theological appreciation and understanding of the theatre, and it is my hope that theology's employment of the theatre does heed Khovacs' advice that "theological commitment to the theatre, however, can only be dramatic to the extent that the theologian learns to hear the multiplicity of the dramatic voice in the moment of performance and is moved by the immediacy of its action."[48] My point, and I would imagine Khovacs would

---

44. *TD* V, 56.
45. *TD* IV, 405.
46. Ibid., 327.
47. *TD* II, 11.
48. Khovacs, "Divine Reckonings," 36.

agree, is that the theatre and/or drama are not to be identified as separate entities from a theological dramaticas. With this said, though, what is being argued is that the proper alignment and relationship should be held, both drama and theology contribute in different ways to our understanding of God's Being-in-act, yet, it is our theology that must be in the forefront of our endeavors. To allow the theatre/drama to guide our practices is the result of a movement from the proper Christocentric perspective to an anthropocentric one whereby the action of humanity is esteemed over and above the action (performance) of the Godhead. There is no denying that the conventions of the theatre allow theology to further its exploration into the knowledge of God, but this is only because both theology and theatre—drama—find reality from the action and Being of the Triune God. Again, the theatre is no mere metaphor for God's interaction with humanity—such interaction is the drama of life—the Theo-drama.

§ Theological Interlude: *The Person of the Spirit in the Theo-Drama*

The attention paid to performance is indeed quite extraordinary in terms of theology, as it centers upon the performance and action of the Trinity in Christ through the Spirit. One area, though, where I do believe Balthasar could be more explicit in the performative reality of the Godhead, is his (Balthasar) characterization and discussion of the person of the Holy Spirit. Often times in the *Theo-Drama*, Balthasar's focus is so heavily Christological that the Pneumatological essence of the drama tends to fade from the performance. This slight fading of the Spirit from the pictured performance is one of the effects of characterizing the Spirit as the "bond of love."[49]

Balthasar's labelling of the Spirit as the bond of love tends toward a de-personalizing of the Spirit thereby detracting from the dramatic interactions between the Spirit, Christ and the Church. In fact, such characterization fails to do justice to Balthasar's own claim that it is the Trinity that is the "last horizon of the revelation of God himself." Furthermore, Balthasar detracts from the overall dramatic reality of theology in his oscillating between the completeness of personhood and the subtle lessening of personhood with regards to his descriptions, and recognition of the mission of the Spirit throughout the Theo-drama. Aligning himself with the Augustinian tradition Balthasar writes, "if Love, in turn, is grasped as the Third Hypostasis, proceeding from both the One who generates/utters and from the Word,

---

49. See chapter 1 of this project, §4.3 for a brief discussion on Barth and the Augustinian influence on Barth's theology of the Spirit.

it becomes clear how profoundly rooted the dialogic principle is in God."[50] Indeed, the dialogic principle is fully in God and through God, but does not the designation of the "Third Hypostasis" as love deny the fullness of personhood?

Balthasar's further development of the dialogue between The Word and creation misses out of the person of the Holy Spirit. "In Jesus Christ this word (scripture) is addressed to us articulately in a way we simply cannot avoid hearing, and it also liberates us and empowers us to give answer—provided that, . . . the word of Jesus penetrates to man's hearing in such a way that he can believe."[51] There is no denying the power of Jesus' word, but because of Balthasar's de-personifying of the Spirit, this power is conspicuously lacking of the presence of the Holy Spirit, which does not actually appear until "the Word of God utters his last."[52] Balthasar does not attempt to offer an explanation of how the power of the word is heard, nor does he explain how belief from hearing becomes a reality. The de-personifying of the Spirit leads Balthasar toward the problematic tension of negating his very premise, of the Spirit being the one who "directs" the action of the play.

Balthasar further examines the unfolding of the Theo-drama through the cosmic mystery of the action and extreme self-surrender of the Son. Such action, which is both "central in the world drama" while attracting "every power hostile to God," culminates in God's glory—a glory that is accomplished "in the Resurrection and exaltation of Jesus," which becomes "the starting point of the outpouring of the Trinitarian Spirit of the—now manifest—love between Father and Son."[53] The question raised through this central point in the world drama is the question of the distinct person of the Spirit—for how is it that He, the Third Person of the Trinity, is both, absent before the Resurrection (one wonders here about the dramatic baptismal account of Jesus and the descending of the Spirit), while also being relegated to the "love manifest between Father and Son?"

Advancing further into the *Theo-Drama*, Balthasar later follows Aquinas when he states that "God the Father effects creation by his Word, who is the Son, and by his love, who is the Holy Spirit."[54] Again, we witness the lingering effects of the Augustinian influence in Balthasar's theology when he relegates the Spirit to the role of love. Instead of reading Romans 5:5 as "the love poured out *by* the Spirit," Balthasar attributes the Spirit as *the*

---

50. *TD* II, 72.
51. Ibid., 73.
52. Ibid., 74.
53. Ibid., 88.
54. *TD* V, 62.

love being poured out. What is more, the Holy Spirit is not simply the love manifested between the Father and Son, but also "the effects of love that God imparts to creatures . . . the Holy Spirit, who is the love of the Father for the Son, is also his love for creature."[55] The subtle neglect of personhood for the Spirit in light of the Augustinian influence exposes possible tension points as to the fullness of the Trinitarian involvement in and upholding of the Theo-Drama. The reason behind such a faulty view of the Godhead is, as Paul Blackham states:

> When (Colin) Gunton pinpoints Augustine's understanding of mediation, we then see why his doctrine of God must take the shape that it did. Because Augustine's doctrine of God began with the divine substance rather than the three Persons, his understanding of the divine substance controls his understanding of the possible roles and actions of the three. The nature of the divine essence determines what the three persons can or cannot do, rather than a specific examination of what the three persons *actually* do or do not do.[56]

Gunton further expounds upon the superficial implications resulting from the Augustinian model of the Trinity, with specific regard to the Holy Spirit; noting that "Augustine's concept of the Holy Spirit as the love which unites the Father and Son is among the most contested of his theologoumena, not only for its apparent derivation, but for the way it appears to sit ill with particular features of the economy."[57] The identification of the Spirit to the love between Father and Son is neither found in scripture nor fully comprehensive of the fullness of the person of the Spirit. In fact, attributing the Spirit to the love denies the full understanding of 1 John whereby God is love. As Gunton remarks, "there is a sense in which Father, Son, and Spirit together are love."[58]

Furthermore, while the bond of love within the communion of the Trinity is essential to the foundation and strength of the Church, as we are brought into this communion through the love poured into our hearts, and called to perform out of such love, the paradigm used by Augustine concerning the Trinity is incomplete in its nature. While acknowledging the bond between Father and Son as being a bond of love, Augustine's talk of the Holy Spirit as being the bond of love between Father and Son is problematic in that it fails to delineate how the Spirit is Himself constituted in

---

55. Ibid., 63.
56. Blackham in Metzger, *Trinitarian Soundings*, 44.
57. Gunton, *Promise of Trinitarian Theology*, 48.
58. Ibid., 49.

His own distinct relations to the Father and Son. Instead of the Spirit being a person amidst the Trinity of beings, He is demoted to an essence or ethereal existence as opposed to one of the three persons constituting the Being of the Godhead.

It seems unclear how the Spirit could be the "bond of love" between the Father and Son in any meaningful way and retain his own personal particularity in the relational dynamic of the Trinitarian life. Such a lack of clarity creates an almost dramatic tension that detracts from the true drama playing out upon the world's stage. Balthasar's problem is not that his lacking in a performative perspective per se, but that his perspective lacks a full theological and performative reality. Rather than characterizing the Spirit as the "bond of love," Balthasar's account finds its truthfulness/faithfulness when remaining bound to the Spirit's mission and personhood. Rather than the bond of love, the Spirit is properly the one who "accompanies the Son's entire mission, shares in the experience of it and, as it were, enfolds this mission in himself."[59] This idea and reality is furthered by Balthasar who writes, "He is simultaneously the Spirit of the Father who surrenders his Son and that of the sacrificed and glorified Son; he is the Trinitarian Spirit, yet he informs the entire 'economy,' and so he contains within himself, in unity, both the movement toward the Cross and the movement from Cross to Resurrection."[60] The recognition of the Spirit's accompanying or interceding performance is that which safeguards Balthasar's thought– the very safeguard that was needed by Barth, who himself was able to move beyond binding the Spirit to the concept of love, in recognizing that it is the Spirit who "makes us ready to listen the Word, that He Himself intercedes with us for Himself, that He Himself makes the speaking and hearing of His Word possible among us."[61]

In the end, while performing exceptionally close to the stage's edge, Balthasar is able to remain faithful to the performative reality of the Trinitarian unity explicitly revealed through the Theo-drama. The Spirit, writes Balthasar, who is "given to believers always embraces the totality—the journey to the Cross, the Passion, the Resurrection and Ascension. Paul says explicitly that the Spirit given to believers recapitulates the entire economy of salvation, since his is the Spirit of the whole historical and pneumatic Christ, crucified and risen."[62] In order for the play to be the play, each of the persons of the Trinity must be recognized by and in their personhood, so

---

59. *TD* IV, 384.
60. Ibid.
61. *CD* I/2, 221.
62. *TD* IV, 384.

as to establish the fullness of unity through the particularity. As Balthasar maintains, the dramatic reality of God's action (revelation, invitation and reconciliation) occurs in and through a Trinitarian event:

> The Son and the Spirit "flow back" into the Father: this is both the self-transcendence of the Persons into the simple identity of essence and the highest bliss of love of the Persons, who are perfected as such in this very self-transcendence. Thus God remains eternal event, yet without temporal becoming.
>
> If the creature is to be able to participate in this event, it can only be through the grace of God and through discipleship of the Son . . . The creature never becomes God substantially, but in the Son's Incarnation, in his *pro nobis*, in his Cross and dereliction, in his Eucharist, the Incarnate One enfolds in his embrace, by the Holy Spirit, everything that is striving toward the Father; he is the "pattern that was and is and will remain for eternity."[63]

Such a dramatization of this Triune performance is that which leads to a more appropriate participation of theology, the Church and the world.

§4 The Character of Theology: A Performative Reality

§4.1 Strange Dichotomy

Theological dramatics are concerned with the character of theology as exposed through its performative reality as revealed through God's threefold act. The performative reality from our performances within the Theo-drama is the opening up of our being; it is "the unveiledness of being." The fullness, or *ideal*, of our personhood is exposed through the revealedness of God's act in Christ, and, as Balthasar maintains, we are "open to this act and this openness to God's all-fulfilling truth," which "is itself the form in which they (humanity) participate in divine truth."[64] It is an act that should propel theology to encourage continuously the Church towards incarnational acts, within her body as well as the world. For the Body of Christ, then, to participate in divine truth is to faithfully perform in God's drama.

Realizing humanity's performance within the "theatre of God's glory" leads towards a performance that finds its truthfulness, and its faithfulness, through its relational reality. Upon the confrontation of the Godhead, humanity enters into the regnum gratiae, and experiences the power of God in Christ through the Spirit (*regnum Christi*). It is in this power that the

---

63. *TD* V, 459.
64. *TL* I, 59; my parenthetical insertion.

possibility of our relational position with God becomes real. Barth points out that God's power is reflected in the experience with the Word of God, which is the beginning of our incorporation into His (Christ's) performance. The Word of God is the "living and abiding Word," the in-breaking of God's veiledness. "All this must be said of the Word of God because the Word of God is Jesus Christ and because its efficacy is not distinct from the lordship of Jesus Christ. He who hears God's Word is drawn thereby into the sphere of the real power of this lordship."[65] Christ's lordship is the motivating power that not only provides the energy, but also, secures the beauty and creativity of the stage's movement. Through the incarnation God makes himself "visible *in* the world as he reveals the Creator who transcends the world, and by the same token he reveals his nearness to man by the very fact of his transcendence."[66] God's immanence and presence upon the stage is the impossible possibility, drawing humanity into His performance so as to reorient the entire performance of the stage. Again, such reorientation only comes through our own *particular* performances, with and through the *universal* performance of humanity. To show love to the "other" is the enfleshment of God's love poured out by the Spirit into the hearts of His fellow performers. It is the actualization of the ideal becoming real.

God's in-breaking brings forth the ideal so as to allow it to become the real. This movement—the ideal becoming the real—initiates and actualizes our becoming, thus transcending the once antagonistic relationship between Creator and creature. Thus, what was once in contradiction is now in union in Christ through the Spirit. Through the performance of Christ, the paradox between humanity and God becomes a constant tension or struggle, rather than an opposition or contradiction.[67] Humanity performs amidst struggle, a conflict borne out of our resistance towards the part we are to play within the cosmic drama. It is no stretch of our imagination to recognize what Balthasar describes as being the "strange dichotomy" between the essence of our person and the actions of our lives.

> Everyone experiences the strange dichotomy between the core of his person (which is not immediately accessible to him) and the role he plays for himself and for society. He is hemmed in by this role and would often wish to break out of it, but he simply cannot; precisely because he is a person, he is *this* particular

---

65. *CD* I/1, 153.

66. *TKB*, 112.

67. See chapter 4 for a fuller discussion of the paradoxical gap. Through the imagination, humanity is able to apprehend that it is from Christ's actions that the paradox of the God-human relationship is transformed.

individual and will always have a *particular* mode of manifestation. But which one is the right one, the one that fits his nature and his inalienable "mission'? It is not something he can produce out of himself *alone*; it arises in part from his reaction to his environment, from personal interaction.[68]

How everyone experiences the strange dichotomy between the essence of his person and the mission he finds for himself and for society is bound up in God's threefold act of revelation, invitation and reconciliation. It is, on the one hand, a determined fact as to how God reveals, invites and reconciles; yet on the other hand, it is the freedom of the creature that allows for the particular playing of the specific role as presented through creation.

Participation in the divine drama stems from the freedom granted in and through creation. From this freedom the creature is able to *improvise* upon the stage. Through improvisation, the performance remains active and dynamic, always providing the opportunity for *true* freedom to be realized. The significance of improvisation stems from its dynamism. J.L. Styan points out that improvisation is "the source of the actor's greatest contribution in any drama." To improvise is to acknowledge one's freedom, yet never in an aimless manner; for as Styan continues, while being a source of tremendous contribution, improvisation is not "a freedom to invent haphazardly, but it can include building upon the written word . . . For the actor, comic business and dialogue are not a matter of memory but of imagination."[69] The overarching aspect of improvisation is the creation of the human actor, by God, to be just that, an actor in God's drama. The stage's freedom is made possible through the fact that God, out of His own freedom, created and sent forth "genuinely free beings (which is bound to cause the philosopher the greatest embarrassment) in such a way that, without vitiating the infinite nature of God's freedom, a genuine opposition of freedoms can come about."[70] Such freedom thus allows for the creature to disrupt "any static notions" of defining the stage, players and audience. Furthermore, through the reality of improvisation, the acting area is opened, thereby allowing a "state of readiness . . . trust and respect for oneself and the other actors. There is alertness and attention. There is fitness and engagement . . . There is an aptitude for altering and playing with status roles, for relating to others, remembering, sustaining, and developing character and sensing the shape of a story."[71] The openness of the acting area, and its incorporation of the

68. *TD* I, 264.
69. Styan, *Drama, Stage and Audience*, 81.
70. *TD* II, 190.
71. Wells, *Improvisation*, 80.

whole of creation, undoubtedly raises questions concerning such a freedom that allows for the participation of non-believers in the play of life. Yet in doing so, these very queries question the power of God to use those who deny His presence or very Being.

Freedom in creation is not freedom if it denies the potential for humanity to attempt to "play God." Sin, claims Balthasar, "*presupposes* freedom and selfhood, but it is not to be *equated* with them." In its sin, humanity does not sink into nothingness or chaos; it does not become a "mere shadow of a shadow as would be the case if creatureliness coincided with sin."[72] Even in our sin, though, we remain active participants in God's drama, able to improvise, both positively (responding yes to God), as well as negatively (responding no to God), as not even sin can remove us from God's presence. Improvisation interpenetrates our being, for, as Styan writes, "at the heart of performance, improvisation is intimately associated with the assumption of a role."[73] In theological terms, positive improvisation manifests itself when the actor has become aware of her ontological reality, that her *mission* is acknowledged in its fullness through her relational reality *in* Christ. Realization of our relational reality *in* Christ should constantly remind us that God desires us to be His covenant partner, not a spectator or observer of His Being-in-act. As Barth maintains, "I cannot simply observe this heavenly-earthly drama of Christ's priestly and kingly work. I myself am involved. If it could be simply observed, this work would no longer be what it is."[74] Thus, through the gift—the grace—of freedom, humanity is able to faithfully engage the stage's action or turn a blind eye to the action in the attempt to distance oneself from the movement.

We are who we are and are becoming through this *strange dichotomy* between the core of our person and the role we play for society. In fact, while conflict has fundamentally been thought to be a necessity of the drama, the struggle of the Theo-drama differs, as it is not a pure conflict but a paradoxical self-giving, that transcends the conflict to find joy. The conflict is not conflict per se but ontological participation; it is one being participating reciprocally with another. Paul Harrison writes that "the fundamental characteristic of drama is not merely conflict, as posited by so many theorists, but moral sacrifice, giving of the self, the gift of Being, and openness on the part of the others to the reception of the gift."[75] Giving of self is only understood dramatically through the Theo-dramatic performance of Jesus Christ, who

---

72. *TKB*, 111.
73. Styan, *Drama, Stage and Audience*, 149.
74. *LJC*, 137.
75. Harrison, "Toward a Dramaturgical Interpretation," 391.

for the sake of His creation, gave himself. Thus, the Theo-drama embodies conflict, self-giving and much, much more, because of its foundation in the Being-in-act of God.

God's Being-in-act is the foundation of the Church's Eucharistic celebration, and thus, its faithful performance. Balthasar writes that "every Eucharistic sacrifice on the part of the Church always proceeds on the basis of a communion with Christ that he has already initiated and has the effect of creating a new and ever deeper communion." Such a deepening of our communion with Christ—the *real* of being *in* Christ—manifests itself as the "Church primarily joins in and assimilates herself to the work of Christ; she is thus privileged to *act*, taking the place reserved for her by Christ, who *suffers* the action of others."[76] It is from the performance of Christ that the Church, and thus humanity, witnesses the ultimate giving of self; a giving that re-humanizes the human, so that she might be able to participate faithfully in God's self-giving act through her own acts of self-giving.

Through the dramatic, theology is provided the tools to perform its mission, as it acts alongside the Church, with both participating in the ongoing event of God. Theology should continue to explore how best to bring the dramatic perspective into theological employment. The Church requires theology to unveil our performative powers and thus, writes Balthasar, "arises our task, which is to draw an *instrumentarium*, a range of resources, from the drama of existence which can then be of service to a Christian theory of theo-drama in which the 'natural' drama of existence (between the Absolute and the relative) is consummated in the 'supernatural' drama between the God of Jesus Christ and mankind."[77]

§4.2 Redemptive Reality

The "supernatural" drama between Creator and creature is one that finds its resolve in the profound performance of the protagonist. The real of being in Christ must encourage and motivate humanity's faithful performance, as our redemptive reality is the fullness of our being—it is our fulfilment. Salvation is "more than being. Salvation is fulfilment, the supreme, sufficient, definitive and indestructible fulfilment of being . . . Since salvation is not proper to created being as such, it can only come to it, and since it consists in participation in the being of God it can come only from God." This act of redemption, this event of salvation, is not our struggle, but God's; and as Barth continues, "it is God that has become man in order as such,

---

76. *TD* IV, 405.
77. *TD* I, 130.

but in divine sovereignty, to take up our case."[78] The once thought of need of struggle for the drama now becomes the beauty of the marriage—the tragedy becoming comedy—made possible through the overcoming of the once recognized paradox of the Creator-creature relationship. This paradox that once overwhelmed history is now the epitome of reconciliation, played out in humanity's performance in Christ through the Spirit. At the very moment the drama would seemingly conclude, when man and woman were expelled from the presence of God, the actions of God actually propel the drama into the reality of hope and reconciliation. Thus, the action and redemptive reality of the drama is that which calls forth humanity's faithful performance, which has moved beyond the paradox into the tension of freedom and faithfulness. The real of today finds its unveiledness in the reality of being *in* Christ so as to move out from Christ into the on-going performances of the stage. Lack of such perspective arises through either unwillingness or blindness towards theology's imaginative powers.

Today, if we allow our imaginative powers to guide our endeavors, we open up the potentiality of comprehending the meaning of truth and being. Such endeavors however, do not occur beyond or outside of us, but from within, or what Balthasar calls *from the middle*. "From the middle" we are able to comprehend the beauty of God's continual movement toward us, whereby we find the truth of Christ, "the space within which finite freedom finds liberation . . . and can attain completion."[79] The truth of finite freedom is the unveiledness of being apprehended by the creature *in* Christ. Yet the creature, as Ben Quash reminds, "can only think towards the truth 'from the middle' of creaturely existence, and this necessarily involves a continuous activity of imaginatively constructive participation, in which we develop our own interpretative readings of God's ways in the world alongside the readings of other people."[80] The relationality of God must continually ignite and fuel our understanding of being. Thus, through revelation, invitation and reconciliation, if we allow, our theological imaginative powers can help us understand the essence and reality of "God with us" so as to encourage, develop and reveal our faithful performances that manifest the truth of "we with God."

It is through the unified work of our heart's thoughts, that is, our imaginative reasoning, that we come to recognize the need for our embodied response to God's revelation and invitation. Through this we grasp the fullness of God's redemptive reality; a reality that while always propelling our

---

78. *CD* IV/1, 8, 12.
79. *TD* III, 19.
80. Quash, *Theology and the Drama of History*, 182.

theological performances, should never lose sight nor fade in our astonishment at the profundity of what it means that God is with us. Such meaning is drawn from the event of revelation and redemption, for as Barth writes:

> At the very point where we refuse and fail, offending and provoking God, making ourselves impossible before Him and in that way missing our destiny . . . forfeiting our right, losing our salvation and hopelessly compromising our creaturely being—at that very point God Himself intervenes as man. Because He is God He is able not only to be God but also to be this man. Because He is God it is necessary that He should be man in quite a different way from all other men; that He should do what we do not do and not do what we do. Because He is God He puts forth His omnipotence to be this other man . . . in our place and our sake.[81]

Through the communion of the Creator and creature, the stage is enlightened in the very action and outpouring of God's redemptive action.

The reality of redemption thus empowers the continual movement of the narrative becoming the drama—the step into and participation with all of life. The becoming of the Biblical narrative into its always present dramatic reality is the movement that allows for the apprehension of the fullness of God's performance, so as to realize the *here and now* of the stage's performance, as illumined by the *not yet* of the stage's encore. This is to say that the essence and profundity of both theology's and humanity's performance comes through the reality that God is dramatically involved—an involvement that sees the fulfilment of action today through the lens of tomorrow. We are reconciled and redeemed as we are incorporated into the perfected performance of Christ. Through the content of revelation—Jesus Christ and the Holy Spirit—we enter into the performative excellence of the Godhead. Our participation in Christ through the Spirit in the eternal act of reconciliation sets the stage for the final act of God's drama—the return of the protagonist Jesus Christ. This return to the stage is the very act that consummates the dramatic opening of humanity, which began at creation, continued with the journeys and covenants of the Jews, and burst into its full manifestation and power with the incarnation, thereby exposing us to the Truth of reality, the fullness of God in His encore presentation.

God's drama incorporates as it consumes all possible drama between God and his creation. God's performance, His place upon the stage is eternal. From the beginning everything takes place in and through the embrace of God, an embrace that is given its fullness through the incarnational

---

81. *CD* IV/1, 12.

performance of Christ, which calls forth further acts of self-giving by those willingly participating in Christ's reconciliatory action. It is through such performances that humanity obtains the ability to understand *true* freedom. Because humanity is created as a reflection or better yet, in the image of a Trinitarian God, it must then reflect the essence and reality of the Trinitarian life. This reflection is manifested in the free movement of the stage—the ability for improvised scenes. That is, scenes whereby participants in Christ actualize their faith through their performances of love toward the "other." Sharing life through the actions of grace and love—whether it is through the local school, local Church, involvement in charity—is the manifestation first, of God's love poured out into our hearts, and second, the freedom of the stage. Such freedom stems from the free revelatory action of Christ which invites the stage to share in His reconciliatory performance. This unfolding dramatic tension beckons humanity's response. It does not allow for neutrality. As Balthasar notes:

> If the performance is to win our unreserved involvement—for it excludes any neutral "observation"—it presupposes that we are unreservedly ready to be carried wherever it takes us, even "where you do not wish to go," into areas that are painful, disturbing and possibly unbearable.[82]

God's action—His performance—allows for two responses: yes or no. There is no in-between with regards to our roles upon the stage, due to the absolute reality of the person of Christ. Because Christ is the "living framework within which every human destiny is acted out" there can be no ambiguity of decision within the human response. "Every human destiny is judged by his (Christ) perfection and saved by his redeeming meaning." The action of Christ incorporates the action of the stage, which concludes Balthasar, ultimately means:

> The individual's own drama can be either crossed out, rejected and "burned"(while the actor himself "will be saved only as through fire': (1 Cor 3:15), or by grace, it can be recognized as a dramatic action within the dramatic action of Christ, in which the actor becomes a "fellow actor," or a "fellow worker" with God (1 Cor 3:9).[83]

Freedom of choice means the ability either to participate in the on-going drama or to refuse to participate in the drama. A refusal does not render one devoid of action, as all in some sense participate within God's theatre.

82. *TD* I, 309.
83. *TD* II, 87.

Instead, as Balthasar has indicated, a negative response to God's invitation results in an "outside performance" that, while will be ultimately rejected, throughout its earthly performance finds itself embedded within a continual performance of mis-steps—flawed lines, missed cues and the like. Instead of allowing oneself to be led through the performative attitude of humility in Christian faith, thereby "making room for God's self-disclosure, opening up the whole area, in purity of heart (Matt 5:8), to the light of God,"[84] an answer of "no" only illumines the tragic result of attempting to be a "one-man show." However, through the availability of *true* freedom, including the creature's freedom to respond negatively to God's invitation, the entirety of the stage's freedom is further exposed. The ability to respond in the negative must be allowed, and as Balthasar maintains, freedom is the "very essence of love;" and because of this, "God cannot and will not withhold such freedom from the chief beings in the world, and this in turn means that, from all eternity, he designs the world in such a way that it includes the eventual misuse of freedom in the form of human (and angelic) sin."[85] This very reality of freedom that allows for either *true* freedom—the creature positively responding to the Creator—or *false* (non-real) freedom—the creature's misuse of freedom—is properly understood through the dynamics of the multiple "plays" within the Theo-drama.

§5 Theological Performance

§5.1 Moving Towards the Core of Performance

A significant reality of participating in the performative mission of Christ is realized in and through the performance of the Church, as she is the one called to share God's revelatory message of an invitation and reconciliation while awaiting the return of her king. In this action of God, His revelation, invitation and reconciliation, the Church witnesses and shares in the glory of God through the performance of Christ in the Spirit. In waiting, the Church should not be thought of as being static or inactive as she has tremendous responsibility towards the world. In light of the aforementioned, today's theologians should remain mindful of the essential need for an interactive performance that includes theology, the Church and society. Bearing in mind this interactive reality heightens our attentiveness to the words of Lesslie Newbigin, who states that, "It is not sufficient for the Church to point to itself and say, 'Here is the Body of the Messiah.' It must point beyond itself

---

84. *TD* II, 125.
85. *TD* V, 99.

to Him who is sole Judge and Savior, both of the Church and of the world. And yet the Church is not *merely* the witness to Christ; it is also the Body of Christ. It is not merely the reporter of divine acts of redemption; it is also itself the bearer of God's redeeming grace, itself part of the story of redemption which is the burden of its message."[86] The importance, then, of today's theological endeavors transcends the walls of the academy, as they are to assist in the perspective and path of the Church. According to Balthasar, in Christ as the Church:

> We discern the unity of "glory" and the "dramatic." God's glory, as it appears in the world—supremely in Christ—is not something static that could be observed by a neutral investigator. It manifests itself only through the personal involvement whereby God Himself comes forth to do battle and is both victor and vanquished. If this glory is to come within our range at all, an analogous initiative is called for on our part. Revelation is a battlefield. Those who do battle on it can only be believers (the Church) and theologians, provided they have equipped themselves with the whole armor of God (Eph 6:11).[87]

There remains a crucial and essential relationship between theology and the Church as the world depends on both.

The Church is the "Eucharistic community which participates in the life of the triune God, who is the only good that can be common to all. Its reality is global and eternal, anticipating the heavenly polity on earth."[88] The Church is the congregation of the faithful who are called by faith to the light of the truth and the knowledge of God whereby in unity of faith, the community, through the Holy Spirit, serves the Head—the Son of God—with their whole heart. This is accomplished through our embodied responses that manifest themselves through explicit acts of love, e.g., money to charity, walking our elderly neighbor's dog, feeding the poor etc . . . . The Church is to perform Christ's love to the world thereby transcending the nation so as to *be* the body of Christ. In this mission, the Church realizes her performance as constituted in the expectation of her proclamation and her action to the world.

We, as the Church, although being distinct from culture, must not lose sight of the reality that we have a likeness with culture due to each one of us being created in the image and likeness of God. Our calling is one that seeks to bear witness to Christ—to participate in the on-going revelation

---

86. Newbigin, *The Household of God*, 103.
87. *TD* IV, 12.
88. Cavanaugh, *Modern Theology*, 269.

that wipes away the blindness in culture. Because of sin "the world ceased to be transparent—a window through which he (man) gazed on God—and it grew opaque; it ceased to be life-giving, and became subject to corruption and mortality . . . The divine image in man was obscured but not obliterated."[89] Thus, the theological performance needed for today—both from the Church and her theologians—is one that participates in Christ's *Eucharistic* and *eschatological* performance.

§5.2 Eucharistic Improvisation

Our faith is realized through its action. The Church is meant to be a dramatic witness to the world, of the living sacrifice made by Christ. Theology is called to do the same. Both acts of sacrifice and surrender form parts of the Eucharistic act of Christ, an act of giving and receiving that insists upon a response. The only true response from theology and the Church is one of reciprocity, in the acceptance of not only sharing in this mission—the self-giving to society and the world—but more importantly, working for the continuation of the mission. As Balthasar points out, "given the plan to bring about creatures endowed with freedom, the ultimate form of this pouring-forth will be that of the Eucharist, which as we know it, is intimately connected with the Passion, *pro nobis*."[90] God's for us is to be actively performed by the Church and her theologians, thereby sharing in the eternal performance of the Redeemer's life.

Christ's Eucharistic act is that which overcomes the chasm created through sin, while never overwhelming His fellow actors. Humanity is incorporated, not forced, into Christ's performance. The Eucharistic aspect of His performance is that which is to be shared in by the Church of Christ. It is an act that does not simply seek to be spoken of but acted out both by God and by humanity. It is highly significant that "the God who has reconciled the world to himself has entrusted the Apostles, and in a wider sense the Church of Christ, with the ministry of reconciliation'(2 Cor 5:18), 'the message of reconciliation' (5:19), so that they can 'work with him' (2 Cor 6:1) in the world in implementing this reconciliation."[91] And this incorporation into God's reconciliatory act is meant to further enliven today's theological endeavors through the sharing of Christ's performance, that is self-sacrificial and for the sake of the "other." Furthermore, as Balthasar maintains:

---

89. Ware, *The Orthodox Way*, 61.
90. *TD* IV, 330.
91. *TD* III, 121.

> While the aim of this collaboration, of course, is to spread the peace of Christ (bought on the Cross) among men, to all individual groups, it is a peace that can only be shared by each person entering into the mind of Christ, that is, into his selflessness and his readiness to affirm others and forgive them—which can only come through self-sacrifice and a plunging into the breach on their behalf.[92]

What Christ's performance does is allow for our theological imaginative powers to move beyond repetition into the realm of improvisation. Through improvisation, we come to witness the full dimensions of our freedom as we are not bound to give an automated response, nor to act according to a step by step structured format, as if simply a machine or robot. "It is not that the text of Scripture is not, or should not be fixed," writes Samuel Wells, but that through improvisation humanity comes to realize that "there is a dimension of Christian life that requires more than repetition, more even than interpretation—but not so much as origination, or creation de novo."[93] Our faithful performances stem from the sphere of improvisation, thereby revealing the gracious freedom presented to the stage, which reveals, the absolute love of Father, Son and Spirit. Drawing from the work of Gerard Loughlin, Wells further explains the importance and profundity of improvisation and its reality in the dramatizing of theology. "When a person enters the scriptural story he or she does so by entering the Church's performance of that story: he or she is baptized into a biblical and ecclesial drama. It is not so much being written into a book as taking part in a play, a play that has to be improvised on the spot."[94] With this said, it must be made clear that the call for improvisation is not the denial of our need for Scripture, but the recognition that, while the parameters of our performances are laid out by Scripture, life will present times and scenes in which we will be required to improvise. These times and scenes are the "plays" within the Play that continue to unfold Christ's Eucharistic performance and its call upon our performance.

As an example of one such "play" Wells points out the improvisation of the disciples, who had to maintain God's particular call to Israel as they were performing (preaching and teaching) in the new context of the Gentile mission, while meeting at the Council of Jerusalem. Building from Wells, then, we can highlight further examples or "plays" that illumine a Eucharistic performance of self-giving and self-sacrifice for the sake of the

---

92. Ibid.
93. Wells, *Improvisation*, 65.
94. Ibid., quoting Gerard Loughlin, *Telling God's Story*.

Chapter Five—Performative Reality

"other." One such example might be the scene played out in Luke 5:18-20. This "play" includes the four men, who, after travelling to the house where Jesus was, and finding it inaccessible due to the crowd, had to improvise in order to serve faithfully their friend. Thus, they scale the house and lower their friend through the roof, so that he would be healed by Jesus.

For another example of such selflessness in act, we can look at Rahab's improvised actions that helped save the lives of the two spies from Shittim. Here, Rahab improvises, when approached by the king of Jericho, by telling the king the previous whereabouts of the men from the sons of Israel, rather than revealing their position on the roof. She goes even further when she not only helps the men escape, but procures the safety and lives of her father's household (Josh 2). The point to be made is that the Biblical account provides a multitude of "plays," where we see a constant need of finding ways to remain faithful to the actions and words of God. Describing the whole of Acts, Jeremy Begbie writes that the action here, was a "stream of new, unpredictable, improvisations."[95]

Christ's performance is the archetype of humanity's faithful performance. He reveals Himself to the stage, and its actors, and invites all to share in His faithful performance. This very performance (revelation, invitation and reconciliation) strikes against the secular conceptions of society, as it calls upon Christ's fellow participants to do the very same. Jesus does not expect the performative reality of the Church to be determined by the world. In fact, Christ's performance can only be understood Biblically and theologically as it goes against the power structures of the world that tend think victory and power come only through abusive and violent means. Yet, Christ "accepts His suffering and rejection freely and obediently in order to refashion the ending of the old Adam into his genuine beginning in the New. This is the mystery of the pro nobis, the mystery of the Eucharist, in which his death on the Cross, which is laid upon him, is transformed from the outset into the 'remedy of immortality.'"[96] Christ's action invites all of the dramatis personae to share in His redemptive performance; and while He is the center of the stage's action, it is never to the denial of his fellow actors.

Christ's performance makes space for each of us to improvise, to trust in Christ's originality so as to participate explicitly in this action. Our improvised participation can occur through such means as community involvement, Church involvement, or even theological discussions that openly engage issues that are contentious, amongst the differing religious and/or theological thoughts, as well as amongst the different denominational

---

95. Ibid., 66, quoting Jeremy Begbie, *Theology, Music, and Time*.
96. *TD* IV, 476.

realities within Christianity. To improvise within the realm of theology is to not try to be original, but to be faithful to Christ's willingness to engage the culture He lived in. His performance is powerful, but not in the way of society.

In his discussion of Christ's dramatic performance, Wells draws out the transformative reality of Christ's performance. Through His performance, Jesus invites humanity to participate in His transforming action. This invitation into the transformation of history through the act of Christ is what Wells characterizes as Jesus "overaccepting." Overaccepting is the profundity of God's interaction with his creation. God does not block or destroy His creation, tossing it away for the sake of another. Instead, He "overaccepts his creation."[97] Ultimately, according to Wells, the significance of our participation in Christ's action manifests itself when "Christians use their imaginations to see how the gifts of creation and culture fit into the story of the way God deals with the world, given that the fundamental decision has already been made—God's decision for humanity and creation in Christ."[98] Elucidating our understanding of the paradox of Christ's power, Wells writes that "his kingship rides not on the power of a horse but on the humility of a donkey. He does not block the people's desire to acclaim him, nor does he accept their idea of kingship: he overaccepts and becomes the servant king."[99]

Christ's "overacceptance" is the emblematic motif of both theology's and the Church's Eucharistic performances. He recognizes His mission upon the stage, which is constituted in His full giving and receiving; and shares this with the whole of creation. Thus, it can be said that because of her participation *en Christōi*, the Church and her theologians do not have to accept and suffer evil. In fact, as Wells notes, "The Church does not simply accept the story of evil. It has a story of its own. The Church's story begins before evil began and ends after evil has ended . . . This story does not accept evil—it overaccepts it."[100]

In Christ there constantly remains the awareness of the other, through a "relaxed awareness." Drawing from the work of Jacques Lecoq, one of the leading practitioners in using improvisation as a way of preparing a script for performance, Wells writes "*La disponibilité* is a condition of relaxed awareness. In this state of awareness, the actor senses no need to impose an order on the outside world or on the imagination; there is openness to

---

97. Wells, *Improvisation*, 134.
98. Ibid., 133.
99. Ibid., 139.
100. Ibid., 113.

both receiving and giving. The actor is at one with the whole context: self, other actors, audience, theatre space."[101] Christ's own drama is one of giving and receiving; He does not impose his way and His order, and in one of His final earthly scenes, He sets the stage for the Church's own *Eucharistic* performance.

Arguably the Cross-event is the greatest and most dramatic performance of Christ's improvisation. In this very scene, Christ freely accepts (receives) the sin of the world, while giving back to creation eternal life. He takes the burden of sin only to return the breath of eternity. Balthasar maintains, that "Christ's real awareness manifests itself in that man's refusal was possible because of the Trinitarian 'recklessness' of divine love, which, in its self-giving, observed no limits and had no regard for itself."[102] Christ's own awareness, as played out through His Eucharistic performance, is that which hinges together theology's (the Church's) faithful performance with the truth of participation. This is to say, that through the willingness to dramatically improvise with Christ, so as to share in His eternal performance, theology will come to realize and be able to perpetuate the reality of the truth-event—Christ's *Eucharistic* performance.

§5.3 Today's Performance within the Play of Yesterday and Tomorrow

Christ's action of His giving and receiving towards humanity is the Christian message, a message that is not static, that is, it is not a "state but an event" such that any interaction with God has to do with "an event, with an act of God." The Eucharistic act of Christ transcends the bounds of time, while embracing the reality of today. As Balthasar notes, "the drama of the Passion, to which the Eucharist belongs, embraces all past and future points of world time."[103] If this is the case that Christ's Eucharistic performance dramatically interacts with today in light of tomorrow's hope, should not the actions of theology and the Church continue to reflect this dynamic reality? If indeed the self-expression of the Godhead is the absolute attention of the world, "whose *passio* in history is as such *actio*,"[104] should not our theological endeavors seek to participate in this performance? Humanity exists not in story form but through its interpersonal dialogue—its intersecting performances. "The history of the world," writes Balthasar, "is a dialogue

101. Ibid., 80.
102. *TD* IV, 329.
103. Ibid., 363.
104. *CD* I/1, 144.

between creation and covenant, kingdom of the world and kingdom of God, Church and culture."[105] Failure to recognize this reality will lead to a discontinuity between theology and society, and between yesterday, today and tomorrow. Today's theological performance should continually remind itself that the Eucharistic performance of Christ, while being the crux of today's action, anticipates "the final act, the eschatology." Thus, in order for the performance of both theology and the Church to remain faithful, it must always have its gaze upon the Cross-event, not to establish another system of theology or doctrine of the Church as "the Cross explodes all systems," but to remain ever mindful of the fact that "God's entire world drama is concentrated on and hinges on this scene. This is the theo-drama into which the world *and* God have their ultimate input; here absolute freedom enters into created freedom, interacts with created freedom and acts *as* created freedom."[106]

God's act of revelation, invitation and reconciliation embraces the entirety of the stage and illumines the whole of history from the tree in which Christ hung. Christ's actions are both *Eucharistic* and *eschatological*, as they are actions of self-giving and receiving that cannot be left in the past nor propelled to the future. This act—Christ's faithful performance—insists upon an equally driven Eucharistic and eschatological performance of theology and the Church; Christ's performance insists upon the Church giving our own self-sacrificial, self-giving performances (e.g., feeding of the poor, standing up for the outcast and downtrodden), while enacting the hope of tomorrow through the performances of today. The reality of such a performance by theology and the Church manifests itself through the acceptance of our performances being ones constituted by the past, present, and future. Because we share in Christ's performance, we must acknowledge the depth of His action upon the world's stage and this depth embraces the whole of history. "His eschatology embraces all continuing chronological time" and as such, "qualitatively determines it. His eschatology is primary: of itself it qualifies the secondary eschatology of those who continue to live on earth whether or not they believe in him."[107] This is the truth exposed through God's Word to humanity, whereby humanity, even amidst this seemingly final scene, is yet again extended the ability to participate in Christ's performance.

All participants in life's drama are incorporated into the dramatic tension of God's faithful performance. Through the multitude of the scenes

---

105. *MWR*, 37.
106. *TD* IV, 318.
107. *TD* V, 20.

(plays) of the Bible, humanity witnesses the unity of God's definitive Word amidst the tensions and joys of reality, while being ever mindful of tomorrow's hope. God's promise, made in the bodily resurrection of Christ, is the eschatological claim made upon theology and the Church—a claim that incorporates the whole of creation. The incorporation of humanity rests upon the playing out of God's continued act of love—the external presentation of His love, who writes Barth, "at the creation of the world and man, at the laying of the presupposition of the covenant, at the preparation of the creature for His grace, is never at a loss for the right ways and means, but whose Word is sufficient to give being and existence to the creature as the object of His love and as the partner of His covenant."[108]

The manifestation of God's promise through Christ's eternal performance is "holistic and all-encompassing." It contains the answers for today's performances, as it is the renewal, the transformation of the entirety of creation. Christ's resurrection is "holistic and all-encompassing: for whole persons, body and soul, for all the networks of relationship in human society that are integral to being human, and for the rest of creation also, from which humans in their bodiliness are not to be detached."[109] It is in light of God's drawing together the fragments of humanity's performances that the claim can be made that the entirety of the Biblical scenes unite in Christ, as He is the center of history and life. And while Christ is the normative of the drama—so concrete a norm that His action has "universal application"—His performance by no means annihilates the performances of others. Christ's performance "leaves the person free to decide; and even as it leaves him free, it points to the source of all true freedom: the Son's readiness to perform the Father's will."[110]

§5.4 The Final Word: Love

God's action through Christ's performance secures the profundity of each human performance, while elevating the one universal performance on the world's stage. This unified and particularized movement is due to God's own unity and particularity. As Balthasar writes, "we see that only a Trinitarian God can guarantee that man will not forfeit his independent being when united with God. God does not put us into a uniform of love. He lets his own love, out of which he has created every man, be reflected in the particular way in which each person loves." Thus, drawing on von Speyr, Balthasar

---

108. *CD* III/1, 231
109. Bauckham, *Cambridge Companion*, 268.
110. *TD* II, 86.

continues, "the unity bestowed by the Lord not only preserves all that is personal, it actually promotes it where hitherto it was hard to recognize;" just as, in the unity of the Trinity, we become aware of the distinction of Persons, "so, in the unity that the Lord bestows upon us, we always discern both his fundamental imprint and our own personal imprint. This is the basis of that eternal dignity which belongs to every human being."[111] It is specifically because Christ is the normative of history that humanity comes to realize its perfection, through its incorporation into Christ's performance. And since Christ is definitive of revelation, the Bible opens of itself. "In Christ, God speaks a final Word (*eschaton logon*), albeit in the midst of the ongoing drama of the world."[112] The spoken eschaton logon exposes the tension raised through God's willingness to bestow freedom upon humanity, thereby securing the profundity of humanity's involvement within His drama, while calling forth its very eschaton logon.

The unfolding action, while seemingly tragic to many, erupts into the joyful praise of reconciliation and redemption through the performance of Christ. However, with this said, it should be noted that such a perspective of the drama—an eschatological perspective of hope—embraces the fullness of life's actions if and only if such action is bound up in the tragicomedy of the Godhead. "Only because Jesus died in loving identification with all" notes Bauckham, "could his resurrection be on behalf of all, opening up for all the way to life with God beyond death."[113] Through His identification with humanity yesterday and today, our performance now, can look to the hope of tomorrow so as to enact its becoming the *real* in Christ through the Spirit. As was argued in chapter four, theology should continue to risk moving deeper in the action of the ideal becoming the real, so as to realize not only the performance of Christ, but our very performance. This movement is elevated through the tragicomedy.

The luminous stage of God's drama, therefore, sheds light upon humanity's darkness while seeking to break through so as to illuminate the goodness and beauty of creation. This drama is that of a tragicomedy. It is paradoxically a tragedy, as on one hand, its ultimate—climactic event—is the tragic event of the cross, while on the other hand, the Cross-event is the most beautiful and glorious event that has broken into the darkness and chaos upon the stage. Christ's *Eucharistic* performance, His self-giving, is simultaneously His *eschatological* performance, His enactment and presentation of heaven's hope for humanity, and this performance stretches across

---

111. *TD* V, 108, quoting von Speyr, *Kath. Briefe*.
112. *TD* II, 124.
113. Bauckham, *Cambridge Companion*, 277.

the strands of history, transforming the tragic performance into the beauty of the comedy, whereby the final act of *The Play* ends in the glorious wedding feast of the bridegroom and His beautiful bride.

Christ's action, as exposed and revealed through His eschatological and Eucharistic performance, unsettles the movement of the stage, so as to re-settle through His call to participate in His reconciled hope. This invitation to share in His hope of tomorrow today moves the tragic into the comedy, for the cross, which rests at the center of the stage, and is the fullness of God's action, represents the "epitome of human cruelty and ugliness" while ultimately being the "manifestation of God's beauty—a beauty that we cannot possess but only suffer," as through such beauty, humanity is "unselfed, thus formed, making possible our reception of charity, the form of all the virtues."[114] Love is the action of the Spirit by which He takes humanity into the fullness of life through the outpouring of divine love. As such, the fullness of humanity shall be apprehended through the Spirit in Christ, for it is through this Trinitarian act—the outpouring of divine love—that Christian hope is realized and enacted. Concerning the reality of tomorrow lived (performed) today, Bauckham writes:

> Christian hope for the future of Jesus Christ promotes the same kind of compassionate and undaunted engagement with reality for the sake of its future in God that Jesus himself practiced and pioneered as far as death, trusting that his way is the way to the kingdom of God . . . It neither over-reaches itself in attempting what can only come from God nor neglects what is humanly possible in God's grace. Sustained by hope of everything from God, it attempts what is possible within the limits of each present . . . It does what can be done . . . here and now, confident that every present will find itself, redeemed and fulfilled in the new creation. Most characteristically of all, it knows that only by expending life in the service of God and God's world can life finally be found secure, hidden with the Christ who is yet to be revealed.[115]

The dramatic call for the community of Christ and its theology is immersed in the eschatological and Eucharistic reality of Christ—a reality that often times draws a reaction from the world and the academy, as the message, or rather, the invitation to share in such a performance, goes against the tendency of a "rationalistic theology" that seeks to remain a distant observer rather than an active participant. However, as Balthasar writes,

---

114. Hauerwas, *Performing the Faith*, 163–64.
115. Bauckham, *Cambridge Companion*, 280.

"the Church's whole destiny proclaims that she belongs to him (Christ) and that her destiny is shaped by his." A destiny, writes Balthasar, which is distinct because "what is particularly visible in Christians, is the fact that their existence is governed by the eschatology of Jesus Christ."[116] Theological performances intent on sharing in the destiny of Christ recognize the severity of responsibility placed within its hands, for as Stephan van Erp notes, "theology itself is also a form of teaching but it is a form of teaching that tests and corrects the teachings of the Church." Expanding further upon the thoughts of Balthasar, van Erp continues, "Balthasar makes little distinction between a theological commentary and a sermon of someone like Origen. Although these theological genres differ in style and form, and perhaps in interest, academic or pastoral, they are explanations of the Word of God and can therefore both be called 'theology.'"[117] The Theo-drama calls forth a participatory mission upon the world's stage from both theology and the Church while always recognizing the inseparable relationship of the two—where one is, so too is the other.

The dramatic reality of theology's message to the Church and to the world is due in fact, to the scandal or "offense" caused by the drama of the Bible. The scandalous nature of the Christian faith is because its message has at its core, "the figure of a crucified teacher in such a way that the teacher becomes the teaching," and this, continues Gunton, "is an offense to the intellect and moral sense of the 'natural' person."[118] Yet through this "natural offense," theology and the Church are exposed to their *perfected ideals*. Through the allowance and movement of the ideal becoming the real, the world witnesses the performance of Christ as played out in His witnesses. The actors *en Christōi*, who are sharing in this eternal drama that is foolishness to those who are perishing (those who continue to respond negatively to Christ's invitation), continue to be empowered by God's final word of love. Such empowerment enables those who have joyfully said "yes" to God's threefold movement to present to Him, and to our fellow participants, our final word of love, through our faithful performances.

---

116. *TD* V, 21.

117. Erp, *Art of Theology*, 93, 97.

118. Gunton, *Actuality of Atonement*, 24.

Concluding Remarks

> There is only room for hope at this point, where we simply can know nothing more. For a Christian, this is no arbitrary hope but one that makes, according to Jesus" command of love, no exception of any of our fellow human beings and lets none of them travel but halfway to the goal and then falter.[1]

§1 What's Done Cannot Be Undone

IT MIGHT IN MANY ways seem anti-climactic or even un-dramatic to attempt to conclude the dialogue offered throughout this project; and in some sense, this is true. However, rather than viewing these last words as the attempt to conclude the project, I hope to offer them as a summary, so as to allow for the potentiality and continuation of this project's premise and argument, always being mindful of Shakespeare's words, "Good reasons must of force give place to better."[2] The hope is that the reasons presented in the dramatizing of theology are those that are secure enough to endure the strains of time so as to contribute positively to our theological endeavors.

As was stated in the introduction, God is Being-in-act and that humanity, and thus, the Church, encounter Him through and in His action, and this action, it has been argued, is dramatic. Moving forward in this understanding was the recognition that the dramatizing of theology presupposes that theology "understands itself to be involved in and committed to the drama which—according to the Bible—is taking place."[3] Theology's involvement in and commitment to the drama is played out when we proclaim God's Word so as to draw the Church continuously back to her source. Theology is "concrete obedience . . . Obedience exists only in the action of a will which submits itself to a higher will . . . As obedience to faith, it obviously stands in relation to the will of God manifested in his revelation; and

---

1. *Ep*, 122.
2. Shakespeare, *Julius Caesar* IV.iii.203.
3. *TD* II, 151.

the will of God so manifested is the reconciliation of man with himself while he speaks, and the leading of man to his redemption. As the God who has spoken in his Son and still speaks through the witness of his servants and messengers, he will also speak today—*today*."[4]

The reality however, of some of theology's presence on the world's stage resembles the man who wanted nothing more than a box to hide in.

"You want a box?" he asked.

"I want a box to hide in," I said.

"Whatta you mean?" he said. "You mean a big box?"

I said I meant a big box, big enough to hold me.[5]

Why the box? Precisely because, continues Thurber, "It's a form of escape," I told him, "hiding in a box. It circumscribes your worries and the range of your anguish. You don't see people, either."[6] Sometimes, theology is quite comfortable remaining locked inside its *theological* box, investigating, arguing and debating amidst its own *box* occupants, thereby leaving alone the Church and society. The box remains inconspicuous because, as Thurber continues, "nobody pays attention to a big box lying on the floor. You could stay in it for days and nobody thinks to look in it, not even the cleaning-woman."[7] On the world's stage, then, this theological box is located in the shadows of the stage, in hopes of not being interacted with by any of the other performers. However, every so often, someone nudges the box and encourages theology to interact. Yet, rather than seeking to participate completely with the entirety of the dramatis personae, theology sometimes simply mimics the actions of Christ, doing just enough to keep people away from continued interest and expectation of the contents and possibilities contained in our theological box. This performance can sometimes give the appearance of our opening up and surrender to the Church and society, but in the end reveals very little of the reciprocal truth of the stage. Instead, the actor (in this case theology), "exploits the movement of self-surrender as a mere means to become even better enclosed within himself."[8] This deepening enclosure of the actor, is, as we are reminded, what both Balthasar and N.T. Wright discuss as being a *spectator* or a mere *observer* as opposed to a faithful performer in God's drama.

4. *T & C*, 302–3.
5. Thurber, *Writings and Drawings*, 304.
6. Ibid.
7. Ibid.
8. *TL*, I, 123.

The question presented to theology, then, is whether or not the Church's theologians are willing to entertain the enactment of theology's dramatization? What has been argued by this thesis is that the Church's faithful performance is manifested through her recognition and realization of her mission. This acknowledgement occurs most effectively through the *dramatizing* of theology. The truth remains that both theology and the theatre are rooted in the relational reality of humanity. "How we as Christians live in our own surrounding cultures" writes Savidge, "overarches the relationship of how we perform theatre, experience theatre as audiences, and use theatre in our worship."[9] Thus, as has been argued throughout the thesis, awareness of the theatre, and theology's interaction with it and the reciprocal truth between the two, stems from humanity's *imago Trinitatis*. Humanity's ontology, which is manifested and performed in the theatre, resembles the theatre, and is thus faithfully attended to through the dramatizing of theology, is constituted by its relationality.

Through theology's becoming, the stage witnesses its faithful performance in God's theatre of glory. It is when the dramatizing of theology is taken as the real that the truth of Christ begins to free the movement of the stage. In other words, when theology explicitly recognizes that our source—Father, Son and Spirit—is Being-in-act, we can and should seek to reciprocate through our own being-in-act. It is through theological action that seeks not simply to investigate or observe God's revelation, invitation and reconciliation, but to participate in this transformative performance, that the Church and society are opened up to the potentiality of their faithful performances.

§2 The Truth Shall Set You Free

Participation in Christ's performance is participation in Truth; it is the answer not only to Pilate's historical query, "what is truth?" but more importantly, the answer to "what is the human?" As discussed in the introduction, the relationship between theology, the Church and society inevitably centers on the meaning of life, that is, "what is the human," or better yet, "who am I?"

Participation in Christ frees humanity, so as to be able to realize its mission, a mission made real through the *analogia relationis*. From the foundation of relation, established in Christ through the Spirit, humanity is invited to participate in the faithful performance of Christ, thereby coming closer to the originality of its identity. As Balthasar points out, "The closer

---

9. Savidge, *Performing the Sacred*, 97.

man comes to this identity, the more perfectly does he play his part."[10] It is from this ontological reality that the truth of our performance moves closer and closer toward its perfected performance.

The truth that has been expressed throughout this project is that God, through His threefold act of revelation, invitation and reconciliation, truly does desire a positive participatory response from the whole of humanity. This recognition is realized when the Church and her theologians give themselves fully to the action of Father, Son and Holy Spirit. Thus, the project's argument:

Chapter 1 acknowledged that as is shown to us in the event of revelation, humanity is confronted with a God whose Being is, *Being-in-act*. The Church's response to this eternal act should also be act. Through our theological acts, we come closer to understanding the essence of being as we participate in God's Being-in-act. Faithful participation in Christ's Being is manifested through our intentional response to God's event of revelation.

Chapter 2 furthered this aspect of action through a look at two models of theology: narrative and dramatic. The intention of such an investigation was to expose us and our practices to the most effective ways to guide the Church, while seeking always to participate in God's Being-in-act. What the chapter argued was that theology best guides the Church and participates in God's threefold act through the active becoming of the narrative into the drama. Through the dramatizing of theology, the Church witnesses the true reality not only of its own becoming, but more, of importantly, the *becoming* of humanity. Again, the *becoming* of theology is facilitated by the becoming of its own model and presentation. That is, in all its endeavors, theology should be act if it is to be faithful to God who is act.

Chapter 3 moved from the models of theology to the expected performance of contemporary theology. As Balthasar writes, "once the eternal God determines to create a world-time characterized by *becoming*, his eternal time will be, of necessity, contemporaneous with every moment of transitory time, and this contemporaneity will be the time 'which, in his grace, God takes to concern himself with us.'"[11] God takes to concern Himself with us, and thus, the call made on contemporary theology is faithfully to guide the Church continuously back to her source, Jesus Christ. This continual turning to Christ is accomplished, as was argued, through the dramatizing of theology. Through this movement, theology and the Church fully realize that "everything is becoming and growing, and therefore it is Christian revelation."[12]

10. *TD* II, 14.
11. *TD* V, 126. Balthasar quoting von Speyr, *Kath. Briefe*.
12. Ibid., 130.

Chapter 4 argued that in Christ creation is opened up to the image of perfected humanity, thereby witnessing the possibility of our perfection, through the *becoming* of the ideal into the real. To enable our becoming, the chapter pushed for the active employment of our theological imaginative powers. The need for the imagination rests within its ability that allows theology to see simultaneously what is and what might yet be for the best. Through the imagination, theology guides the Church into envisaging the possibilities of tomorrow so as to participate in its performance today. Tomorrow's *ideal* only becomes today's *real* when theology not only imagines such action but actively seeks to participate in this faithful performance.

Chapter 5 highlighted the fact that theology's faithful performance brings the Church and humanity closer to grasping what it means to be a performer in God's drama. Theology's mission is the guidance of the Church, and thus, humanity, back to Christ. Such movement is the glorification of God which, is "continually being reached—and only *because* it has already been reached we can reach it anew. Becoming coincides with being."[13] Theology, the Church, and humanity all find their faithful performances in Christ through the Spirit. All Christian teaching proceeds from the reality of Christ, His incarnation, life and work, death, resurrection and ascension, which is "by no means mythical and speculative but sober and historical; this dramatic performance illuminates that truth and meaning of his Cross, and behind it, of his entire Incarnation."[14] It is this very performance that theology is called to participate in, so as to guide the Church and humanity, back to our source in order to illuminate God's self-giving love to the world.

§3 How Now Shall We Live?

As indicated in the introduction, the purpose, therefore, of theological dramatics is to raise the question and awareness of the location and reality of life's dramatic action. The point made through Hans Urs von Balthasar's *Theodramatik* is not one of a revival for the Christian theatre, or its denial, but to bring into center stage "the *drama intrinsic to divine salvation*."[15] Drawing from this perspective, we can begin to apprehend how the drama of life is fully embodied in, and explored through, the *Theologica Dramaticas*. Drama illumines and exposes the foundational element of life *in Christ through the Holy Spirit*. This illumination is the performance that, as Balthasar continues to remind theology and the Church, "will no doubt

13. *TD* V, 131.
14. *TD* V, 52.
15. Nichols, *No Bloodless Myth*, 23.

challenge our personal and social sense of 'ought' through its positive or negative models."[16]

Contemporary theology is in continuous need of the re-humanizing power of Christ's dramatic interaction, so that we might actively participate in God's reconciliatory and redemptive love. The effects of modernity and the post-Christian movement upon contemporary theology subtly influence our theological practices so that at times, there tends to be a separation of our words and deeds; a separation that creates words that are absent of action. Instead of theology realizing the gospel and its proclamation through word *and* deed, much of the time we desire our theological box, as opposed to an active role in God's drama. The result of such desires often times manifests in our overlooking the participatory reality of the gospel, for the sake of analysis, observation or exegesis of its narrative.

What is needed in society today is not simply for the Church to raise issues that the lowly and downtrodden are affected by, or call for the rich and powerful to be humble, as important as these actions are. Instead, what is needed is for the Church to share life with the lowly and downtrodden, the outcasts, the rich and powerful; the *other* and to encourage participation in God's drama by the entire dramatis personae. That is, theology remains obedient to its call through its overt performance of incorporation. Jurgën Moltmann writes that such incorporation is realized through the "anticipation of Christian hope, which is, vital and effective only when we act on behalf of those who have no future. When believers, the firstfruits of the new creation . . . take up their cross, they anticipate the future of redemption."[17] Thus, as Balthasar maintains, "the eschatology of the future and the theology of the cross are interwoven."[18] It is in light of this that theology should continue to remind the Church, that just as Jesus incorporates the whole of humanity into His performance, so too should the Church and her theologians. The Church's faithful performance occurs through her willingness and push to participate in Christ's reconciliatory performance, through the incorporation of the *other*.

> As a fellow human being with us, Jesus can do no other than draw other human beings into his unique and incomparable work. And so he calls others to join with him in the special task of continuing his work. From the very beginning, in the call of the Twelve, Jesus gave a share in his authority both before the Passion ("Do this') and after it ("Whose sins you shall forgive

---

16. *TD I*, 266.
17. Moltmann, *Zukunft der Schopfun*, 63-64: as quoted by Balthasar, *TD V*, 171.
18. *TD V*, 171.

... '), drawing them ever more deeply into his own mission. In this way he made them capable as well of drawing others into his special mission. We must see all these aspects together, as intimately bound up with each other, if we want to perceive, at least to some extent, the mystery of the fruitfulness of the continued life of the incarnate Word—called the Church—without abridgment.[19]

The source of all theology must be appropriate to its matter—the revelation, invitation and reconciliation of God in Christ through the Spirit. It has been argued, then, that on this basis, it is through the Theo-drama that the Church is able to realize her being, which is a being rooted in covenantal communion with the Triune God, and in that, with the whole of humanity. Through this relational reality, the Church is graciously gifted the performance of participation in Christ's reconciliatory action. We have "the *obligation* to hope for the salvation of all."[20] Through God's revelation, invitation and reconciliation the Church is empowered and commanded through its *hope*, which, writes Balthasar, is the result of love that "*hopes for everything* (1 Cor 13:7)."[21] The Church's faithful performance in God's drama occurs only through our participation in Christ's performance, which is a performance that enlivens the stage with hope. Thus, while theology cannot answer the question, whether *all* will be reconciled, we should be mindful of Balthasar's words that "I cannot do otherwise than hope for the reconciliation of all men in Christ. "Such unlimited hope is not only permitted to the Christian, it is *commanded*."[22] Obedience to God's command and call for participation in His redemptive performance empowers theology to continuously refer the Church back to her source, so as to ultimately bear witness to Christ through the Holy Spirit to the world, thereby faithfully participating in the Theo-drama.

19. *Ep*, 113.
20. Ibid., 122.
21. Ibid., 123.
22. Ibid., quoting Hermann-Joseph Lauter, *Pastoralblatt*.

Bibliography

Adam, James. *The Republic of Plato.* Cambridge: Cambridge University Press, 1902.
Allen, Diogenes, and Eric O. Springsted. *Philosophy for Understanding Theology.* London: Westminster John Knox, 2007.
Alter, Robert. *The Art of Biblical Narrative.* New York: Basic, 1981.
———. *The World of Biblical Literature.* New York: Basic, 1992.
Aristotle. *Aristotle on the Art of Poetry.* Translated by Ingram Bywater. Oxford: Clarendon, 1962.
———. *Poetics.* Translated by Malcolm Heath. London: Penguin, 1996.
———. *Rhetoric.* vol. 22. Translated by J. H. Freese. London: Harvard University Press, 1926.
Artaud, Antonin. *The Theater and Its Double.* Translated by Mary Caroline Richards. New York: Grove, 1958.
Auerbach, Erich. *Mimesis: The Representation of Reality in Western Literature.* Princeton: Princeton University Press, 2003.
Augustine. *The Anti-Pelagian Writings.* Edited by Philip Schaff. A Select Library of the Nicene and Post-Nicene Fathers of the Christian Church, First Series 5. Grand Rapids: Eerdmans, 1956.
———. *The City of God against the Pagans.* Translated by R. W. Dyson. Cambridge Texts in the History of Political Thought. Cambridge: Cambridge University Press, 1998.
———. *Confessions.* Translated by Henry Chadwick. Oxford: Oxford University Press, 1998.
———. *Homilies on the Gospel of John.* Edited by Philip Schaff. A Select Library of the Nicene and Post-Nicene Fathers of the Christian Church 7. Grand Rapids: Eerdmans, 1980.
———. *On Christian Doctrine.* Translated by D. W. Robertson Jr. New York: Bobbs-Merrill, 1958.
———. "On Free Will." In *Augustine: Earlier Writings,* edited by John H. S. Burleigh. Philadelphia: Westminster, 1979.
———. "The Trinity." In *The Works of Saint Augustine: A Translation for the 21st Century,* edited by John E. Rotelle. New York: New City, 1990.
Avis, Paul. *God and the Creative Imagination: Metaphor, Symbol and Myth in Religion and Theology.* London: Routledge, 1999.
Bakhtin, M. M. *The Dialogic Imagination: Four Essays.* Edited by Michael Holquist. Translated by Caryl Emerson and Michael Holquist. Austin: University of Texas Press, 1981.
———. *Speech Genres and Other Late Essays.* Translated by Vern W. McGee. Austin: University of Texas Press, 1986.

Baldry, H. C. *The Greek Tragic Theatre*. New York, 1971.
Balthasar, Hans Urs von. *Epilogue*. San Francisco: Ignatius, 2004.
———. *Explorations in Theology*. Vol. I, *The Word Made Flesh*. Translated by A. V. Littledale and Alexander Dru. San Francisco: Ignatius, 1989.
———. *Explorations in Theology*. Vol. II, *Spouse of the Word*. San Francisco: Ignatius, 1993.
———. *Explorations in Theology*. Vol. III, *Creator Spirit*. San Francisco: Ignatius, 1993.
———. *Explorations in Theology*. Vol. IV, *Spirit and Institution*. San Francisco: Ignatius, 1994.
———. *The Glory of the Lord*. Vol. I, *Seeing the Form*. Translated by Joseph Fessio and John Riches. San Francisco: Ignatius, 1983.
———. *Love Alone is Credible*. Translated by D. C. Schindler. San Francisco: Ignatius, 2004.
———. *My Work: In Retrospect*. San Francisco: Ignatius, 1993.
———. *Theo-Drama: Theological Dramatic Theory*. Vol. I, *Prolegomena*. Translated by Graham Harrison. San Francisco: Ignatius, 1988.
———. *Theo-Drama: Theological Dramatic Theory*. Vol. II, *Dramatis Personae: Man in God*. San Francisco: Ignatius, 1990.
———. *Theo-Drama: Theological Dramatic Theory*. Vol. III, *Dramatis Personae: Persons in Christ*. San Francisco: Ignatius, 1992.
———. *Theo-Drama: Theological Dramatic Theory*. Vol. IV, *The Action*. San Francisco: Ignatius, 1994.
———. *Theo-Drama: Theological Dramatic Theory*. Vol. V, *The Last Act*. San Francisco: Ignatius, 1998.
———. *Theo-Logic*. Vol. I, *Truth of the World*. Translated by Graham Harrison. San Francisco: Ignatius, 2000.
———. *Theo-Logic*. Vol. II, *Truth of God*. San Francisco: Ignatius, 2004.
———. *Theo-Logic*. Vol. III, *The Spirit of Truth*. San Francisco: Ignatius, 2005.
———. *A Theology of History*. San Francisco: Ignatius, 1994.
———. *The Theology of Karl Barth: Exposition and Interpretation*. Translated by Edward T. Oakes. San Francisco: Ignatius, 1992.
———. *Prayer*. San Francisco: Ignatius, 1986.
———. *Presence and Thought: Essay on the Religious Philosophy of Gregory of Nyssa*. San Francisco: Ignatius, 1995.
———. *Unless You Become Like This Child*. San Francisco: Ignatius, 1991.
Banks, R. A. *Drama and Theatre Arts*. London: Hodder and Stoughton, 1985.
Barth, Karl. *The Christian Life*. Translated by G. W. Bromiley. Edinburgh: T. & T. Clark, 1981.
———. *Church Dogmatics*. Vol. I/1, *The Doctrine of The Word of God*. Edited by G. W. Bromiley and T. F. Torrance. Edinburgh: T. & T. Clark, 1975.
———. *Church Dogmatics*. Vol. I/2, *The Doctrine of The Word of God*. Edinburgh: T. & T. Clark, 1956.
———. *Church Dogmatics*. Vol. II/1, *The Doctrine of God*. Edinburgh: T. & T. Clark, 1957.
———. *Church Dogmatics*. Vol. II/2, *The Doctrine of God*. Edinburgh: T. & T. Clark, 1957.
———. *Church Dogmatics*. Vol. III/1, *The Doctrine of Creation*. Edinburgh: T. & T. Clark, 1958.

———. *Church Dogmatics*. Vol. III/2, *The Doctrine of Creation*. Edinburgh: T. & T. Clark, 1960.
———. *Church Dogmatics*. Vol. III/3, *The Doctrine of Creation*. Edinburgh: T. & T. Clark, 1961.
———. *Church Dogmatics*. Vol. III/4, *The Doctrine of Creation*. Edinburgh: T. & T. Clark, 1961.
———. *Church Dogmatics*. Vol. IV/1, *The Doctrine of Reconciliation*. Edinburgh: T. & T. Clark, 1956.
———. *Church Dogmatics*. Vol. IV/2, *The Doctrine of Reconciliation*. Edinburgh: T. & T. Clark, 1958.
———. *Church Dogmatics*. Vol. IV/3 *The Doctrine of Reconciliation*. Edinburgh: T. & T. Clark, 1961-2
———. *Church Dogmatics*. Vol. IV/4, *The Doctrine of Reconciliation*. Edinburgh: T. & T. Clark, 1969.
———. *Dogmatics in Outline*. Translated by G. T. Thomson. New York: Harper Perennial, 1959.
———. *The Epistle to the Romans*. Translated by Edwyn C Hoskyns. New York: Oxford University Press, 1968.
———. *Evangelical Theology: An Introduction*. Translated by Grover Foley. New York: Holt, Rinehart, and Winston, 1963.
———. *God Here and Now*. Translated by Paul M. van Buren. London: Routledge, 2003.
———. *God in Action*. Translated by E. G. Homrighausen and Karl J. Ernst. New York: Roundtable, 1963.
———. *The Humanity of God*. Translated by John Newton Thomas and Thomas Wieser. Richmond, VA: John Knox, 1960.
———. *Learning Jesus Christ Through the Heidelberg Catechism*. Translated by S. C. Guthrie. Grand Rapids: Eerdmans, 1981.
———. "Liberal Theology: Some Attributes." *Hibbert Journal* 59 (1961) 213–18.
———. *Theology and Church*. Translated by Louise Pettibone Smith. New York: Harper & Row, 1962.
———. *The Theology of John Calvin*. Translated by Geoffrey W. Bromiley. Grand Rapids: Eerdmans, 1995.
———. *The Word of God and the Word of Man*. Translated by Douglas Horton. New York: Harper, 1957.
Bartholomew, Craig G., and Michael W. Goheen. *The Drama of Scripture: Finding Our Place in the Biblical Story*. Grand Rapids: Baker Academic, 2004.
Bauckham, Richard. "Christology Today." *Scriptura* 27 (1988) 20–28.
———, ed. *God Will Be All In All: The Eschatology of Jürgen Moltmann*. Edinburgh: T. & T. Clark, 1999.
Begbie, Jeremy S., ed. *Sounding the Depths: Theology Through the Arts*. London: SCM, 2002.
———. *Theology, Music and Time*. Edited by Colin Gunton and Daniel H. Hardy. Cambridge Studies in Christian Doctrine 4. Cambridge: Cambridge University Press, 2000.
Berkouwer, Gerrit Cornelis. *The Triumph of Grace in the Theology of Karl Barth*. London: Paternoster, 1956.
Bial, Henry, ed. *The Performance Studies Reader*. 2nd ed. London: Routledge, 2007.

Bockmuehl, Markus, ed. *The Cambridge Companion to Jesus.* Cambridge: Cambridge University Press, 2001.

Bonhoeffer, Dietrich. *Christ the Center.* Translated by John Bowden. New York: Harper & Row, 1966.

———. *The Communion of Saints.* New York: Harper & Row, 1963.

———. *The Cost of Discipleship.* Translated by R. H. Fuller. New York: Simon and Schuster, 1995.

———. *Creation and Fall: A Theological Exposition of Genesis 1–3.* Translated by John W. de Gruchy and Douglas S. Bax. Dietrich Bonhoeffer Works 3. Minneapolis: Fortress, 1997.

———. *Ethics.* New York: MacMillan, 1955.

Braaten, Carl E., and Robert W. Jenson. *In One Body: Through the Cross.* Grand Rapids: Eerdmans, 2003.

———. *Our Naming of God: Problems and Prospects of God-Talk Today.* Philadelphia: Fortress, 1989.

Brecht, Bertolt. "A Short Organum for the Theatre." In *Brecht on Theatre: The Development of an Aesthetic,* 179–208. Translated by John Willett. New York: Hill and Wang, 1992.

Bromiley, Geoffrey William. *Introduction to the Theology of Karl Barth.* Edinburgh: T. & T. Clark, 2000.

Brook, Peter. *The Empty Space.* New York: Penguin, 1968.

Brown, David. *Discipleship and Imagination: Christian Tradition and Truth.* Oxford: Oxford University Press, 2000.

———. *God and Mystery in Words: Experience through Metaphor and Drama.* Oxford: Oxford University Press, 2008.

———. *Tradition and Imagination: Revelation and Change.* Oxford: Oxford University Press, 1999.

Calvin, John. *Institutes of the Christian Religion.* Edited by John T. McNeill. Translated by Ford Lewis Battles. The Library of Christian Classics 20–21. Philadelphia: Westminster, 1960.

———. *Truth for all Time: A Brief Outline of the Christian Faith.* Translated by Stuart Olyott. Edinburgh: Banner of Truth, 1998.

Carr, David. "Narrative and the Real Word." *History and Theory* 25 (1986) 117–31.

Cavanaugh, William T. *Being Consumed: Economics and Christian Desire.* Grand Rapids: Eerdmans, 2008.

———. "Killing for the Telephone Company: Why the Nation-State Is Not the Keeper of the Common Good." *Modern Theology* 20/2 (April 2004) 243–74.

Chapp, Larry. *The God Who Speaks: Hans Urs von Balthasar's Theology of Revelation.* San Francisco: Catholic Scholars, 1996.

Chia, Roland. *Revelation and Theology: The Knowledge of God in Balthasar and Barth.* New York: Lang, 1999.

Clark, Tony. *Divine Revelation and Human Practice: Responsive and Imaginative Participation.* Eugene, OR: Cascade, 2008.

Cobley, Paul, ed. *The Communication Theory Reader.* New York: Routledge, 1996.

Coleridge, Samuel T. *Biographia Literaria.* Vol. 1. Edited and translated by J. Shawcross. Oxford: Oxford University Press, 1958.

Craigo-Snell, Shannon. "Command Performance: Rethinking Performance Interpretation in the Context of Divine Discourse." *Modern Theology* 16/4 (October 2000) 475–94.
Cuddon, J. A. *A Dictionary of Literary Terms*. London: Penguin, 1979.
Davies, Oliver. *The Creativity of God: Word, Eucharist, Reason*. Cambridge: Cambridge University Press, 2004.
———. "The Lordship of Christ: Freedom, Command and Sacrifice." Paper presented at ITIA seminar, St. Andrews University, May 2, 2008.
Davis, Tracy C., ed. *The Cambridge Companion to Performance Studies*. Cambridge: Cambridge University Press, 2008.
Dawn, Marva. *Powers, Weakness, and the Tabernacling of God*. Grand Rapids: Eerdmans, 2001.
Dearborn, Kerry. *Baptized Imagination: The Theology of George MacDonald*. Aldershot: Ashgate, 2006.
Delgado Morales, Manuel. *The Calderonian Stage: Body and Soul*. London: Associated University Presses, 1997.
Derrida, Jacques. *Acts of Literature*. Edited by Derek Attridge. London: Routledge, 1991.
———. *Acts of Religion*. Edited by Gil Anidjar. London: Routledge, 2001.
———. *The Derrida Reader: Writing Performances*. Edited by Julian Wolfreys. Lincoln: University of Nebraska Press, 1998.
———. *Of Grammatology*. Translated by Gayatri Chakravory Spivak. Baltimore: Johns Hopkins Press, 1998.
———. *On the Name*. Translated by David Wood and John P. Leavey. Stanford: Stanford University Press, 1995.
———. *Religion*. Edited by Gianni Vattimo. Translated by David Webb. Stanford: Stanford University Press, 1998.
———. *Specters of Marx: The State of the Debt, the Work of Mourning, and the New International*. London: Routledge, 1994.
Diller, Kevin. "Does Contemporary Theology Require a Postfoundationalist Way of Knowing?" *SJT* 60/3 (2007) 271–93.
Djuth, Marianne. "Veiled and Unveiled Beauty: The Role of the Imagination in Augustine's Esthetics." *Theological Studies* 68 (2007) 77–91.
Dyrness, William A. *Reformed Theology and Visual Culture: The Protestant Imagination from Calvin to Edwards*. Cambridge: Cambridge University Press, 2004.
Eichrodt, Walter. *Theology of the Old Testament*. Translated by J. A. Baker. London: SCM, 1961.
Elwell, Walter A., ed. *Evangelical Commentary on the Bible*. Grand Rapids: Baker, 1989.
Erp, Stephan van. *The Art of Theology: Hans Urs von Balthasar's Theological Aesthetics and the Foundations of Faith*. Leuven: Peeters, 2004.
Esslin, Martin. *An Anatomy of Drama*. London: Temple Smith, 1976.
———. *Brecht: A Choice of Evils; A Critical Study of the Man, His Work and His Opinions*. London: Eyre & Spottiswoode, 1959.
———. *Samuel Beckett: A Collection of Critical Essays*. Englewood Cliffs, NJ: Prentice-Hall, 1965.
———. *The Theatre of the Absurd*. Harmondsworth, UK: Penguin, 1980.
Geertz, Clifford. *The Interpretation of Cultures*. New York: Basic, 1973.
Giddens, Anthony. *Central Problems in Social Theory: Action, Structure and Contradiction in Social Analysis*. Berkeley: University of California Press, 1979.

———. *The Constitution of Society: Outline of the Theory of Structuration*. Berkeley: University of California Press, 1986.

———. *Modernity and Self-Identity: Self and Society in the Late Modern Age*. Stanford: Stanford University Press, 1991.

Green, Garrett. *Imagining God: Theology and the Religious Imagination*. Grand Rapids: Eerdmans, 1989.

Guder, Darrell, ed. *The Continuing Conversion of the Church*. Grand Rapids: Eerdmans, 2000.

———. *Missional Church: A Vision for the Sending of the Church in North America*. Grand Rapids: Eerdmans, 1998.

Gunton, Colin. *Act and Being: Towards a Theology of the Divine Attributes*. London: SCM, 2002.

———. *Actuality of Atonement: A Study of Metaphor, Rationality and the Christian Tradition*. Edinburgh: T. & T. Clark, 1988.

———. *A Brief Theology of Revelation*. Edinburgh: T. & T. Clark, 1995.

———. *The One, The Three, and The Many: God, Creation and The Culture of Modernity*. The 1992 Bampton Lectures. New York: Cambridge University Press, 1994.

———. *The Promise of Trinitarian Theology*. 2nd ed. London: T. & T. Clark, 2003.

———. *Theology through the Theologians*. London: T. & T. Clark, 1996.

———. *Triune Creator: A Historical and Systematic Study*. Grand Rapids: Eerdmans, 1998.

Harris, Max. *The Dialogical Theatre*. London: Macmillan, 1993.

———. *Carnival and Other Christian Festivals: Folk Theology and Folk Performance*. Austin: University of Texas Press, 2003.

———. *Theatre and Incarnation*. Grand Rapids: Eerdmans, 2005.

Harrison, Paul M. "Toward a Dramaturgical Interpretation of Religion." *Sociological Analysis* 38 (1977) 389–96.

Hart, Trevor. *Faith Thinking: The Dynamics of Christian Theology*. Downers Grove, IL: InterVarsity, 1995.

———. "Imagination for the Kingdom of God? Hope, Promise, and the Transformative Power of an Imagined Future." In *God Will Be All in All: The Eschatology of Jürgen Moltmann*, edited by R. J. Bauckham, 49–78. Edinburgh: T. & T. Clark, 1999.

———. *Regarding Karl Barth*. Carlisle, UK: Paternoster, 1999.

———. "A Suspicion Observed: Christian Responses to the Imagination." Paper delivered at Wheaton College, April 2008.

Hart, Trevor, and Steven Guthrie, eds. *Faithful Performances: Enacting Christian Tradition*. Ashgate Studies in Theology, Imagination, and the Arts. Aldershot: Ashgate, 2007.

Hauerwas, Stanley. *Community of Character*. Notre Dame: University of Notre Dame Press, 1981.

———. *Performing the Faith*. Grand Rapids: Brazos, 2004.

———. *With the Grain of the Universe: The Church's Witness and Natural Theology*. Grand Rapids: Brazos, 2001.

Hauerwas, Stanley, and L. Gregory Jones, eds. *Why Narrative? Readings in Narrative Theology*. Eugene, OR: Wipf & Stock, 1997.

Hauerwas, Stanley, and William H. Willimon. *Resident Aliens: Life in the Christian Colony*. Nashville: Abingdon, 1989.

Healy, Nicholas J. *The Eschatology of Hans Urs von Balthasar: Being As Communion*. Oxford: Oxford University Press, 2005.
Horton, Michael S. *Covenant and Eschatology: The Divine Drama*. Louisville: Westminster John Knox, 2002.
Hunsinger, George. *Disruptive Grace: Studies in the Theology of Karl Barth*. Grand Rapids: Eerdmans, 2000.
———. *For the Sake of the World*. Grand Rapids: Eerdmans, 2004.
———. *How to Read Karl Barth*. Oxford: Oxford University Press, 1991.
Hütter, Reinhard. *Suffering Divine Things: Theology as Church Practice*. Grand Rapids: Eerdmans, 2000.
Irenaeus. *Against Heresies*. In *Irenaeus of Lyons*, edited by Robert M. Grant. Early Church Fathers. New York: Routledge, 1996.
Iser, Wolfgang. *The Fictive and the Imaginary: Charting Literary Anthropology*. Baltimore: Johns Hopkins University Press, 1993.
Jenson, Robert. *God after God: The God of the Past and the God of the Future, Seen in the Work of Karl Barth*. New York: Bobbs-Merrill, 1969.
———. "How the World Lost Its Story." *First Things* 36 (October 1993) 19–24.
———. *Systematic Theology*. Vol. 1, *The Triune God*. Oxford: Oxford University Press, 1997.
———. *Systematic Theology*. Vol. 2, *The Works of God*. Oxford: Oxford University Press, 1999.
———. *The Triune Identity*. Philadelphia: Fortress, 1982.
Jeremias, Joachim. *The Parables of Jesus*. Translated by S. H. Hooke. New York: Scribner's, 1962.
Johnson, Samuel. *On Shakespeare*. Edited by W. K. Wimsatt. New York: Hill and Wang, 1960.
Johnson, Todd E., and Dale Savidge. *Performing the Sacred: Theology and Theatre in Dialogue*. Grand Rapids: Baker Academic, 2008.
Johnstone, Keith. *Impro: Improvisation and The Theatre*. London: Methuen Drama, 1989.
Kaufman, Gordon D. *In Face of Mystery: A Constructive Theology*. Cambridge, MA: Harvard University Press, 1993.
———. *Theological Imagination: Constructing the Concept of God*. Philadelphia: Westminster, 1981.
Kearney, Richard. *Poetics of Imagining: Modern to Postmodern*. Edinburgh: Edinburgh University Press, 1998.
Kelly, J. N. D. *Early Christian Doctrines*. Francisco: HarperCollins, 1978.
Kennedy, Andrew. *Six Dramatists in Search of a Language: Studies in Dramatic Language*. London: Cambridge University Press, 1975.
Khovacs, Ivan. "Divine Reckonings in Profane Spaces: Towards a Theological Dramaturgy for Theatre." PhD diss., St Mary's College, University of St. Andrews, 2006.
Kierkegaard, Søren. *The Concept of Anxiety: A Simple Psychologically Orienting Deliberation on the Dogmatic Issue of Hereditary Sin*. Translated by Reidar Thomte and Albert Anderson. Kierkegaard's Writings 8. Princeton: Princeton University Press, 1980.
———. *Philosophical Fragments*. Princeton: Princeton University Press, 1959.

———. *Practice in Christianity*. Kierkegaard's Writings 20. Princeton: Princeton University Press, 1991.

———. *The Sickness Unto Death: A Christian Psychological Exposition for Upbuilding and Awakening*. Translated by Howard Vincent Hong and Edna Hatlestad Hong. Kierkegaard's Writings 19. Princeton: Princeton University Press, 1980.

King, Martin Luther, Jr. *The Measure of a Man*. Minneapolis: Fortress, 2001.

LaCugna, Catherine Mowry. *God for Us: The Trinity and Christian Life*. San Francisco: Harper San Francisco, 1991.

Leeuw, Gerardus van der. *Sacred and Profane Beauty: The Holy in Art*. New York: Holt, Rinehart & Winston, 1963.

Longenecker, Bruce, ed. *Narrative Dynamics in Paul: A Critical Assessment*. Louisville: Westminster John Knox, 2002.

Ludwig, Nita. "The Drama of Salvation: An Essay on Conflict, Crisis and the Search for Meaning in Christianity." *Epiphany* 1/3 (Spring 1981) 43–53.

Luther, Martin. *Concerning Christian Liberty*. Translated by W. A. Lambert. Minneapolis: Fortress, 2003.

———. *Martin Luther: Selections from His Writings*. Edited by John Dillenberger. Garden City, NY: Doubleday, 1961.

———. *Lectures on Romans*. Translated by Wilhelm Pauck. The Library of Christian Classics 15. Philadelphia: Westminster, 1961.

Lynch, William. *Christ and Prometheus: A New Image of the Secular*. Notre Dame: University of Notre Dame Press, 1970.

MacIntyre, Alasdair. *After Virtue*. Notre Dame: University of Notre Dame Press, 1981.

Marcus Aurelius. *Meditations*. Translated by Gregory Hays. New York: Random House, 2003.

Martin, Wallace. *Recent Theories of Narrative*. Ithaca: Cornell University Press, 1994.

McCormack, Bruce L., and Gerrit W. Neven, eds. *The Reality of Faith in Theology Studies on Karl Barth: Princeton-Kampen Consultation 2005*. Bern: Peter Lang, 2007.

McIntyre, John. *Faith, Theology and Imagination*. Edinburgh: Handsel, 1987.

———. *The Shape of Pneumatology*. London: T. & T. Clark, 2004.

Metzger, Paul. *Consuming Jesus*. Grand Rapids: Eerdmans, 2007.

———. "The Sorcerer's Apprentice and the Savior of the World: Space, Time, and Structural Evil." *Cultural Encounters: A Journal for the Theology of Culture* 1 (Winter 2004) 85–95.

———, ed. *Trinitarian Soundings in Systematic Theology*. London: T. & T. Clark, 2005.

———. *The Word of Christ and the World of Culture: Sacred and Secular through the Theology of Karl Barth*. Grand Rapids: Eerdmans, 2003.

Moltmann, Jürgen. *The Crucified God*. Minneapolis: Fortress, 1993.

———. *God in Creation: A New Theology of Creation and the Spirit of God*. The Gifford Lectures, 1984–1985. San Francisco: Harper & Row, 1985.

———. *Theology of Hope: On the Ground and the Implications of a Christian Eschatology*. Translated by James W. Leitch. New York: Harper & Row, 1967.

———. *The Trinity and the Kingdom*. Minneapolis: Fortress, 1993.

———. *The Way of Jesus Christ: Christology in Messianic Dimensions*. Translated by Margaret Kohl. Minneapolis: Fortress, 1993.

Murphy, Francesca A. *Christ the Form of Beauty: A Study in Theology and Literature*. London: T. & T. Clark, 1995.

———. *The Comedy of Revelation: Paradise Lost and Regained in Christian Scripture.* London: T. & T. Clark, 2000.
———. *God is Not a Story: Realism Revisited.* Oxford: Oxford University Press, 2007.
———. "Inclusion and Exclusion in the Ethos of von Balthasar's Theo-Drama." *New Blackfriars* (January 1998) 56–64.
———. "On Finding the Whole within the Part: A Reassessment of William Lynch's *Christ and Apollo: The Dimensions of the Literary Imagination*." *Literature and Theology* 3/2 (July 1989) 242–50.
———. "The Sound of the Analogia Entis: An Essay on the Philosophical Context of Hans Urs von Balthasar's Theology, Part I and Part II." *New Blackfriars* (November 1993) 508–21 and (December 1993) 557–65.
———. "Whence Comes this Love as Strong as Death: The Presence of Franz Rosenzweig's 'Philosophy as Narrative' in von Balthasar's Theo-Drama." *Literature and Theology* (September 1993) 227–47.
Murphy, Michael. *A Theology of Criticism: Balthasar, Postmodernism, and the Catholic Imagination.* Oxford: Oxford University Press, 2008.
Newbigin, Lesslie. *The Gospel in a Pluralist Society.* Grand Rapids: Eerdmans, 1989.
———. *The Household of God.* New York: Friendship, 1954.
Newell, Philip. *Shakespeare and the Human Mystery.* New York: Paulist, 2003.
Nichols, Aidan. *Divine Fruitfulness: A Guide though Balthasar's Theology beyond the Trilogy.* London: T. & T. Clark, 2007.
———. *No Bloodless Myth: A Guide Through Balthasar's Dramatics.* Washington, DC: Catholic University Press of America, 2000.
———. *Say It Is Pentecost: A Guide Through Balthasar's Logic.* Washington, DC: Catholic University Press of America, 2001.
———. *Scattering the Seed: A Guide Through Balthasar's Early Writings on Philosophy And the Arts.* T. & T. Clark, 2006.
———. *The Word Has Been Abroad: A Guide Through Balthasar's Aesthetics.* Washington, DC: Catholic University Press of America, 1998.
Niebuhr, Reinhold. *The Nature and Destiny of Man: A Christian Interpretation.* 2 vols. Gifford Lectures, 1939. New York: Scribner's, 1951.
Niebuhr, H. Richard. *The Meaning of Revelation.* New York: Macmillan, 1941.
Niebuhr, H. Richard, and Richard R. Niebuhr. *Faith on Earth: An Inquiry into the Structure of Human Faith.* New Haven, CT: Yale University Press, 1989.
Nietzsche, Friedrich. *The Twilight of the Idols.* In *The Portable Nietzsche*, edited and translated by Walter Kaufmann. New York: Penguin, 1976.
Nouwen, Henri J. M. *Can You Drink the Cup?* Notre Dame: Ave Maria, 2006.
———. *The Return of the Prodigal Son.* New York: Doubleday, 1992.
———. *The Selfless Way of Christ.* Maryknoll, NY: Orbis, 2007.
———. *The Wounded Healer.* New York: Doubleday, 1979.
Nuttall, A. D. *A New Mimesis: Shakespeare and the Representation of Reality.* New Haven, CT: Yale University Press, 2006.
Oakes, Edward T., and David Moss, eds. *The Cambridge Companion to Hans Urs von Balthasar.* Cambridge: Cambridge University Press, 2004.
O'Donnell, John. *Hans Urs von Balthasar.* Edited by Brian Davies. Outstanding Christian Thinkers. Collegeville, MN: Liturgical, 1992.
Partridge, Michael. "The Diversity of Theology in a 'Lifescape' of God-with-us." Paper presented at ITIA Seminar, University of St Andrews, October 2, 2009.

Quash, Ben. *Theology and the Drama of History*. New York: Cambridge University Press, 2005.
Rae, Murray. "The Ethics of Jesus or, Why Christian Values are a Bad Idea." *Cultural Encounters: A Journal for the Theology of Culture* 3/2 (Summer 2007) 47–64.
Ratzinger, Joseph. *Introduction to Christianity*. London: Burns & Oates, 1969.
Richardson, Kurt Anders. *Reading Karl Barth*. Grand Rapids: Baker Academic, 2004.
Riches, John, ed., *The Analogy of Beauty: The Theology of Hans Urs von Balthasar*. Edinburgh: T. & T. Clark, 1986.
Sailhamer, John H. *The Pentateuch as Narrative*. Grand Rapids: Zondervan, 1992.
Sartre, Jean-Paul. *The Devil and the Good Lord*. New York: Vintage, 1960.
Sayers, Dorothy. *The Greatest Drama Ever Staged*. London: Hodder & Stoughton, 1938.
Schechner, Richard. *Performance Studies: An Introduction*. London: Routledge, 2002.
———. *Performance Theory*. 2nd ed. London: Routledge, 2003.
Schindler, David L., ed. *Hans Urs von Balthasar: His Life and Work*. San Francisco: Ignatius, 1991.
Schleiermacher, Friedrich. *The Christian Faith*. Edited by H. R. Mackintosh and James Stuart Stewart. Edinburgh: T. & T. Clark, 1989.
Scola, Angelo. *Hans Urs von Balthasar: A Theological Style*. Grand Rapids: Eerdmans, 1995.
Shakespeare, William. *The Poems*. Edited by David Bevington. New York: Bantam, 1988.
———. *The Riverside Shakespeare*. Edited by G. Blakemore Evans. Boston: Houghton, 1974.
Shepherd, Simon, and Mick Wallis. *Drama/Theatre/Performance*. London: Routledge, 2004.
Smail, Tom. *The Giving Gift: The Holy Spirit in Person*. Lima, OH: Academic Renewal, 2002.
Smith, James K. A. *Speech and Theology: Language and the Logic of Incarnation*. Routledge, 2002.
———. "Staging the Incarnation: Revisioning Augustine's Critique of Theatre." *Literature and Theology* 15/2 (June 2001) 123–39.
Stanford, Michael. *An Introduction to the Philosophy of History*. Oxford: Blackwell, 1998.
Stanislavski, Constantin. *An Actor Prepares*. Translated by Elizabeth Reynolds Hapgood. London: Methuen Drama, 2008.
Styan, J. L. *Drama, Stage and Audience*. London: Cambridge University Press, 1975.
Tambling, Jeremy. *Narrative and Ideology*. Buckingham: Open University, 1991.
Thompson, John. *The Holy Spirit in the Theology of Karl Barth*. Allison Park, PA: Pickwick, 1991.
Thurber, James. "A Box to Hide In." In *Writings and Drawings*, edited by Garrison Keillor, 304–6. New York. Penguin Putnam, 1996.
Torrance, James B. *Worship, Community and The Triune God of Grace*. Downers Grove, IL: InterVarsity, 1996.
Torrance, Thomas F. *Theology in Reconstruction*. London: SCM, 1965.
Vanhoozer, Kevin J. *The Drama of Doctrine*. Louisville: Westminster/John Knox, 2005.
———. *First Theology: God, Scripture and Hermeneutics*. Leicester: Apollos, 2002.
———. *Is There a Meaning in this Text?* Grand Rapids: Zondervan, 1998.

———. "The Voice of the Actor: A Dramatic Proposal About the Ministry and Minstrelsy of Theology." In *Evangelical Futures: A Conversation on Theological Method*, edited by John G. Stackhouse, 75-86. Grand Rapids: Baker, 2000.
Volf, Miroslav. *After Our Likeness: The Church as the Image of the Trinity*. Grand Rapids: Eerdmans, 1998.
Ward, Graham. *Barth, Derrida, and the Language of Theology*. Cambridge: Cambridge University Press, 1995.
Ware, Kallistos. *The Orthodox Way*. Crestwood, NY: St. Vladimir's Seminary Press, 1995.
Watson, Francis. *Text and Truth: Redefining Biblical Theology*. Edinburgh: T. & T. Clark, 1997.
Webster, John, ed. *Barth's Moral Theology: Human Action in Barth's Thought*. Edinburgh: T. & T. Clark, 1998.
———. *The Cambridge Companion to Karl Barth*. Cambridge: Cambridge University Press, 2000.
———. *Karl Barth*. London: Continuum, 2004.
———. *Word and Church: Essays in Christian Dogmatics*. Edinburgh: T. & T. Clark, 2001.
Wedel, Theodore. *The Drama of the Bible*. Cincinnati: Forward Movement, 1965.
Wells, Samuel. *Improvisation: The Drama of Christian Ethics*. Grand Rapids: Brazos, 2004.
White, Alan R. *The Philosophy of Action*. Oxford: Oxford University Press, 1968.
White, Alfred D. *Bertolt Brecht's Great Plays*. New York: Barnes & Noble, 1978.
Williams, Raymond. *Drama from Ibsen to Brecht*. London: Hogarth, 1993.
Wolterstorff, Nicholas. *Art in Action: Toward a Christian Aesthetic*. Grand Rapids: Eerdmans, 1980.
———. *Divine Discourse: Philosophical Reflections on the Claim that God Speaks*. Cambridge: Cambridge University Press, 1995.
Wright, N. T. *The Last Word: Beyond the Bible Wars to a New Understanding of the Authority of Scripture*. San Francisco: HarperCollins, 2005.
———. *The New Testament and the People of God*. Minneapolis: Fortress, 1992.
Zizioulas, John. *Being Is Communion: Studies in Personhood and the Church*. Crestwood, NY: St. Vladimir's Seminary Press, 1985.
———. *Eucharist, Bishop, Church: The Unity of the Church in the Divine Eucharist and the Bishop During the First Three Centuries*. Brookline, MA: Holy Cross Orthodox, 2001.

Author Index

Artaud, Antonin, 16, 20, 70, 76–77, 81, 94, 103, 129–30,
Auerbach, Eric, 19
Augustine, 43, 140–43, 185
Avis, Paul, 138

Balthasar, Hans Urs, 1–3, 17–18, 20, 49, 65, 86, 97, 109, 112–16, 151, 155, 177–83, 187–88, 201–2, 211
Barth, Karl, Chapter 1, 3, 19, 37, 56, 68, 85–86, 91, 98, 106, 112–16, 153–54, 176, 190–92, 203
Bartholomew Craig, 117–18
Bauckham, Richard, 61–62, 128, 149–50, 172, 204–5
Beckett, Samuel, 74–76, 79–81,
Begbie, Jeremy, 199
Blackham, Paul, 185
Brecht, Bertolt, 16, 75, 78, 86, 100,
Brook, Peter, 12, 51, 66n40, 74–75, 86, 100–101,
Brown, David, 15–16, 65, 88, 139

Carlson, Marvin, 8, 11–12
Cavanaugh, William, 94–95, 196
Coleridge, Samuel, 138

Davies, Oliver, 113, 115n96
Dyrness, William, 146

Giddens, Anthony, 62
Goheen Michael, 117–18

Green, Garrett, 117, 138,
Gunton, Colin, 34, 96, 185, 206

Harris, Max, 10, 68, 119–20
Hart, Trevor, 9–10, 69, 82, 101, 115, 121, 129, 144–45, 163–64
Hauerwas, Stanley, 31, 63, 65, 105–6, 118–19
Horton, Michael, 118

Irenaeus, 30, 40–41,

Jenson, Robert, 37
Johnson, Todd, 13, 66, 72–73
Johnstone, Keith, 138, 152

Khovacs, Ivan, 2, 13, 71, 73, 139, 142–43, 177–83
Kierkegaard, Soren, 103,

MacDonald, George, 138, 146
McCormack, Bruce, 28–29,
McIntyre, John, 45–46, 136, 146
Metzger, Paul, xi–xiii,
Moltmann, Jurgen, 121–22, 212

Newbigin, Leslie, 195–96
Nichols, Aidan, 15, 20, 67, 90–92, 123–24, 131–33, 162–63

Quash, Ben, 107, 113, 173–75, 192

Sailhamer, John, 107-9,
Savidge, Dale, 13, 66, 72-73, 209
Sayers, Dorothy, 113,
Schechner Richard, 9-12, 14, 69
Schwobel, Christoph, 48
Shakespeare, William, 70-71, 107, 207
Shepherd Simon, 9, 66, 72
Stanislavski, Constantin, 16-17, 74, 95, 102, 104, 126, 136-37, 147, 155
Styan, J.L., 13, 189-90

Thompson, John, 24, 28-29, 31, 44-45
Thurber, James, 208
Torrance, T.F., 38, 97-98,

Vanhoozer, Kevin, 2, 57n6, 82, 107, 116-17, 175

Wallis, Mick, 9, 66, 72
Webster, John, 6
Wells, Samuel, 63-65, 84, 189, 198-201
Wright, N.T., 96, 110-12, 208

Subject Index

actor, 1, 3, 13, 17, 74–75, 95, 100–104, 126, 142, 143, 147, 152, 155, 158, 175, 179, 182, 189–90, 194, 200–201, 208
analogy, 5, 76, 96, 121–22
being, 5, 113, 123, 160–61
faith, 5, 160,
relations, 112–14, 121–24, 157, 160–61, 169, 209

becoming, 18–19, 22, 39, 57, 65–68, 70, 77, 85, 91, 95, 102, 105–6, 121–24, 126, 131, 137, 147–48, 151, 153, 156, 162–63, 167, 179, 187, 190, 210–11

Church, 10, 13–15, 24, 26–27, 32, 48–49, 53–55, 75, 86–89, 97, 104, 114, 120, 123, 139, 145, 150, 153, 169, 175, 182–83, 185, 187, 191, 195–202, 210, 213
communal, 33, 36, 47, 71, 73, 173, 191, 196
covenant, 29, 32, 43, 68, 83, 100, 112, 120, 147, 161, 168, 190, 202–3
creativity, 64, 138, 188,
culture, 84, 150, 196–97, 200, 202, 209

doctrine, 20, 24, 44–45, 47–48, 51, 53, 64, 71, 88, 96, 102, 116, 136, 142, 176, 185, 202
drama, 1–4, 8, 12–16, 20, 50–56, 64–68, 70–74, 76–81, 83, 87–88, 92–94, 96, 99–102, 110–14, 128, 133, 142, 150, 156, 169–70, 174–79, 189–91, 202–4, 207, 210–11

dramatizing of theology, chapter 3, 4–5, 14–15, 19, 21–22, 25, 49–51, 53, 55, 58, 66–70, 73, 82–86, 126, 139, 167, 170, 172–80, 198, 207, 209–210

Eucharistic, 55, 147, 171, 191, 196–206
eschatological, 14, 55, 67, 127, 131, 134, 136, 157, 179–80, 197–206

faith, 6, 8, 10, 24, 31, 33, 39–40, 42–43, 52, 64–65, 72, 85, 108–9, 113, 117, 143–44, 147, 152–54, 160–61, 164–65, 170–71, 173, 194–97, 206, 207,

God
act, 3, 7–8, 10, 19, 25–28, 30–44, 47–55, 64, 68, 84, 88, 97–98, 103–4, 106, 109, 115, 117–19, 122, 135, 153, 156, 170–71, 176, 181–82, 187, 191, 193, 197, 201, 203
Being-in-act, 1, 14, 21, 27–32, 35, 44, 46–49, 63, 67, 86, 97–98, 106, 112, 123, 162, 167, 171, 178–79, 181, 183, 190–91, 207, 209–210
event of revelation, 14–15, 19, 21, 24–27, 29–36, 42, 44–45, 49, 51, 53–54, 90, 93, 153, 162, 179–80, 193, 210
Father, 19–20, 23, 26, 29–30, 34–38, 40, 42–45, 52, 99, 128–29, 133, 151, 159, 176, 182, 184–87
for us, 28–32, 47, 55, 92, 173, 187, 197

God *(continued)*
  Holy Spirit, 8, 19–20, 29, 32, 34, 37, 41–46, 51–52, 83, 97–98, 108, 114, 118, 120, 128, 148, 150, 162, 164–66, 176, 180, 183–87, 193, 196, 211, 213
  Son, 19–20, 29–30, 32, 34, 38–41, 43–45, 100, 111, 118, 121, 128, 133, 149, 151, 159, 165, 170–71, 176, 182, 184–87, 196, 208. *See also* Jesus Christ
  Trinity, 20, 22, 24, 26, 29, 31, 34, 36, 41, 47, 57, 72, 97–98, 120, 135, 151–52, 158, 161, 171, 175–76, 182–83, 185–87, 203–4
  unity and distinction, 33–45
God's drama. *See* Theo-drama
grace, 3, 5–6, 27, 29, 32–33, 35, 39–41, 48, 50, 54, 63, 68, 88, 98, 112, 114–15, 120, 128, 140, 157, 160, 164, 168–69, 172, 182, 187, 190, 194, 196, 203, 205, 210

hope, 46, 78–79, 81, 125–26, 129–31, 134, 136–37, 146, 152, 158, 164, 180, 192, 201–2, 204–5, 207, 213
humanity, 1, 3, 6–8, 13, 19, 21–22, 26, 28–32, 34–55, 60–61, 66–67, 71–75, 77, 82–83, 87, 92–95, 97–99, 102, 106–7, 111, 115, 118–20, 123–24, 128, 130, 132–35, 147–57, 160–63, 167–70, 173–74, 178–83, 187–91, 194, 197–98, 200–205, 209–210, 213

identity, 16, 46, 56, 61–62, 64–65, 72, 74, 78, 112, 120–21, 124, 126n4, 128, 131–32, 155, 158–62, 175–77, 209–210
imagination, chapter 4, 45n101, 46, 74, 108, 188, 189, 200, 211
imago Trinitatis, 7, 132, 149, 169, 209
improvisation, 152, 189–90, 198–201
incarnation, 45, 49, 63–64, 68, 70, 72–73, 77, 83, 93, 97n24, 99, 102–3, 114–16, 119–20, 122, 127, 143, 146–50, 152–53, 155, 157–59, 162–63, 166, 171, 179, 187–88, 193, 211

Jesus Christ, 3–4, 6, 8, 18–19, 23, 28–29, 34–36, 38–41, 45n101, 51–52, 55, 56, 57n6, 60–62, 64, 68–70, 72, 77n75, 78–79, 82–83, 87, 91–95, 97–104, 107–8, 109n71, 111–12, 114–15, 121–24, 125, 128–36, 147, 149, 151–53, 157–59, 165, 172–74, 176, 180, 187–95, 197, 201–3, 204–6, 209–210, 213

language, 20–21, 45n101, 47, 50, 54, 56, 58–60, 70–71, 75–76, 78, 81, 87–88, 94–96, 102–4, 105–8, 110–13, 115, 117, 144, 173
love, 23, 26–27, 29–32, 37, 39, 42–46, 54, 68, 78, 84–85, 90, 98, 111, 121–22, 133–34, 142, 155, 157, 164, 176, 181, 183–87, 194–96, 203–6

mission, 18, 22, 86, 94, 99, 104, 116, 124, 125–26, 131–32, 135, 151–55, 157–62, 165, 168–69, 173, 175, 178, 1180, 183, 189–91, 195–98, 200, 206, 209, 211, 213

narrative, 50n119, 58–70, 76, 87–88, 91, 94, 97, 99, 105–110, 113–19, 150, 165–66, 172, 193

participation, 1, 7–8, 15, 18, 20, 22–23, 30, 31–33, 38, 39, 42–44, 50–54, 56–57, 63–70, 77, 85–89, 95, 98–99, 103–5, 107, 109, 111–12, 115, 119, 129, 130–32, 137, 146–47, 151–54, 156, 158, 160–61, 168–69, 170–74, 176, 179, 189–93, 199–201, 209, 212, 213
performance, 3, 5, 8–12, 15, 19–20, 22, 36, 50–55, 56–57, 62–64, 66, 71–76, 82–89, 91, 93–95, 98–100, 101, 103–4, 105–7, 109, 111–12, 121–23, 128–30, 131–36, 147–53, 164–66, 168–72, 174–83, 187–97, 209–213
personhood, 18, 62, 69, 74, 78, 83, 88, 91, 103, 110, 112, 120, 121–23, 131–32, 135, 146, 156, 158, 163,

Subject Index

167, 168, 172, 173, 178, 180, 182–86, 187
praxis, 7–8, 72, 171, 173, 181

redemption, xii, 29–30, 92, 116, 118–19, 130, 162, 173, 191, 193, 196, 199, 204, 208, 212
relational, 6, 33–34, 36, 47, 60, 71–72, 91, 96, 110, 112–13, 115, 119–22, 124, 128, 131–32, 136, 145, 150, 154, 157–62, 165, 168–70, 172–74, 177, 186, 187–88, 190, 192, 209, 213
role, 8, 15, 33, 46, 50, 54, 63, 68, 70, 74–75, 83, 86, 88, 94, 97, 99–100, 102, 108, 110, 122–23, 131, 150–52, 155, 158–62, 169, 175, 180, 188, 190, 212

salvation (drama of), 14, 26, 29–30, 34, 42, 50, 52, 67, 75, 83, 87, 92, 99, 116, 122–23, 149, 168–69, 173, 180, 186, 191, 193, 211, 213
Scripture (Biblical script), xi, 8, 10, 14, 20, 35, 41, 47, 52, 56, 58, 66, 70, 73, 77–81, 85–89, 97, 102–3, 105–6, 108–9, 113–18, 123, 150, 178, 184, 188, 198, 200
stage. *See* world stage
story, 50n119, 54, 56–64, 66, 68, 71, 77, 85–87, 91, 94, 104, 105–7, 109–112, 116–19, 150, 165–66, 168, 189, 196, 198, 200, 201

theatre, 4, 9, 12–16, 50–52, 55, 64, 66n40, 68, 71–76, 78–81, 83, 85–86, 91, 94–95, 100–101, 103, 109, 119, 124, 139, 140, 142, 147, 151–52, 155–56, 167, 168–70, 176, 177n31, 180–83, 194, 201, 209, 211
theatre of God's glory, 41, 50, 55, 76, 78, 86, 101, 111–12, 115, 149, 152, 157, 169, 187, 209
Theo-drama (God's drama), xi, xii, 2–4, 14, 18n72, 19, 25, 49, 54, 66–67, 82, 85–86, 90, 92, 94, 97n24, 98, 100–101, 105, 108, 116, 121, 123, 132, 167, 170–71, 187–213
theology, 5–7, 19, 24, 46, 48, 51–53, 70–71, 76–81, 86–89, 93–95, 104, 109–110, 147–48, 152, 176, 179–80, 182, 187–91, 193, 195–203, 206, 209, 211–13
threefold movement, 3, 15, 25, 50–51, 53, 62, 68–70, 84–85, 90, 96, 112, 122–24, 127, 130–36, 180, 187, 189, 206, 210
revelation, 1–4, 6–7, 14–15, 19, 23, 25–27, 30, 33–34, 38, 42, 56, 67, 97–98, 106, 109, 113, 115, 117, 119, 123, 128 131–32, 135, 139–40, 145, 151, 155, 157–58, 162–63, 170, 171, 173–74, 176, 179–81, 187, 192–93, 195–96, 202, 204, 207, 209, 213
invitation, 2, 6, 11, 15, 20, 22, 23, 25–26, 31, 40, 42, 52, 63, 68, 73, 82, 91, 95, 97, 99, 100, 107, 123–24, 128, 130, 132–34, 139, 151, 157, 162, 170, 174, 180, 187, 192, 195, 200, 202, 209, 213
reconciliation, 3, 8, 15, 22, 25–26, 28–29, 36, 38, 40–41, 52, 54, 68, 91, 99, 101, 123–24, 128–29, 134–36, 139, 151–53, 157, 162, 170, 174, 176, 179, 187, 192–93, 195, 197, 202, 204, 208–9, 213

world stage, xi-xiii, 3, 6–9, 13–14, 17–20, 22, 38n66, 40n77, 46, 49–54, 63, 66n40, 67, 69, 70–71, 73, 76–79, 81–84, 87–88, 90, 92–93, 94–97, 99–101, 103–4, 106, 108–9, 111–13, 116, 118–20, 122, 128, 130, 132, 135–37, 139, 146, 149–50, 152–59, 161, 163, 165, 167, 169–70, 172–74, 176, 178, 180, 182, 186, 188–89, 192–94, 199–206, 209, 211, 213

Scripture Index

Joshua
2	199

Matthew
22:37–39	23
25	69–70
28:18	69

Luke
4:18	52n127
5:18–20	199
10:25–37	85

John
7:16	35
7:17	84, 174
8:13f	174
8:31f	84

Acts
19:29	13n51

Romans
5:5	43, 45, 184

1 Corinthians
3:9	194
3:15	194
4:9	13n51, 91
13:7	213

2 Corinthians
1:3	129
1:22	164
3:2–3	51n121
5:5	164
5:18–19	197
5:20	52n127
6:1	197
7:6	129
10:5–7	109n71

Ephesians
1:10	68, 129
1:14	164
4:15	84

Hebrews

4:12	103
9:28	52n127
10:23–24	78
10:32–34	77

1 John

185

Revelation

19:6–7	179
21:3–4	179
22:13	99

www.ingramcontent.com/pod-product-compliance
Lightning Source LLC
Chambersburg PA
CBHW072023240426
43667CB00044B/2265